Impossible Puzzle Films

Impossible Puzzle Films

A Cognitive Approach to Contemporary Complex Cinema

Miklós Kiss and Steven Willemsen

EDINBURGH
University Press

©Edinburgh University Press is one of the leading university presses in the UK. We publish academic books and journals in our selected subject areas across the humanities and social sciences, combining cutting-edge scholarship with high editorial and production values to produce academic works of lasting importance. For more information visit our website: edinburghuniversitypress.com

Edinburgh University Press Ltd
The Tun – Holyrood Road
12 (2f) Jackson's Entry
Edinburgh EH8 8PJ

First published in hardback by, Edinburgh University Press 2017

Typeset in Garamond MT Pro by
Servis Filmsetting Ltd, Stockport, Cheshire,
printed and bound in Great Britain by
CPI Group (UK) Ltd, Croydon CR0 4YY

A CIP record for this book is available from the British Library

ISBN 978 1 4744 0672 7 (hardback)
ISBN 978 1 4744 3197 2 (paperback)
ISBN 978 1 4744 0673 4 (webready PDF)
ISBN 978 1 4744 0674 1 (epub)

Contents

Acknowledgements

Our ideas about cinematic narrative complexity have been in development for quite some time, and our sincere thanks extend to all of those who helped, encouraged and contributed to the thoughts that found their way into this book. We are grateful for teachers, colleagues and ex-colleagues, students and friends – at the Arts, Culture, and Media Department, The Groningen Research Institute for the Study of Culture (ICOG) and the Research Centre for Arts in Society of the University of Groningen, at the University of Pécs and at the University of Jyväskylä – for their trust, support and generosity in reflecting and sharing their expertise: Barend van Heusden, László Tarnay, Ágnes Pethő, Balázs Varga, Jarmo Valkola, Annie van den Oever, Annelies van Noortwijk, Julian Hanich, Susan Aasman, Anna Backman Rogers, Thijs Lijster, Tom Slootweg, Vincent Ros, Krina Huisman, Ari Purnama, Martin Rossouw, Gert Jan Harkema, Sjoerd-Jeroen Moenandar, Thomas van den Berg, Tamás Csönge, the students of the Contemporary Complex Cinema Masters course and the members of the late Shadows Film Club in Groningen.

We are especially grateful to Liesbeth Korthals Altes for her expert readership and straightforward remarks throughout many stages of the manuscript, but most importantly for her unflagging openness and hearty enthusiasm in discussing our points in the making. We also wish to extend our sincere gratitude to Marco Caracciolo, Jan Alber and Gábor Kiss for their thorough reviews and insightful comments on the penultimate version of this book; their critical questions and illuminating observations enabled us to strive for greater precision as well as clarity in our argumentation.

This book also benefited from several open lectures, public talks and personal conversations during which we tested many of the ideas with regard to complex film experiences. On this note, let us thank Marina Grishakova of the University of Tartu, as well as Markus Kuhn and Jan Horstmann of the University of Hamburg for their kind invitations, colleagues at the Society for the Cognitive Study of the Moving Image (SCSMI) for their always erudite comments, and also our critical friends – Ed Tan, Charles Forceville, Jason Mittell, Henry Bacon, Torben Grodal, John Bateman, William Brown,

Stefan Iversen, Henrik Skov Nielsen, Hilary Dannenberg, Karin Kukkonen, Maarten Coëgnarts, Peter Kravanja, Steffen Hven, Maria Poulaki, Jelena Rosic, Sebastian Armbrust, Ana Carolina Bento Ribeiro, Katalin Bálint and Brendan Rooney – with whom we had the additional pleasure of discussing our forming ideas personally.

We are indebted to our commissioning editor at Edinburgh University Press, Gillian Leslie, without whose vote of confidence and friendly management this book would not have been possible. Many thanks also go out to the whole editing team at Edinburgh University Press, mostly to Richard Strachan, Eddie Clark, Emma Rees, Anna Stevenson and Rebecca Mackenzie, for their time, energy and professional guidance in bringing this project to fruition. Finally, we are also particularly grateful to the anonymous reviewer for offering the opportunity to pre-empt some criticism during revision, and from whose intellectual input this book benefited greatly.

Introduction

A man is sitting in his favourite armchair, green velvet upholstery with a high headrest, reading the final chapters of a book he had begun to read a few days before. He keeps his cigarettes close at hand to be able to fully immerse himself in the story, and sits with his back to the door of his study. The tranquil scenery is underscored by the study's window that looks out upon a park planted with oaks. Once he opens the book, his memory retains the familiar names and images of the characters with ease. Engrossed by the story, he disengages, line by line, from the surrounding reality, and gently slides into the fictional world . . . A man and woman meet secretly in a cabin. The woman kisses the man, but he resists her passion. He has deadly business ahead. After going over their cold-blooded plans once more, they split up. Leaving the cabin with a dagger hidden against his chest, the man follows a path, lined by trees, leading to a house. It is getting dark. He enters the house and, following the woman's instructions, arrives at the door of a large room. With the knife in his hand, he looks inside and sees a man, his back to the door, sitting in an armchair of green velvet upholstery with a high headrest, reading a novel.

Those who know Julio Cortázar's 1956 mind-bending short story *Continuidad de los parques* (*Continuity of Parks*) will probably remember the shock of realising that the reading character *in* the story shares the fate of the character he is reading *about*: that the reader of Cortázar's novel reads about a character who is reading about a character that becomes this reading character's murderer. The impossible transgression between the telling and the told could suggest a collapse of ontological boundaries; a train of thought that even seems to imply the unsettling idea that the threatened fictional reader actually could also be the novel's actual reader – that is, he could also be *us*. But wait a minute. Is there really a murder taking place in the story at all? More importantly, are we even sure that the fictional reader and the threatened reader are the very same character? After all, what if the fictional reader's high-backed armchair covered in green velvet is only very similar but not identical to the one in which the other, threatened reader sits? What if the story is only a narrative mise-en-abyme, without a short-circuit among its embedded levels? And if there is such a narrative breach between the telling and the told, how to make sense of this anomaly?

Although Cortázar's story can be read as an implausible scenario, unlikely in fiction but possible in reality (a huge coincidence among similar rooms, chairs and readers), most people will probably read it as a *conceivable impossibility*, only 'possible' in fiction (a paradoxical confrontation between identical elements from the embedded story and the story that frames it). Readers are therefore likely to find themselves facing one of two key questions: what to do with this *ambiguity* balanced by Cortázar's polysemous telling; or, if one goes with the mind-bending suggestion of transgressed narrative levels, how to handle the *paradoxical impossibility* presented in this fictional story. After all, on the one hand, it is hard to imagine someone taking the short novel's suggested impossibility seriously, and by that questioning his or her well-founded beliefs about the world – about time's chronology and irreversibility, about human beings' uniqueness, or about the ontological difference between actual readers and fictional characters. Yet, due to their obvious impossibilities and baffling experiences, stories like Cortázar's do potentially trigger various implied meanings, connotative interpretations and imaginative possibilities. Readers may feel that the novel's aim is to blur the line between fiction and reality, to comment on immersion and the power of storytelling, to mock passive readership, and so on. But one can also read this type of intricate stories very 'literally'. Many impossible but seemingly realistic stories skilfully tempt us into their diegetic worlds, presenting them as highly immersive, potentially logically coherent and perfectly inhabitable. These stories often present themselves as 'puzzles' to be solved, luring us into figuring out what is going on, and by what laws their storyworld and story logic work. Narratives like this may also invite us to engage in 'meta-fictional' appreciation and reflection, marvelling at the cleverly designed narrative gears at work and making us aware of our own involvement and interpretive activity when construing such worlds of fiction.

In short, the tangled fiction in Cortázar's intricate narrative design purposely generates various possible questions for its readers. These questions are in many respects related to the topics explored in this book. What we aim to find out is *what such puzzling and enigmatic stories do* and *how viewers make them work*. What difficulties do they pose? What is engaging about these stories' challenges, and what do readers and viewers draw from these experiences?

Why would one take such clearly fictional scenarios seriously in the first place? What keeps an audience guessing about logical and coherent solutions to these otherwise impossible plots? Or, on the contrary, when would one give up on deciphering such puzzling mysteries? Under what conditions do viewers abandon a rationalising and problem-solving approach, and exchange it for, for instance, a more metaphorical or symbolic reading? Ultimately, our questions are about what makes these stories *complex* beyond being simply *complicated*. Although the topics might be similar, our aim is different from Cortázar's. We are interested in the effects of these 'impossible' stories in the context of cinematic storytelling, where such narrative forms seem to be increasingly used. Moreover, it is our ambition to provide systematic answers to these questions and to reveal what is hidden in 'the continuity of parks': an engaging narrative art experience that is ultimately about experiencing *complexity* itself.

I.1 IN THIS BOOK

This book's main topic is the palpable trend of *narrative complexity in contemporary cinema*. As many critics and scholars have noted, over the last two decades a significant and distinct group of contemporary movies has offered specific kinds of viewing experiences that seem to be all about complexity. Naturally, complexity in relation to film can have many different meanings and manifestations. Films can present complex stories (convoluted stories of classic noirs and neo-noirs), complex emotions (from Alexander Payne's subtle psychology to Kim Ki-duk's eccentrics), complex visuals (from meticulously staged mise-en-scène to stylistic overloads of CGI effects), complex interpretive possibilities (see, for example, William Brown (2014) on Abbas Kiarostami), or complex systems (as in Maria Poulaki's work (2011, 2014) on Omar Naim, Matteo Garrone or the Coen brothers' cinema). Among these many options and aspects, our focus will be restricted to formal-structural complexity in stories and storytelling.[1] Hence, whenever this book makes reference to 'complex films', this is shorthand for fiction films featuring some kind of *narrative complexity*. We certainly do not intend to deny all other constituents of the cinematic experience (such as cinematography, style, sound, mise-en-scène or acting) the ability to evoke complexity in viewing experiences. But this book focuses on the specific aesthetic engagement of *story-related*

---

[1] It should be stressed that our use of the term 'complexity' is intended to be value-free: we do not wish to convey any normativity that could be implied in the notion (for instance as being superior to 'simplicity') and will not consider complexity in narrative to be in any way an intrinsically 'good' or 'bad' quality.

complexity, and for the sake of this focus, we only analyse matters of film style or sound to the degree that these take on explicit relevance in relation to issues of narrative.

Complex story structures have been notably abundant in mainstream cinema over the past two decades: from the reversed amnesia neo-noir plot of Christopher Nolan's *Memento* (2000) through the riddling dream logic of David Lynch's *Mulholland Drive* (2001) to the time-travel paradox of Rian Johnson's *Looper* (2012), recent film history has seen the emergence of a range of films, both surprising cult hits and major blockbusters, making clever use of confusing plots. It is films such as these that we want to understand better or, rather, the type of *viewing experiences* that they offer. Therefore, instead of examining the possible meanings and thematic variations of complex films, and besides refining existing taxonomies based on these movies' recurring formal-structural features, we will primarily investigate the *cognitive-psychological impact* of formally complex narratives. This book analyses how different types of complex movies can evoke varieties of viewing effects. Our investigation attempts to identify these effects as caused by different kinds of *cognitive puzzlement*. We also aim to explain the positive mental responses that seem to (somewhat paradoxically) accompany such confusing viewing experiences. After all, complex stories do not seem to fit the picture of ordinary narrative enjoyment; people tend to think of stories as having a function to organise human experience, or to mimetically communicate and provide clear and life-like access to the emotions and experiences of others (whether fictional or actual). But *confusing* narratives seem to upset this 'ordinary' organising function. They often even problematise the access to the basic mimetic level of actions and emotions in which viewers normally immerse themselves. So why then do confusing films fascinate large audiences worldwide?

In this book, we will explore and discuss possible reasons for the engaging potential of narrative complexity in film, drawing from various fields (narrative theory, embodied-cognitive theory, cognitive sciences, psychology, media theory and game studies). To better understand the viewing experiences that complex films provide, we aim to bring together three branches of theorising in particular. These are, firstly (and most obviously) *film studies* and the work that has been done on narrative complexity, both with regard to contemporary audiovisual culture and in a broader film historical perspective (for instance, regarding the narrative experiments of the European modernist art films of the 1960s). Secondly, we draw from *literary theory* and *cognitive narratology*, as these fields have offered some very insightful work relating to storytelling, story structures, story comprehension and complication, as well as more general thinking about narrativity as a key tool of the human mind to organise data and make sense of events. The most recent findings from cognitive narratology have not often been brought into dialogue with the question of complexity in film studies, and we find this encounter to be very fruitful for thinking about complex story experiences. Thirdly, our study connects to work from the paradigm of *cognitive sciences*, as we aim to understand the kinds of (embodied-)cognitive activities that are implicated in making sense of complex stories. Cognitive approaches entered film and literary studies from the 1980s and 1990s onwards. These approaches have handed humanities scholars models and theories that describe how people interact with and make sense of both fictional-mediated and real-world situations. For us, such theories provide a basis to think further about how various complex films may challenge or even obstruct these processes. In this book, we contend that complexity does not only lie in intricate narrative structures themselves, but should also be analysed as *cognitive effects* and *experiences* that such formal disruptions bring about in viewers. Hence, we do not intend to define 'complexity' as an objective property of a film, but rather propose to see it as an effect that emerges (or that can emerge) from the rich dynamics between a film and its viewer. This *cognitive reconceptualisation* of complexity forms one of the book's core aims.

Throughout this study, we will illustrate our findings by analysing different types of complex film in relation to these theories and approaches; each chapter will open with a brief illustrative case study, foreshadowing the theoretical issues it precedes. Ultimately, the aim of this book is to explore and understand the appeal of the cognitive struggles that result from disorientingly complex narrative experiences.

Chapter 1 briefly introduces the trend of narrative complexity in contemporary cinema. It concisely positions narrative complexity within broader shifts in the audiovisual media landscape, including the relation to recent developments in a techno-economical context, as well as this changing context's impact on modes of viewing. This introductory chapter also briefly reviews existing studies on taxonomies that have so far offered *formal-structural approaches* to narrative complexity.

Chapter 2 focuses on a *cognitive approach* as a pertinent method to address complex narratives' 'difficult' viewing experiences. As we argue, complexity does not only lie in a story's formal composition itself, but is best understood in terms of how the narrative hinders viewers' comprehension and meaning-making routines. Noticing that some films pose more conspicuous impediments to sense-making efforts than others, in this section we differentiate movies in regard to their relative complexity in cognitive terms – that is, their ability to cause various states of cognitive puzzlement and trigger diverse mental responses in their viewers. The cognitive approach will lead us to reconsider the classificatory accuracy of existing concepts, such as the umbrella term of *puzzle film*. From there on, we propose more refined categories within the overarching division of narrative complexity, aiming to discern between different types of film that offer various degrees of complexity.

Among these emerging options, we will concentrate on the distinct group of what we call *impossible puzzle films*. This category comprises narrative movies that are characterised by pervasive paradoxes, uncertainties, incongruities and ambiguities in the narration, and which, as a consequence, tend to elicit a state of ongoing cognitive confusion throughout the viewing experience. Examples include David Lynch's *Lost Highway* (1997), *Mulholland Drive* (2001) and *Inland Empire* (2006) (the 'Los Angeles trilogy'), Richard Kelly's *Donnie Darko* (2001), Shane Carruth's *Primer* (2004), James Ward Byrkit's *Coherence* (2013) as well as confusing loop narratives such as Nacho Vigalondo's *Los cronocrímenes* (*Timecrimes*) (2007), Christopher Smith's *Triangle* (2009) or Quentin Dupieux's *Réalité* (*Reality*) (2014). These impossible puzzle films will be the focal point of this book, particularly because, through the distinct viewing effects of their highly confusing stories, they foreground cinematic experiences of 'genuine' complexity, often for the sake of complexity itself.

Chapter 3 describes how impossible puzzle films create paradoxical, incongruent or impossible narrative experiences. To understand the nature of the confusion these films create, this chapter adopts Leon Festinger's original theory on the psychological state of *cognitive dissonance* (1957). We argue that the perplexing effects of impossible puzzle films can be understood as cognitive dissonances. These films strategically evoke and maintain *dissonant cognitions* in their viewers through internal incongruities (contradictions in their narration) and projected impossibilities (narrative structures or elements that disrupt the elementary knowledge, logic and schemas that viewers use to make sense of both real life and fiction). Along with more recent insights from embodied-cognitive sciences and narratology, cognitive dissonance theory offers us a tool to explain the effects that impossible puzzle films have on viewers.

In consequence, Chapter 4 addresses how these effects of cognitive dissonance incite in viewers an *urge to make meaning*, and therefore asks how viewers cope with dissonant experiences in narrative fiction. In this chapter, we offer an overview of the different *interpretive strategies* and *hermeneutic manoeuvres* that viewers may utilise to 'tame' troubling or puzzling dissonances in narrative artworks. Regarding the reception and interpretation of highly complex stories, we aim to answer relevant questions such as 'How do viewers usually make sense of or assign meaning to contradictory and impossible narrative elements?', 'What kinds of interpretive activity do these challenging films evoke in viewers?' and 'How do such interpretive activities shape our viewing experiences?'.

Chapter 5 returns to the formal make-up of impossible puzzle films, asking how they regulate viewer responses to their excessive complexities. In this section we address two specific questions: 'How do impossible puzzle films cue certain sense-making and meaning-making operations over others?' and 'How do they keep viewers hooked on trying to solve their ultimately unsolvable puzzles?'. In line with these questions, a significant portion of the chapter will be dedicated to a *comparative perspective* on the storytelling mode of impossible puzzle films and that of (modernist) art cinema. Art cinema, as a narrative mode, has used complex means similar to its contemporary counterpart, but, as we will demonstrate, has generally done so to different ends. We will argue that impossible puzzle films draw from both the tradition of (modernist) art-cinema and classical narration, but remain fundamentally rooted in the latter by carefully balancing their pervasive complexities with more classical elements of mainstream film storytelling.

Finally, in Chapter 6, our exploration concludes with an outlook on the reasons why viewers may find narrative complexity *engaging* or even *attractive*. As a kind of outro, here we offer hunches (and by that we hope to incite further research) regarding the possible reasons why viewers may be fascinated by such confusing story experiences. After all, why would anyone want to engage with complex puzzles that perhaps cannot even be solved? The final aim of this book is to disclose this peculiar appeal – the pleasures and fascinations of engaging with highly complex, cognitively challenging if not confusing experiences of impossible puzzle narratives.

CHAPTER 1

Contemporary Complex Cinema

The joy of the technological media revolution is that it has proved viewers like shows that are reassuringly complicated . . . They want to be able to pause and reflect about what's happened, to watch something that's chewy.

Stuart Murphy, Entertainment Director of Sky, interviewed
by Sarah Hughes (2015)

On 2 October 1988, during his regular sleepwalking nights, schizophrenic Maryland teenager Donald Darko (Jake Gyllenhaal) meets a mysterious man wearing a creepy rabbit costume. Frank, the giant bunny, informs Donnie that the world will end in twenty-eight days, six hours, forty-two minutes and twelve seconds. While Donnie is still outside, a huge passenger plane engine crashes through the Darkos' roof, destroying Donnie's bedroom. Notwithstanding the curious fact that no plane or engine has been reported missing, had Donnie not been sleepwalking, he would have been killed. Haunted by Frank, the intro-verted Donnie gradually becomes the school's unruly troublemaker. After sunset, he turns into a radical rebel. One night he floods his high school, while on another evening, he burns down the home of a local celebrity (revealing the man's hidden child porn dungeon). Despite his violent acts, Donnie makes new friends and seemingly enjoys his new-found status. He starts dating a new girl in town, Gretchen (Jena Malone), and, after Frank makes him curious about time travel, makes contact with the school's science teacher, Mr Monnitoff (Noah Wyle). Monnitoff gives Donnie a book, The Philosophy of Time Travel, *written by former teacher Roberta Sparrow (Patience Cleveland), alias 'Grandma Death', the freak of the town. As the film unfolds, we see pages from this book that expounds on the possibility of time travel, including some cryptic notes about tangent universes and alternative realities (these regularly appearing scenes are available only in the director's cut of the film). As part of his night-time hallucinations, Donnie starts to see fluid light tunnels streaming out of people's chests, anticipating their future acts. His own emerging light tunnel leads him to his father's closet, revealing a gun . . . 29 October – one day remains. While his parents are away, Donnie and his sister hold a Halloween party. Realising that there are only hours left before Frank's apocalyptic prophecy, Donnie and Gretchen decide to visit Grandma Death. When they arrive, they run into the school's bullies, who are attempting to rob Sparrow's house. In the heat of the fight that spills into the street, a speeding car comes out of nowhere and runs Gretchen over, leaving her dead. The car is driven by a boy called Frank (James Duval), wearing an eerie rabbit costume for the Halloween party – an exact copy of Donnie's hallucination. Using his father's gun, Donnie kills Frank and drives off with the lifeless body of Gretchen . . . It's dawn, the time is up and as a sign of an imminent apocalypse, a dreadful vortex cloud forms over the town. While peacefully contemplating the unfolding events, Donnie spots his returning mother's plane. The next moment we see that due to violent turbulence, one of the plane's engines breaks free and falls into the vortex . . . Fast-rewind, all events of the last 28 days reverse and we're back at 2 October. At midnight the huge engine of the plane crashes into Donnie's bedroom and kills him . . . The next morning Gretchen rides her bike to the wrecked house, learning about the fate of some guy called Donnie. The film ends with a déjà vu moment between her and Donnie's mother. They wave at each other kindly, even though they have never met before.*

Richard Kelly's 2001 cult hit *Donnie Darko* is one of the early trendsetter examples that brought an opaque story to a wide audience. Drawing on the beloved high-school teen genre, the movie builds a realistic world with its own intrinsic scientific laws that closely corresponds to – but also disturbingly subverts – our known physical reality. The necessary explanations of the workings of these fictional laws unfold partially in the film itself (thanks to the appearance of Stephen Hawking's 1988 pop-science book *A Brief History of Time*) but, more remarkably, also across a variety of supplementary paratexts that surrounded the film: clues could be found on its official website,[1] in an abundance of DVD extras and commentaries, by scrutinising differences in the theatrical and director's cut versions, and even through Roberta Sparrow's fictitious book *The Philosophy of Time Travel*, from which excerpts were released in the film's DVD box. Initially failing at the box-office (the film had a limited release, a month after 9/11), *Donnie Darko*'s 'cult-hit' status actually emerged precisely thanks to this richly built paratextual aura, which, by utilising the novel affordances of technological changes in media consumption and online interaction, amplified the film's full experience. A director's cut DVD was released in 2004, and an extended, paratext-packed version – including twenty minutes of clue-studded extra footage – followed in 2005. Arguably, without these extensions, the film would be even more puzzling. One might even look at these officially designed supplements as compensating tools for the film's arresting complexity.

---

[1] Quite progressively for its time, the official website of the film incorporated, among other things, audio, visual and audiovisual materials, luring fans into active investigation of the film's puzzling universe. The site was built as a kind of non-linear hypertext, giving navigational and investigative freedom to the user-viewer. The original URL is now unavailable; the entire site has been archived at http://archive.hi-res.net/donniedarko/ (Van den Berg and Kiss 2016).

Instead of concentrating on this film's specific diegetic enigma,[2] let us start with some more fundamental interrogations regarding general aspects of the complex puzzles that films like *Donnie Darko* offer. How and when did such story complexity enter mainstream film and television? What are the basic forms and mechanisms of these complex film experiences? And, more essentially, what is this 'complexity' that we are talking about in the first place?

1.1 COMPLEX CONDITIONS: THE RESURGENCE OF NARRATIVE COMPLEXITY

Let us start with a concise statement: *narrative complexity is a trend in contemporary cinema and television*. Both components of this assertion require some brief explanation.

By *narrative complexity* we mean a kind of structural-constructional complexity in storytelling logic.[3] This complexity can be witnessed through the increasing popularity of what critics and scholars have called *database, multilinear, forking-path, fractal, episodic, alternative-plot, cubist, loop, modular, multiple-draft, multiform, multiple-embedded, hyperlink* or otherwise formally unconventional narratives.

Also, one can justifiably speak of a *trend* – or at least a 'certain tendency'[4] – in terms of the profusion and 'mainstreamification' of complex stories in film and television. This trend emerged in the mainstream in the mid-1990s, and, as the below text box illustrates, arguably persists to the present day. Even though narrative complexity has not eclipsed more traditional forms of narration and representation, being only one among many parallel trends in contemporary audiovisual storytelling, it is likely that this period of film and television history 'will be remembered as an era of narrative experimentation and innovation, challenging the norms of what the[se] medium[s] can do' (Mittell 2015: 31).

---

[2] According to probably the most thorough among the film's explanatory sites (www.donniedarko.org.uk/explanation/), Kelly's movie fantasises on a possibility of a tangent universe (created at midnight on 2 October) parallel to the film's primary reality. Being an occasional and unstable time-construction in an alternative reality, a tangent universe lasts only for a few weeks (in this case a bit longer than twenty-eight days), but, upon its collapse, might have catastrophic consequences for the primary world. Gradually understanding the situation and accepting his role in it, Donnie sacrifices himself (according to Sparrow's explication, he is endowed with supernatural powers and is the only person who could prevent the apocalypse): he restores the time-construct of the primary world by throwing a jet engine into the vortex, and therefore saves his family and, indeed, the whole world from apocalyptic destruction.

[3] The word 'complex' is rooted in the Latin *plectere*, meaning *to weave* or *to entwine*.

[4] In deference to François Truffaut's famous essay 'A Certain Tendency of the French Cinema' (1976 [1954]), Thomas Elsaesser acknowledges the complex trend as 'certain tendency' in contemporary cinema (2009: 14).

Trailing the immense success of Quentin Tarantino's *Pulp Fiction* in 1994, the current trend of narrative complexification started with sporadic examples of progressive films such as Alejandro Amenábar's *Abre los ojos* (*Open Your Eyes*) or David Lynch's *Lost Highway*, both from 1997, and continued through trendsetter threshold movies like Tom Tykwer's *Lola rennt* (*Run Lola Run*) (1998), David Fincher's *Fight Club* (1999), David Cronenberg's *eXistenZ* (1999), Spike Jonze's *Being John Malkovich* (1999) and *Adaptation* (2002), Christopher Nolan's *Memento* (2000), Michael Walker's *Chasing Sleep* (2000), Lynch's *Mulholland Drive* (2001), Richard Kelly's *Donnie Darko* (2001), Michel Gondry's *Eternal Sunshine of the Spotless Mind* (2001), Cameron Crowe's *Vanilla Sky* (2001), Jee-woon Kim's *Janghwa, Hongryeon* (*A Tale of Two Sisters*) (2003), Christoffer Boe's *Reconstruction* (2003), or Shane Carruth's *Primer* (2004). In recent years this tendency has culminated in an abundance of manifestations in art-cinema, midcult and mainstream platforms alike. Titles may include Emmanuel Carrère's *La moustache* (2005), Marc Forster's *Stay* (2005), John Maybury's *The Jacket* (2005), Lynch's *Inland Empire* (2006), Csaba Bollók's *Miraq* (2006), Nacho Vigalondo's *Los cronocrímenes* (*Timecrimes*) (2007), John August's *The Nines* (2007), Mennan Yapo's *Premonition* (2007), Charlie Kaufman's *Synecdoche, New York* (2008), Jaco Van Dormael's *Mr. Nobody* (2009), Christopher Smith's *Triangle* (2009), Thomas Jane's *Dark Country* (2009), Martin Scorsese's *Shutter Island* (2010), Abbas Kiarostami's *Copie conforme* (*Certified Copy*) (2010), Duncan Jones's *Source Code* (2011), Jack Heller's *Enter Nowhere* (2011), Nolan's personal projects like *The Prestige* (2006) as well as his 'complex narrative blockbuster[s]' (Campora 2014: 36) such as *Inception* (2010) and *Interstellar* (2014), Rian Johnson's *Looper* (2012), Tom Tykwer and the Wachowskis' *Cloud Atlas* (2012), Richard Ayoade's *The Double* (2013), Danny Boyle's *Trance* (2013), Denis Villeneuve's *Enemy* (2013), James Ward Byrkit's *Coherence* (2013), Dennis Iliadis' *+1* (2013), Bradley King's *Time Lapse* (2014), Paul Thomas Anderson's *Inherent Vice* (2014), Michael and Peter Spierig's *Predestination* (2014), Quentin Dupieux's *Réalité* (*Reality*) (2014), Michael Hurst's *Paradox* (2016), Isti Madarász's *Hurok* (*Loop*) (2016) and so on. Beyond the general tendency of enhanced playfulness in the storytelling sophistication of television series and serials across their genres (Johnson 2006), popular shows like *Lost* (J. J. Abrams et al. 2004–10), *Fringe* (J. J. Abrams et al. 2008–13) and recently *Person of Interest* (Jonathan Nolan 2011–), *12 Monkeys* (Travis Fickett and Terry Matalas 2015–) or the second season of the neo-noir *True Detective* (Nic Pizzolatto 2015) have embraced radical forms of narrative complexity, further underlining the trend's widespread domestication.

In the wake of the popularisation of narrative complexity in film, an abundance of scholarly works has scrutinised the development and permanence of the trend from a variety of perspectives (see, among others, Bordwell 2002a; Branigan 2002; Young 2002; Eig 2003; Everett 2005; Mittell 2006, 2015; Staiger 2006; Lavik 2006; Berg 2006; Panek 2006; Diffrient 2006; Cameron 2008; Simons 2008; Elsaesser 2009; Buckland 2009a, 2014a; Ben Shaul 2012; Poulaki 2011; Kiss 2012, 2013; Klecker 2013; Campora 2014; Ghosal 2015; Coëgnarts et al. 2016). As Allan Cameron notes, providing one of the most comprehensive overviews of the complex narrative development in the cinematic context, it has become apparent that 'popular cinema has displayed a turn towards narrative complexity . . . The resurgence of this type of formal experimentation became particularly prominent following the success of Quentin Tarantino's *Pulp Fiction* (1994)' (Cameron 2008: 1). Indeed, the contemporary tendency of narrative complexity in popular cinema is best characterised as a 'resurgence'; after all, as David Bordwell laconically puts it, 'nothing comes from nothing' in film narration (Bordwell 2006: 75). The present-day innovative movies that push the limits both of narrative expression and of their viewers' cognitive and interpretive abilities do operate 'within a tradition', one 'that demands a balance between innovation and adherence to norms' (ibid.: 103). Certainly, narrative complexity is not an entirely new phenomenon in film history. One can think for example of the intricate stories and story paths found in 1940s film noirs (ibid.: 72–103), or of the narrative experiments of the European 'modernist' art cinema in the 1950s, 60s and 70s (Kovács 2007: 120–40; Bordwell 1979). As this book too will demonstrate, many contemporary complex films have partially borrowed or adapted strategies from these earlier traditions of cinematic storytelling. What is new, however, is that the current trend seems to be significantly more pervasive and widespread than these earlier traditions, manifesting itself across multiple genres and platforms, and in both national and international cinemas.

Narrative complexification in contemporary mainstream film has proven to be a significant and enduring tendency. Although this book does not aim (or claim) to untangle the various reasons that have led to this trend, in the below we will attempt to concisely sketch some of the contextual factors that form the background against which the mainstream success of complex films can be understood. The reasons behind the comeback of this trend are various but cumulative, and seem to have been mainly propelled by changes in (1) *technological* and (2) *economic* conditions (see, among others, Manovich 2001; Kinder 2002; Mulvey 2006; Mittell 2006, 2009, 2010, 2015; Lotz 2007; Cameron 2008; Gillian 2010; Johnson 2006; Ang 2011; Kiss 2012; Buckland 2014b), resulting in shifts both in film *viewership* (addressed in section 1.2) and in larger *formal* trends within (post-)classical film narration (see section 1.3).

Considering the *technological aspects* (1), complex films not only respond to, but also play with and capitalise on the novel affordances of technological advancements. The growing consumer access to technological goods – for example, to broadband internet, fuelling participatory engagement, granting connection to online communities and creating collective intelligence; or to time-shifting technologies, materialised in diversely advanced analogue (VHS) or digital (Laserdisc, DVD, Blu-ray, VOD) versions of home cinemas – has given *agency* and *control* to the viewer. The traditional passive role of viewers-as-spectators, which asked audiences to submit themselves to the time-bound conditions and conventions of the cinematic screening, has been upgraded with more (inter-)active potential. As the example of *Donnie Darko* illustrated, complex narratives often require such technical augmentation; for instance, filmic puzzles and enigmas incite activity in viewers who engage in collective deciphering and share their explanations on online message boards – performing what Jason Mittell called the 'forensic' mode of fandom (2009). Complex narratives also invite close and controlled tinkering, allowing viewers to embrace time-shifting technologies' support in pausing, rewinding and replaying films and television shows. One early example, regarding a (then) 'particularly complex' television series, *A Very British Coup*, is discussed by Brad Chisholm, who describes the show's complexity as 'a high shots-per-minute ratio and an obsession with placing dialogue from one scene over the images of another' (Chisholm 1991: 394). Chisholm interprets these qualities as conscious choices of the producers who 'seem to have fashioned their program to be watched on a VCR delay-tape, so that a viewer could regularly rewind and take second looks' (ibid.: 394). Chisholm already understood that '[d]ifficulty can be offset and complexity conquered by taping programs and watching them at the viewer's pace' (ibid.: 401). Today, such realisations almost sound like truisms. Moreover, filmmakers nowadays commonly design their narrative experiences in ways that allow for (if not prey upon) an interplay between these technical and narrative dimensions. For instance, Charlie Kaufman, one of the most notable screenplay writers and filmmakers associated with complex story experiments within Hollywood filmmaking, talks openly about the strategy he follows: 'what I try to do is infuse my screenplays with enough information that upon repeated viewings you can have a different experience' (Johnson 2006: 164). Chan-wook Park, director of the cult hit *Oldeuboi* (*Oldboy*) (2003), similarly admits that he made his film 'with the DVD viewers in mind so that they could watch it several times and discover new elements each time' (Thanouli 2009b: 218).

The mindful cooperation between technological and authorial innovations has impacted audiences' behaviour; their changes in attitude, in turn, further encouraged narrative experimentation. Contemporary consumers of art are well-equipped to handle (and, what is more, often demand) narrative challenges beyond the often easy-to-access, linear and transparent experiences of the classical mode of film narration.[5] Arguably, our everyday experiences with new and increasingly sophisticated technological affordances and flows of information inspire more and more complex stories and modes of storytelling. For example, doppelgänger and other schizophrenic stories and their corresponding narrative modes – multilinear, forking-path or loop – are said to be prompted by our customary practice of digital lossless copying, our familiarity with hyperlink and database logic, the habitual virtualisation of our selves through varied avatars on videogame and other online platforms, and our routine in the creation and maintenance of different social media profiles to express the diversity of our *multiple characters*, both professional and private. Producers of audiovisual fiction embrace the novel affordances of technological advancements and meet with the challenge of the new demands from viewers who have been precisely trained by such technical innovations. They set out to experiment with narrative modes, complexifying forms and structures and often 'designing a cultural form explicitly to train the cognitive muscles of the brain' (Johnson 2006: 56).

The strategy of making films rely heavily on multiple viewings has strong ties to the industry's *economical demands* (2). By introducing the idea of 'rewatchability value', Steven Johnson identifies 'repeatability' as one of the most essential characteristics of contemporary audiovisual programmes. Johnson has derived his finding by analysing the evolution of principles that govern US broadcast television programming. We have already summarised Johnson's study elsewhere:

> During the late sixties and the seventies, a safe principle governed the narrative schedules of prime-time television. Thinking about addressing the widest possible audience, NBC's 'Least Objectionable Programming' philosophy followed a cautious rule prioritising the formula of the 'lowest common denominator' in their viewers' tastes (Klein 1971). With the new technological platforms and opportunities, the abounding appearance of specialised, 24/7 broadcasting television channels and, last but not least, with the quick exhaustion of possibilities that the rule permitted, the faint-hearted encompassing principle of the LOP model became obsolete. Although aiming for the same economic outcome, the 'Most Repeatable

---

[5] In this book we use *classical narration* to refer to the dominant 'Hollywood-type' of story-driven, mimetic and immersive narrative mode, most thoroughly defined by Bordwell 1979; Bordwell 1985: 156–204; Bordwell et al. 1985. Comparing classical film narration against art-cinema narration, section 5.2 will provide a more specific definition of classical narratives' transparent, causal and goal-oriented representations.

Programming' model established and, more importantly, allowed new strategies. Arm-in-arm with these changes of the media landscape, 'the MRP model cultivates nuance and depth; it welcomes "tricks"' (Johnson 2006: 162), generally, it opens its governing principles beyond a one-dimensional emotional gratification. (Kiss 2012: 44)

As the example of the success of a screenwriter like Kaufman proves, television's 'M[ost] R[epeatable] P[rogramming] model has infiltrated Hollywood' (Johnson 2006: 163). By playing with viewers' habitual comprehension, 'tricks' in storytelling and story logic encourage repeated viewing, thereby raising the rewatchability value of complex narratives. Taking on the concept of 'two-tiered system of communication' (Carroll 1982), 'multiple entry point' strategies create excuses for a repeated viewing when permitting "access" to the film emotionally and intellectually' (Elsaesser 2011: 248). Whether it is about merely misleading, temporarily confusing or outright lying to the audience, unreliable and twist-narratives knowingly capitalise on viewers' feeling of competence, if not their vanity, as their disbelief that they missed something or that they were outsmarted by the film can lure them back to the box offices. And if not there, audiences may leave their money in regular and online stores, buying physical copies or renting and streaming digital versions of films and television shows. Getting around the elusive flow of scheduled cinematic screenings or television broadcasts, the harnessing of proprietary control holds the promise that a repeated viewing might lead to essential revelations – answering acute questions, resolving pressing ambiguities or at least discovering vital clues – that might have escaped attention during first-time viewing. Often, as exemplified by the case of *Donnie Darko*'s belated cult success, DVD and Blu-ray sales or iTunes, Hulu or Netflix rentals outweigh box-office revenues.

We leave it to those who are specialised in these contextual nexuses to determine whether recent technological alterations and economical recalibrations *reflected* (Everett 2005), *encouraged* (Johnson 2006), were *answered by* (Buckland 2014b), *extended in* (Cameron 2008), *feedbacked* (Hayles and Gessler 2004), *set the stage for*, *impacted* or simply *coincided with* (Mittell 2015) the changes in contemporary narrative modes. In this book, we will instead focus on different questions, particularly relating to why many viewers are engaged in (if not attracted by) the specific viewing *experiences* that complex film narratives offer. While the apparent success, in terms of box-office earnings and viewer ratings, might justify why producers and filmmakers invested money and energy in making these films and television series and serials, an explanation about *how* complex programmes evoke an effect on viewers, and the reasons *why* audiences value their narrative experimentation, is lacking.

1.2 COMPLEX CINEMA AS BRAIN-CANDY FOR THE EMPOWERED VIEWER

With regard to *viewing modes*, complex film narratives take aim at an audience that is used to these rapidly changing techno-economical conditions. The recent *puzzle films* (Buckland 2009a, 2014a), *mind-game films* (Elsaesser 2009), *mindfuck movies* (Eig 2003) or perhaps *mind-tricking narratives* (Klecker 2013) seem to offer cinematic brainteasers. That is, they seem to be 'movies that are "playing games"' (Elsaesser 2009: 14) mostly for the game's sake. Naturally, beyond their self-contained games and genre-limited issues, such playful puzzles can ultimately also be seen as addressing certain 'epistemological problems (how do we know what we know) and ontological doubts (about other worlds, other minds) that are in the mainstream of the kinds of philosophical inquiry focused on human consciousness' (ibid.: 15). Nevertheless, at the heart of the matter, the playfulness of these puzzle films also offers a new deal to the audience, one that is certainly unusual in the history of mainstream cinema and that can be said to possibly stimulate more active or devoted modes of viewership.

There seems to be a close connection between the emerging trends in what one might call 'participatory' film viewing and narrative complexification; that is, between audiences' increased need for active and participatory viewing modes on the one hand, and narrative intricacy, attractive complexity and other means of challenging viewer competences on the other. The recent trend of puzzle films seems to support arguments that highlight a transition from the *naive* and *informed* passivity (Carroll 1982) that characterised traditional film viewing, to more *empowered* positions (Elsaesser 2011: 260) of interactive, actively devoted, *pensive* (Bellour 1987 [1984]) and *possessive* (Mulvey 2006: 161–80), even *forensic* (Mittell 2009) viewership. Laura Mulvey astutely sketches this shift as a transformation of a voyeuristic spectator (Mulvey 1975) to a curiosity-driven viewer, whose needs to decipher 'respond to the human mind's long-standing interest and pleasure in solving puzzles and riddles' (Mulvey 2006: 191). Registering the same transition, Thomas Elsaesser aptly notes that in many contemporary complex films the fictional pact with the viewer is no longer based on 'identification, voyeuristic perspectivism and "spectatorship"' (Elsaesser 2009: 37). Rather, these films set out to elaborate and test known textual forms, narrative tropes and story motifs, providing 'brain-candy' to the viewer – an expression that Elsaesser (ibid.: 38) borrows from Malcolm Gladwell (2005). Indeed, by designing narratives that allow 'cognitive workouts' (Johnson 2006: 14), complex plots offer forensic playgrounds of participatory experiences for the viewer. One might even suggest that the joint effect of the 'mainstreamisation' of complexity and the upgraded roles of new viewership contributes to the fading distinction between professional and 'amateur narratologists' (Mittell 2006: 38; 2015: 52). In both a seminal article, 'Narrative Complexity in Contemporary American Television' (2006), and a comprehensive book, *Complex TV* (2015), Jason Mittell demonstrates how television viewership has been 'upgraded' through the interaction between complex forms of serialised television and the possibilities offered by new media. While television networks slowly began to capitalise on transmedia storytelling across traditional screens and new media platforms (through accompanying websites, videogames and so on), viewers too quickly adapted to the digital era, sharing their experiences, interpretations and puzzle-solving activities on blogs and other podiums of social media. Television writers, in turn, having found a way to bind viewers more strongly to their serial narratives, showed increasing interest in employing narrative puzzles and complexities to elicit such participation and online discussion.

Narrative complexity, in both television and film, seems to encourage this intensified participation from viewers: 'In contrast to . . . accidental difficulty, difficulty by design invites the viewer to engage in a narrative that is purposely obscured, impeded, or otherwise made hard to assimilate' (Chisholm 1991: 391). The success of many complex narratives in both film and television is often ascribed to the effective stimulation of an active viewer response. For instance, in his work on director David Lynch, Dennis Lim looks back on the perhaps surprising success of the highly complex *Mulholland Drive*, noting that

> [a]udiences who responded to *Mulholland Dr.* loved it precisely for its unique architecture as a puzzle movie that required some degree of assembly in the viewer's head. The online magazine *Salon* ran a piece titled 'Everything You Were Afraid to Ask about *Mulholland Drive*,' untangling the film's narrative threads and mapping out its cosmology; various websites, some maintained to this day, went even deeper, parsing the significance of minor characters and the symbolism of individual objects. The cult that emerged around *Mulholland Dr.* bespoke a participatory engagement with fiction, a collective hunger – to solve, decode, demystify – that Lynch had tapped into with *Twin Peaks*. (Lim 2015)[6]

---

[6] Lim further acknowledges how the popularity of Lynch's mysteriously puzzling film was embedded in the broader trend of narrative complexification that was becoming particularly apparent around the time: 'Fractured, elliptical stories were not new to cinema – they were in fact the stock in trade of modernist giants like Alain Resnais and Michelangelo Antonioni – but *Mulholland Dr.* coincided with a mounting appetite for narrative complexity. Audiences were by then accustomed to the shifting time signatures of Quentin Tarantino's movies, or to the gentler fissures in the films of the Polish director Krzysztof Kieślowski, who explored the cosmic patterns of interlocking lives in *The Double Life of Véronique* (1991) and the *Three Colors* trilogy (1993–4). The rug-pulling trickery of hits like *The Usual Suspects* (1995) and *The Sixth Sense* (1999) popularized the notion of narrative as a game; Christopher Nolan's reverse-chronology *Memento*, another amnesia neonoir, was released several months before *Mulholland Dr.*, and temporal loops were becoming an increasingly common device, in such films as *Donnie Darko* (2001), *Primer* (2004), and *Déjà Vu* (2006)' (Lim 2015).

In many complex films, the 'invitation' for active investigation is even extended, rather literally, as part of an overt game that these films set out to play with the viewer. While the first uttered words in Nolan's *The Prestige* – 'Are you watching closely?' – are a modest plea for the viewer's attention, the very beginning of Louis Leterrier's *Now You See Me* (2013) – 'Come in close! Closer! Because the more you think you see, the easier it'll be to fool you' – offers a highly self-conscious invitation, overly confident in its authorial mastery of the game. All things considered, one could even go as far as claiming that narrative complexity is a novel invitational strategy, which upgrades television and film's traditionally offline – 'cool' and 'hot' – media (McLuhan 1964) with some possibility of (inter-)activity that characterises the 'sizzling' new media.

1.3 NARRATIVE TAXONOMIES: SIMPLE, COMPLEX, PUZZLE PLOTS

Lastly, in conclusion to this introduction, we would like to briefly discuss some of the work that has been done on the *formal* study of narrative complexity in contemporary cinema. Multiple works have aimed at understanding how contemporary complex films differ from classical narration by problematising or modulating traditional modes of narrative representation. The question of 'classification' is often central to these studies: can contemporary complex films still be said to belong to the 'same old' category of *classical narrative cinema* – the dominant paradigm of popular film storytelling from which they seem to originate? Or does their complexity go beyond classical storytelling standards and principles, deserving recognition as an altogether new phenomenon with distinct formal strategies, conventions and viewing routines? Theorists like Eleftheria Thanouli have argued that these films belong to a *post-classical* mode of film narration. Among a number of tendencies, post-classical narratives are said to display traits of 'hypermediacy', are characterised by a high degree of 'self-consciousness' and exhibit 'a complex and multi-faceted system of time that problematises the natural progression of real time with the aid of numerous technical devices' (Thanouli 2006: 191). Comparable claims have been made with regard to narrative complexity through more specific labels such as *complex narratives* (Staiger 2006; Simons 2008), *modular narratives* (Cameron 2008), *mind-game films* (Elsaesser 2009) or *multiform narratives* (Campora 2014), while in his 2009 and 2014 anthologies Warren Buckland branded these movies as *puzzle films*. Particularly the latter term requires some elaboration – not least because of its presence in the title of this book.

Although for Buckland, and for several others, 'puzzle films' serves to denote the specificity of contemporary complex movies, it must be noted that the concept also has a broader historical context. While as a *phenomenon* 'puzzle film' appeared first in the mid-1910s in the form of German filmmaker Joe May's 'Preisrätselfilme' or 'prize-puzzle-films' (Pehla 1991; Canjels 2011),[7] and later, in the mid-1920s, as 'Rebus-Filme', short animated crossword puzzles by Paul Leni,[8] the *term* 'puzzle film' stems from Norman N. Holland's 1963 article entitled 'Puzzling Movies', in which he referred to a new genre of European art films of the late 1950s and early 1960s. According to Holland, a movie like Ingmar Bergman's *Det sjunde inseglet* (*The Seventh Seal*) (1957) or Alain Resnais' *L'année dernière à Marienbad* (*Last Year at Marienbad*) (1961) 'puzzles, disturbs, presents us with an emotional riddle, but puts it in an intellectual and aesthetic context' (Holland 1963: 24). Almost half a century later, reflecting on the emerging trend within contemporary mainstream cinema, 'puzzle film' has been resurrected as a distinct category of narrative in several film publications (Panek 2006; Bordwell 2006; Klinger 2006; Mittell 2006), after which a new use of the term received full acknowledgement in Buckland's anthologies (2009a; 2014a). While for Holland, the heady intellectual and aesthetic contexts of 'puzzling films' primarily offered a vehicle for the expression of complex *emotional*, philosophical and psychological contemplations – in short, issues in cinematic modernism (Kovács 2007) – today's narrative complexification seems to aim at eliciting *cognitive* puzzles, primarily for the puzzle's sake.

According to Buckland, the term 'puzzle film' should be used to distinguish contemporary complex films as a novel category of popular film storytelling. For him, the 'puzzle plot' represents a distinct 'third type of plot that comes after [the simple and] the complex plot' (Buckland 2009b: 3). Puzzle films, he argues, are 'intricate in the sense that the arrangement of events is not just complex, but complicated and perplexing; the events are not simply interwoven, but entangled' (ibid.: 3). We find this definition of the puzzle plot rather general. It lacks a precise characterisation, apart from adjectives

[7] 'The first *Preisrätselfilm, Das Verschleierte Bild von Groß-Kleindorf* ([Joe May] 1913), dealt with a female statue that aroused many men, but when the statue was covered up after some incidents it suddenly disappeared. The film stopped there and asked the audience the question, 'who might have stolen the statue?' The moviegoer had to guess the outcome. Answers could be sent to the *Berliner Tageblatt* and other local newspapers, and for each film there was prize money of 8,500 Marks. The following week the solution could be seen in the cinemas' (Canjels 2011: 27).

[8] The short-lived (between 1925 and 1927) German genre of *Rebus-Film*, or, as an advertisement in the period journal *Der Kinematograph* named it, the 'crossword puzzle film' is often considered to be a precursor of today's interactive screen media: 'upon buying their tickets, spectators received puzzle cards which they filled out based on visual clues screened before the feature film and could check against the "solutions" segment shown a week later' (Cowan 2010: 197).

like '*complex*', '*perplexing*', '*interwoven*' or '*entangled*', while the spectrum of case studies also seems to remain rather broad. Hence, in our view, the argument for the specificity of these films (whether formally, experientially or film-historically) should require further clarification. Both Cornelia Klecker and Matthew Campora have similarly questioned this definition, and specifically the usefulness of such an all-encompassing classification. While for Klecker '*puzzle film* does little more than replace the vague concept of complex storytelling' (Klecker 2013: 128), Campora notices that 'gaps in the conceptual work as well as a lack of specificity in some of the analysis . . . has led to a profusion of labels and categories' (Campora 2014: 5). Already in the introduction to the first anthology, Buckland acknowledges the looseness of the puzzle film label, stating that the term's '"unity" is of course outweighed by the diversity of each film' (Buckland 2009b: 6). Later, in his 2014 *Introduction*, Buckland further nuances the term: referring to Anjan Chakravartty's classification theory, he suggests a 'polythetic definition', a definition based on the '"possession of a clustered subset of some set of properties, no one of which is necessary but which together are sufficiently many"' (Chakravartty 2007, 158)' (Buckland 2014b: 13).

Yet another question remains: whether such a lenient classification is able to maintain the claim that puzzle plot extends 'far beyond' the Aristotelian traditional complexity concept (Buckland 2009b: 2). While *simple plots* – by maintaining seamless chronology, straightforward action-reaction-based causality, character integrity, and tight narrative continuity and coherency – are 'excessively obvious' (Elsaesser 2009: 37), *complex plots*, according to the Aristotelian tradition, are

> simple plots with the additional qualities of 'reversal' and 'recognition' . . . Reversal and recognition introduce a new line of causality into the plot: in addition to the actions and events motivated and caused by characters, there's the plot's additional line of causality that exists over and above the characters. Reversal and recognition are not obviously carried out by characters; they are imposed on the characters and radically alter their destiny. The addition of a second line of causality that introduces reversal and recognition is what, for Aristotle, makes the complex plot complex. (Buckland 2009b: 2)

Buckland's argument for the novelty of the puzzle plot has been disputed by David Bordwell. Downplaying contemporary narrative intricacies as 'part of business as usual', Bordwell sees puzzle films' complications as remaining within the Aristotelian complex paradigm (2006: 73). Moreover, Bordwell and Kristin Thompson have the impression that most puzzle films like '*Inception* might be complicated rather than complex' (2013: 53). In their view, many 'puzzle plots' are kept within the classical confines by a *narrative coherency*, maintaining a balanced representation by countering complexity's cognitive challenges with an adherence to classical norms and unity. Indeed, many of the film narratives that are currently being filed under the header of 'complex' seem to remain fairly classical. As we will examine more closely in the next chapter, most of these films embed their complicating techniques in a highly classical structure, or, in other cases, ultimately integrate their interwoven paths, resolve their gaps or offer solutions for the challenges they pose. In so doing, such films maintain most of the core principles of classical film storytelling, albeit in an intensified manner (see Kiss 2013: 247). Once more, Buckland argues to the contrary, claiming that 'the complexity of puzzle films far exceeds Aristotle's meaning of complex plot' (Buckland 2009b: 1). In Elsaesser's words, '[w]hat once was "excessively obvious" must now be "excessively enigmatic"' (Elsaesser 2009: 37). Yet one may wonder whether this applies to all the films filed under the denominator 'puzzle films'. After all, what does 'excessively enigmatic' mean, for instance, in Kar-wai Wong's 2000 *Fa yeung nin wa* (*In the Mood for Love*) or in Tom Tykwer's *Run Lola Run?* It seems to us that Buckland's seminal anthologies group together variously complex movies that do not only use a wide variety of different storytelling *techniques*, but which can also be said to provide significantly dissimilar *experiences*. One can easily argue that films such as Lynch's *Lost Highway*, Ye Lou's *Suzhou he* (*Suzhou River*) (2000), Stephen Daldry's *The Hours* (2002), Chan-wook Park's *Oldboy* or Kar-wai Wong's *2046* (2004) – to name just a few of the discussed titles – pose completely different cognitive (and hermeneutic) challenges. Our view, which leans towards Bordwell's standpoint, is that the complexity that Buckland claims to his puzzle film definition seems to be too permissive; the *excess* of complexity that should characterise and define the specificity of 'puzzle plot' is not always present in the films discussed. For example, against their own claim that contemporary puzzle plots should be distinguished from the Aristotelian notion of complexity, Buckland's anthologies incorporate some fairly common and rather Aristotelian reversal and recognition-based cases – see, for example, Eleftheria Thanouli on *Oldboy* (Thanouli 2009b) or Daniel Barratt on *The Sixth Sense* (Barratt 2009). These films show little to no baffling or pervasive story complexity, especially when compared to David Lynch's or Charlie Kaufman's significantly more 'puzzling' films. As we will argue in the following chapter, our understanding of a film being a complex puzzle is stricter and sharper than that of Buckland's heterogeneous group. Moreover, we also mark out different gradations of complexity within the 'complex' or 'puzzle film' category, which will lead us to our discussion of the subset that we will call 'impossible puzzle films'. It is by taking a narrower definition of 'complexity' that we aim to ensure that the term remains analytically meaningful in relation to film narratives.

At this point we would like to make clear that given the particular interest and analytical angle of this book, we will refrain from partaking in the more general discussion about the usefulness of distinguishing between labels like *classical* (Bordwell et al. 1985), *post-classical* (Wyatt 1994; Thanouli 2006, 2009a) or even *post-post-classical cinema* (Elsaesser and Buckland 2002). In this book, we will not aim to tie – at least not in terms of their definitions – already precarious terms like *simple, complex* or *puzzle* narratives to these highly debated categories of different *classical narrative modes*. While many would see the contemporary trend of complex films as part of – and actually an argument for asserting – (post-)post-classical developments, one could also take Bordwell's moderate position, and see today's formal-structural complexification as *narrative variations* on classical principles, or as part of cinema's more general 'stylistic intensification' (Bordwell 2002b).[9] According to this cautious view, many of the variously complex films' *formal-narrative intensifications* do *not* reject classical storytelling aims and standards, but offer playful or challenging variations on them. We will in fact argue that most contemporary complex narratives are in some ways dependent on principles and conventions of classical film narration. As we will later see (particularly in Chapter 5), even the most confusingly complex films often still rely on classical narrative elements to mobilise familiar viewing routines and retain immersion and engagement.[10]

All in all, we may agree that formal-narrative complexification – as a trend or tendency, rather than as an altogether new narrative mode – might not amount to a sea change that washes away deeply cemented modes of classical filmmaking and film viewing. However, we are also confident in registering that the palpable trend causes more than a tiny ripple, and, in many cases, can be said to encompass significant deviations from traditional forms of classical narrative film viewing. This is certainly the case for the specific subset of complex movies on which this book is focusing – what we have called

---

[9] In his seminal paper Bordwell writes about the visual style that characterises mainstream cinema at the turn of the millennium. He defines intensified continuity as a new style within the mainstream that amounts to an intensification of existing techniques: 'Intensified continuity is traditional continuity amped up, raised to a higher pitch of emphasis' (Bordwell 2002b: 16). The list of features includes the more rapid editing, the bipolar extremes of lens lengths, the more close-ups in dialogue scenes and the free-ranging camera movement.

[10] Be aware that the disagreement between the views of Bordwell and Elsaesser and Buckland is only of a gradual kind: what for Bordwell is a mere intensification of the ever-prevailing classical values (Bordwell 2002b) is for Elsaesser and Buckland something that already goes beyond the classical paradigm: 'the post-classical is not the non-classical or the anti-classical, but the excessively classical, the "classical-plus"' (Elsaesser and Buckland 2002: 39).

the 'impossible puzzle films' – and for these films' subversive approach to mainstream narration, which seriously challenges classical norms, yet without overthrowing them altogether.

In sum, simple, complex, puzzle or impossible puzzle films can be (and often are) studied and classified by the degree to which they complicate the relationship between their stories and storytelling modes, or through careful narrative and stylistic analyses that can lead to arguments for their interrelation in terms of classical and (post-)post-classical modes of representation. However, in this book, rather than focusing on such formal typologies, we will only reconceptualise them, aiming to primarily address variously complex films in terms of fundamental differences in the *viewing experiences* they offer. Our particular attention to cinematic 'cognitive poetics' will lead us to an alternative classification that will be able to account for the diverse kinds and degrees of complexity across various films. Such a cognitive approach will also allow us to identify a specific set of highly complex popular films that have so far remained untheorised, which we will call 'impossible puzzle films'. In the next chapter we embark on this endeavour, introducing the cognitive approach as an alternative and productive method for explaining the challenges and pleasures that complex films pose in the viewing experience.

CHAPTER 2

Cognitive Approach to Contemporary Complex Cinema

The word 'puzzle' is probably derived from the Middle English word *poselet*,
meaning 'bewildered, confused'.

Marcel Danesi (2002: 27)

*A colourful, many-layered, copy-pasted composite image shows jolly couples doing the jitterbug
dance. Cheering sounds replace the upbeat music, and the overexposed face of a smiling blonde
woman (Naomi Watts) is superimposed on the scene. Suddenly all the fun stops. We are in
a dark room and our blurry point of view, underscored by someone's heavy breathing, slowly
sinks into a red pillow . . . Following the film's credits, a violent scene unfolds: while being
driven up Los Angeles' Mulholland Drive at night, a young dark-haired woman (Laura
Harring) is threatened by two men with a gun. Before they can kill her, another car crashes
into their limousine, leaving the men dead and the woman in shock and suffering from
amnesia. Going down into the city, she finds refuge in a vacant apartment. An aspiring
blonde actress, Betty Elms (Naomi Watts), arrives at the same apartment and discovers
the stranger. The confused woman calls herself 'Rita', although she quickly admits to Betty
that she is unable to remember her real name. She can also not account for a large quantity
of cash and a mysterious blue key that they find in her handbag. Plunging into the city, the
two women embark on a sinister quest to find Rita's identity and story. Through its many
sub-plots that saturate the events of the search, the film dives into the shadowy abyss of LA,
including an absurd film casting, a clumsy hitman, a mysterious cowboy and a terrifying
dark creature behind a restaurant. First these scenes seem unrelated – excesses in Lynch's
trademark offbeat style – however they all gradually become pieces of the puzzle in Betty
and Rita's joint exploration. It turns out that Betty's casting success is barred by the mob's
predestined choice of Camilla Rhodes (Melissa George), the hitman is actually looking for
'the brunette' Rita, the cowboy is connected to one Diane Selwyn about whom Rita suddenly
remembers and the creature is . . . well, he is most probably an utterly destitute homeless man
lurking behind Winkie's snack bar. When Betty and Rita visit Diane Selwyn's apartment,
they find only a woman's decaying corpse, lying on the bed. The same evening, Betty and Rita
sleep together and attend an eerie performance at the Club Silencio. Shaken by the powerful
performance, Betty reaches for a tissue but finds a small blue box in her bag. Back home they
search for Rita's key, but before they can open the box, Betty disappears. Rita finds the key
and fits it into the lock on the box, and, as the camera zooms into it, the opened box falls on*

the floor. . . . A loud knock on a door wakes up Diane Selwyn (also Naomi Watts). She is a failed and miserable wannabe actress, living in the shadow of her former lover, star Camilla Rhodes (this time Laura Harring). The urgent knock came from her neighbour, who has come over to pick up her belongings, except for a blue key that remains on Diane's table. Living alone and depressed, Diane is tormented by hallucinations of painful memories of the past, specifically about a party at Mulholland Drive where Camilla mocked her cruelly, kissing another girl (the 'original' Camilla Rhodes played by Melissa George) and announcing her marriage to a film director (who previously failed to cast her Betty-self). Jolting back to reality, we find Diane at Winkie's diner getting served by a waitress called Betty (Missy Crider). She is negotiating with a shady hitman about killing Camilla. As she hands over a large quantity of cash, the hitman promises Betty that she will receive a blue key as a sign of Camilla's death. Back at her apartment, the key is on the table; the guilt-stricken and mentally broken Diane runs to her bed, reaches for a gun and shoots herself . . . An overexposed image of the smiling Betty and Rita is superimposed on the city of dreams. *The soundtrack ends while a woman at the club softly whispers 'silencio'.*

If we were to attempt to illustrate the confusing effects of excessive complexity in storytelling, it would be hard to find a better (and more discussed) example than David Lynch's *Mulholland Drive*. How to find someone's identity in a story that repeatedly changes its characters' integrity? How to tease out the film's various strands when their exact relationship remains underdetermined and if the events presented are cyclically repetitive, interlocked and sometimes contradictory? How (and why) should we distinguish dreams and fantasies from reality? In this book, we do not promise or aim to untangle exceedingly intertwined plots, and nor do we provide any revealing, foolproof solutions – there are more than enough analytical and interpretive attempts out there.[1] What we are interested in, rather, are the dazzling narrative games that such films play with us, their baffled viewers, through subverting the standard building blocks of the story.

Having briefly contextualised the contemporary trend of complexification in film storytelling and the way in which it encourages viewer activity, this chapter introduces an approach through which we can study the *experiential effects* of formal narrative complexity. Although we build on historical, technological, industrial-economical, media-archaeological and socio-cultural perspectives of narrative complexification, we will not seek to address these backgrounds of the general shifts that result in *pensive, possessive, forensic* and other empowered modes of viewership; rather, we aim to learn more about

---

[1] Among the better ones is Matthew Campora's overview, highlighting three possible options when reading *Mulholland Drive* as 'fragmented, subjective realist', 'supernatural' or even 'surrealist or trance film' (Campora 2014: 78–84, 84–8, 75–8).

the psychology of viewing experiences underlying the trend of narrative complexification.

Turning the emotional and philosophical riddles of art-cinema narratives (Holland 1963) into cognitive-hermeneutic 'mind games' (Elsaesser 2009), contemporary complex films arguably restore the original meaning and function of puzzles. According to puzzle historian Marcel Danesi (2002), puzzles on the whole are brainteasers that resonate with the deep-seated human 'puzzle instinct' – a universal 'disposition' that is best understood as part of a general and inherent need for sense-making. If we see complex films as puzzles that problematise or test viewers' sense- and meaning-making processes, then the (embodied-)cognitive approach, which describes human cognition as a problem-solving activity (Eysenck and Keane 2005: 1), seems to offer a particularly suitable mode to study their mental challenges. Embodied-cognitive theory aims to explain and describe the ways in which we make sense of and interact with our environment, whether with everyday real life or with mediated fiction. Films work through a tacit dependence on viewers' cognitive abilities and dispositions (perception, emotions, comprehension, memory), as well as on knowledge and routines that most viewers share (for example, conventions, narrative schemas, real-world knowledge). Narrative complexity, we contend, can be understood as emerging from this relation. It is first and foremost a *viewing effect* – a 'cognitive puzzlement' that occurs when a film obstructs or suspends its viewer's construction or comprehension of the story. In this book, we aim to understand and describe experiences of narrative complexity from this perspective: as emerging between the formal make-up of a narrative artwork and the activities of a 'model' viewer.[2] Cognitive theory provides theoretical vocabulary, models and empirical evidence to understand what kinds of processes and knowledge structures actual viewers use when making sense of narratives. We will build on these findings, models and concepts to advance a 'cognitive poetics' (see, for instance, Stockwell 2002; Tsur 2008) of narrative complexity, the goal of which is to provide an insight into how formal features of an artwork are able to evoke psychological and aesthetic effects.

---

[2] In our conceptualisation of this 'model spectator', we aim to pursue primarily the universal and shared operations relevant to most viewers' narrative sense-making. We thus attempt to focus on the cognitive processes that underlie or precede individual beliefs, competences or interpretive stances. In terms of acculturation, however, we assume a viewer who holds a worldview that is more or less in line with the scientific worldview of modern Western culture, and who is also familiar with the basic conventions of film and audiovisual storytelling (since the films that we discuss arguably also assume and address viewers educated in and familiar with mediated audiovisual environments and narratives). It should be noted that for the sake of elementariness, this model spectator is for now not gendered.

Contemporary cinematic complexity can be understood as a narrative instrument aiming to provide a cognitive playground. As the example of *Mulholland Drive* illustrates, complex films use various narrative techniques to entertain our 'cognitive surplus' (Shirky 2010) – from achronological temporalities to impossible spaces, and from unreliable and contradictory narration to convoluted metaleptic structures of stories embedded in stories. There are also significant differences in the *degrees* to which these techniques are implemented in diversely complex narratives. This can range from a single, diegetically motivated technique in an otherwise classical narrative embedding (such as the black hole story logic of *Interstellar*) to more radical and disconcerting narrative structures (as in *Mulholland Drive*). How, then, might one establish any unity, or at least create conceptual clarity, across the considerable corpus of variously complex films? In this book, rather than just focusing on the various formal features of different films, we will also investigate how films use narratively complex techniques to create a range of different *viewing effects*. By emphasising viewers and viewing experiences, we argue that the heart of complexity does not lie in intricate narrative structures by themselves, but in the *felt experience and cognitive effect* that such compositional disruptions can create.

This chapter outlines our cognitive approach to narrative complexity in three sections. First, section 2.1 introduces and elucidates the embodied-cognitive framework. Readers who are already familiar with the embodied-cognitive theory and its contribution to study of the narrative arts can consider simply glancing over this part, or skipping directly to 2.2. There we utilise the delineated cognitive approach, enumerating the different storytelling features of complex film narratives and theorising how these features work against viewers' cognitive processes and routines. This section thus connects the formal and the experiential dimensions, aiming to get a grip on how various formal devices make up the 'ingredients' of complex narrative viewing experiences. Finally, in section 2.3, we return to the issue of 'classifying' different complex films (as also discussed in 1.3). Here we argue that a cognitive approach can help to create more clarity and precision across the somewhat muddled category of 'complex' films. We suggest a primarily experiential – rather than strictly formal – approach which differentiates movies with regard to their relative complexity and different viewing experiences. This ultimately also brings us to the so far theoretically untouched category of what we call 'impossible puzzle films', a specific subset of contemporary complex films that offer pervasive, highly confusing experiences of complexity. These will be the focal point of this study on cinematic narrative complexity. But first, let us begin by providing a general introduction to the cognitive approach and its embodied extension, proposing it as a suitable and advantageous framework to assess the experiences and effects of complex cinema.

2.1 WHY AN (EMBODIED-)COGNITIVE APPROACH?

With a technical and aesthetic capacity of strong simulation, films create diegetic worlds that, in their spatial and temporal suggestion, seem analogous to our everyday reality. Cinematic realism's illusion of reality, which manifests in near-tangible experiences, makes viewers forget that films are nothing else but rays of light and patterns of shadows (or dense digital pixels) on a flat and lifeless screen. In a similar way to music, film has no materiality, at least not on its primary level of experience. Viewers watch and hear cinematic illusions with their eyes and ears, but experience them with their bodies and minds. Films may confuse us, scare us or make us laugh. Such emotional and cognitive states are products of the combination of our own involuntary and conscious activities, facilitated by the amalgam of our universally shared, socially acquired and individually shaped experience. To put it simply, by paraphrasing the title of Joseph D. Anderson's (1998) ground-breaking contribution to the field, the cognitive approach exchanges the traditional look at *movies as illusions of reality* for an attempt to come to terms with the *reality of the cinematic illusion*. On the other hand, films should not just be characterised as illusions, or at least immersed viewers do not perceive and experience them as such.[3] In Torben Grodal's thought-provoking words, '*film does not possess a semblance of reality*; it is not an illusion, as has been claimed by numerous film scholars and critics; on the contrary, *film is part of reality*' (Grodal 2009: 10). In fact, Grodal's ecological-evolutionary view turns inside out the traditional Coleridgean demand that characterises one's engagement with fiction, reconsidering the long-established idea of 'suspension of disbelief' (Coleridge 1975 [1817]: 169) as a 'suspension of belief' (Grodal 2009: 154). According to this view, since our primary disposition is tied to reality perception ('seeing is believing'), and cinema, by presenting reality-like moving images, builds on this disposition, the extra effort that viewers need to make is not suspending their disbelief, but rather suspending their belief in order to treat films as not being part of their actual reality. Hannah Chapelle Wojciehowski and Vittorio Gallese similarly claim that '[t]he aesthetic experience of art works [is] more than a suspension of disbelief, [and] can be thus interpreted as a sort of "liberated embodied simulation"' (Wojciehowski and Gallese 2011: 17).

The cognitive approach to film attempts to deliver explanations about how viewers resonate with cinematic 'illusions', about how they suspend their default reality-beliefs and create meanings out of the combination of

---

[3] Of course a lot depends on how we define and conceptualise illusion. For one, Murray Smith (2011) would argue that even the most immersed viewers still remain aware (however latently) of the illusion of representation.

their spontaneous and conscious reactions to audiovisual stimuli. Its main scientific interest is to investigate how a viewer's perceptual and cognitive system facilitates comprehension and emotion during the viewing of a film. This approach is about understanding the way one experiences and understands movies, analogous to the way one engages with other aspects of the environment. The cognitive study of film aims to offer descriptive models about behaviourism's 'black box' – about the functioning of the mind and other meaning-making faculties. More precisely, it focuses on how viewers' involuntary and rational-practical problem-solving processes shape understanding and interpretation in aesthetic and mediated contexts. The approach is scientific, but not 'scientistic'; a certain science-based rigour is part of the cognitivist method, but it should remain careful to avoid deterministic or reductionist claims. It is not in opposition to cultural and other interpretive approaches; on the contrary, it aims to provide a solid ground for such inquiries. Its *bio-cultural* scope is neither universalist nor cultural-relativist (Grodal 2007; Boyd 2009; Boyd et al. 2010). A bio-cultural approach acknowledges both influences of *nature* (given embodied and cognitive properties) and *nurture* (learned skills and developmental adaptations). It 'stresses both common evolved understandings and our human ability to refine understanding through our evolved capacity to share so much via culture' (Boyd 2009: 253). Moreover, when applied to film studies, the results of any naturalistic, evidence-based inquiries also need to be evaluated and interpreted in light of traditional film-scholarly concepts and expertise. The cognitive-based approach to film can thus be summarised as a science-based mode of observing, describing and interpreting how the relation between artworks and viewers 'works'.

Through its in-depth study of midrange problems, the 'piecemeal theory' of the cognitive approach (Carroll 1988) initiated a general shift of investigative focus within film studies: it directed interest towards viewer activity, while moving away from an exclusive focus on the material aspects of works of art as well as from the 'sweeping' hermeneutic programmes of cultural studies and speculative social-constructivist views that characterised the dominant theoretical tradition of film studies in the 1970s and 1980s. Despite its ambition of changing analytical gears, its mode of inquiry is not a full changeover of approaches but a mere extension of methods. Cognitive approaches advocate a *naturalistic, rational* and sometimes *empirical* study of both the perceptual and the hermeneutic activities of viewers. In describing the novelty of the approach, David Bordwell uses the label *naturalistic* to 'signal the effort to draw on evidence and research frameworks developed in domains of social science: psychology, but also linguistics, anthropology, and neuroscience' (Bordwell 2013: 47). In a rather energetic effort to distinguish

the cognitive perspective from the previous theoretical tradition, Gregory
Currie identifies the approach as a *rational* one.[4] For him 'rationalism names
a movement which values argument and analysis over dogma and rhetoric'
(Currie 2004: 170). As for being *empirical*, in the introduction of their *Cognitive
Media Theory* anthology, Ted Nannicelli and Paul Taberham importantly note
that 'the method by which cognitivists typically analyse and critique hypotheses is *not* empirical testing, but rather "testing" against *experiential* evidence –
in particular, our intuitions – as well as logical reflection' (2014: 16). Indeed, a
cognitive inquiry, even when ultimately geared towards empirical verification,
does not always have to be an empirical study itself. Cognitive studies can
be (and frequently are) theoretical, as theories and models are first needed
to provide the basis for further experiential or experimental verification.
This book too is not an empirical study itself, but in its analytical method
and scholarly attitude, it does aim to be in compliance with the above views,
drawing on and applying findings from cognitive sciences to conceptualise
the processes of viewers' engagement with narrative artworks in a rational
and partially naturalistic manner.

Although it is not incompatible with formalist and structuralist investigation, the cognitive approach also changes the primary, object-oriented
question of the formal-structural mode of study from its 'What is it made
of?' to the more viewer-oriented 'How does it work?'. While formalist and
structuralist analyses describe *fixed and objective* structures in film texts, the
cognitive mode takes a step back and also considers the *flexible and transient*
mental processes that precede and enable formal-narrative viewing and analysis in the first place.

The revised inquiry of the cognitive perspective has consequences not
only for the *mode* of study, but also for the *definition* of the objects studied.
Concerning our primary interest in narrative complexity, the change in
scholarly approach has an effect on the way one looks at both 'narrativity' and
'complexity'. Starting off from the former, in Edward Branigan's cognitively
versed explanation, *narrative* can refer both to the result of storytelling or
comprehension and to the process of perception and construction (Branigan
1992: 3). This view of narrative as a cognitive process, rather than an object
property, has risen to prominence in the study of narrative since the 1980s
in particular. In the words of Branigan, we can consider 'narrative' a way of
perceiving: 'an *attitude* we adopt when confronted by something that is a *representation* of something else' (ibid.: 3), and a cognitive strategy for 'organizing

---

[4] 'Rational' should not be misread as 'conscious', as the cognitive approach is of course
equally interested in the unconscious and cognitively impenetrable aspects of the meaning-
making process.

spatial and temporal data into a cause-effect chain of events with a beginning, middle, and end' (ibid.: 3). As Nitzan Ben Shaul summarises,

> [t]he cognitive psychological approach maintains that popular narrative films engage viewers because they invite them to witness and experience as satis-fying a process akin to that of knowledge construction. Carroll [1985], for example, suggests that beyond the relative ease with which we understand film sounds and images, the narrative spatial and temporal organization of audiovisual stimuli into a cause-effect chain leading to closure appeals to us, because it caters to our cognitive perceptual mode of making the world intelligible through a question-answer process. In his view, narrative films are particularly appealing because, unlike real-life situations, these movies use framing, composition, and editing to raise clear questions and provide upon closure full answers to all of the questions raised, a process that hardly gets satisfied in real life. (Ben Shaul 2012: 20)

If we follow this understanding, then *complex* film narratives appear as audio-visual stimuli that pose a challenge to this default viewer activity of moulding experiences and information into an intelligible form. Complex films hinder viewers in their routine of constructing a coherent and determinate causal chain of events (as one is likely to experience when watching *Mulholland Drive*). Hence, when we suggest defining complexity as a *felt experience*, we mean a confusion that follows when a story seems to block or problematise (in whatever way) our mental construction of it, or at least demands from us significantly more cognitive effort than usual to make sense of it. Moreover, as we will see, this reception-oriented reconceptualisation allows us to estab-lish some conceptual clarity among different types of complex films.

In short, narrative complexity is not just an abstract structure or object property that has to be mapped by narratological description, but also a very experiential effect resulting from viewers' engagement with a narrative work of art. Complexity therefore should be understood as an effect arising from cognitive activities – or, rather, the obstruction thereof. If human cognition is a problem-solving activity, then the required amount of invested cognitive effort is approximately proportional to the degree of the given situation's – evoked and felt – complexity. Of course, complexity can in this sense also be the result of many different factors beyond story comprehension. Again, we do not intend to privilege narrativity as the only constituent of complex expe-riences (to some degree, narrative can be seen as an organisational cognitive tool that serves to *reduce* the complexity of our everyday lives), but, as recent film history has shown, narrative complexity forms a particularly popular and effective way of complicating the viewing experience.

The *embodied* extension of the cognitive approach has become one of the most significant additions of the 'second generation' (Lakoff and Johnson

1999) of cognitive sciences. By challenging early computational and disembodied views of first-generation *cognitivism*, the embodied approach acknowledged and scrutinised the human body's and the lived environment's formative role in cognition. Second-generation cognitive sciences have shifted attention towards what have been called 'E approaches' to cognition. These approaches understand cognition as *embodied* (working on and in the organism as a bodily being); informed by *emotion* (rather than merely propositional or linguistic; abstract knowledge structures, for instance); *ecological* (placing understanding in a natural evolutionary context); *embedded* (an environment co-shapes and constitutes cognition); *engaged* (acting in an environment occurs intentionally, guided by specific affordances); *extended* (cognitive processing might be literally extended into the environment); *emergent* (cognition emerges from dynamic interactions between brain, body and environment); and *enactive* (cognisers make their idiosyncratic worlds as a result of the activities afforded by their specific bodies and particular environmental constraints).[5]

In essence, the current generation of cognitive sciences thus asserts that our minds are *embodied*, and that our bodies are *situated*. Let us first explain what these claims mean in general and, consequently, what they entail for a cognitive approach to film and narrative specifically.

Firstly, our brain is *embodied* in the sense that cognition depends upon experiences of a body with specific physiological characteristics and sensory-motor capacities. Differences in bodies and sensory-motor capacities result in different perceptual systems, which ultimately lead to different cognitions. As Warren Buckland aptly summarises Thomas A. Sebeok's (1994) theory of the biosemiotic self: '[d]ue to the variation in the biological make-up of each species, it is plausible to argue that different species live in different sensory worlds' (Buckland 2003: 95). In embodied cognition, *proprioception* describes one's feeling and understanding of one's own specific, bodily determined existence, allowing for grasping basic spatial relations (like 'back-front', 'centre-periphery', 'part-whole', 'inside-outside' and so on). Second-generation approaches have drawn links between what they called these basic 'embodied image schemata' and the formation of higher-order abstract concepts in human language and thinking. As Mark Johnson notes, basic 'image-schematic structures of meaning . . . can be transformed, extended, and elaborated into domains of meaning that are not strictly tied to the body' (Johnson 1987: 44–5). As we will soon see, this claim also holds relevance with regard to narrative.

Our embodied brain is also fundamentally *situated*; as we do not live in a

---

[5] For an overview of 'E approaches' see Daniel D. Hutto and Patrick McGivern's 'How Embodied Is Cognition?' (2014).

vacuum, our surrounding space is vital to cognition, assigning reason and meaning to our proprioceptive awareness in terms of our personal dimensions, movements and possible actions. The term 'exteroception' refers to one's awareness of one's own environmental situatedness, which is a bodily understanding of the actual environment's physical limitations, allowing for understanding elementary spatial affordances (such as 'up-down', 'links', 'paths', 'forces' and so on). This exteroceptive extension of the embodied mind has given rise to an understanding of cognition as 'enacted' (Thompson 2010: 13–15) through a mind fundamentally embedded in an environment that offers concrete affordances and stimuli.

According to Vittorio Gallese and Michele Guerra, there are '*at least* three types of embodiment related to cinema: i) film style as embodiment; ii) acting style as embodiment; iii) viewer's responses to filmed bodies and objects as embodiment' (Gallese and Guerra 2012: 206 – our emphasis). Beyond the more plausible and well-researched bodily resonation with acting agents that results in simulated identification with fictional characters,[6] there are also less apparent, often pre-conscious engagements through which one can make embodied contact with cinematic stimuli. In our contribution (Kiss 2015) to Maarten Coëgnarts and Peter Kravanja's anthology on the cinematic impact of the embodied cognition thesis (Coëgnarts and Kravanja 2015a), we added a fourth type to the possible co-operations: by exposing the relation between narrative form and embodied cognition, we have been specifically interested in answering Richard Menary's vital question of 'how the thoughts, feelings, and perceptions of the minimal embodied and ecologically embedded self give rise to narratives' (Menary 2008: 75). We based our argument on the so-called *image schemas*, on the kind of bodily rooted dynamic patterns that internally organise our experience and on their influential role in the initiation and maintenance of *narrative schemas*, as formal gestalts through which one gains comprehensive access to different forms of (film) narratives.

Continuous motoric and bodily interactions with the environment result in a certain regularity within one's perception. Such recurring world-explorations assemble into predictable patterns, even at an early age, and thus create a sense of coherence and structure. Habitualised bodily interactions

---

[6] The theory of viewers' bodily resonation with onscreen characters is based on the neuro-scientific evidence for a particular class of 'mirror' neurons (first discovered in the pre-motor cortex of the macaque monkey). 'Mirror neurons are premotor neurons that fire both when an action is executed and when it is observed being performed by someone else (Gallese et al. 1996; Rizzolatti et al. 1996) . . . The same motor neuron that fires when the monkey grasps a peanut is also activated when the monkey observes another individual performing the same action' (Gallese 2009: 520). In essence: '[a]ction observation causes in the observer the automatic activation of the same neural mechanism triggered by action execution' (ibid.: 520).

reinforce this sense of coherence and structure, and give rise to clustered knowledge frameworks of mental schemas. By building on available (originally rather disembodied and propositional) psychological theories of *schemas* (Bartlett 1932; Rumelhart 1975), *frames* (Minsky 1975) and *scripts* (Schank and Abelson 1977), cognitive linguist George Lakoff and philosopher Mark Johnson have coined the term *kinaesthetic image schemas* (Lakoff 1987: 271–5), or simply *image schemas* (Johnson 1990 [1987]). Following Johnson's (1990: 23) guideline, we use the terms *schema, embodied schema, image schema* and *kinaesthetic image schema* interchangeably. Proprioceptive (the feelings of one's own body) and exteroceptive (the kinetic affordances that the body allows in the physical environment) explorations mentally solidify as CONTAINER, SOURCE-PATH-GOAL, LINK, FORCE, BALANCE, UP-DOWN, FRONT-BACK, PART-WHOLE and CENTRE-PERIPHERY image schema constructions. In the bodily determined human mind, these skeletal structures function as top-down governing filters for one's perception, and as primary organisational frames for comprehension.

Additionally, invoking Johnson's renowned phrasing, 'image-schematic structures of meaning . . . can be transformed, extended, and elaborated into domains of meaning that are not strictly tied to the body' (Johnson 1990: 44–5). In this book, we contend that the same holds with regard to narrative. This means, we argue, that elementary embodied image schemas are *blended* (Fauconnier and Turner 2002), *binded* (Lakoff and Johnson 2003) or *transfigured* (Spolsky 2007) into narrative schemas.[7] As a next step, these narrative schemas may turn into higher-order, conventional story schemas, such as those described by Algirdas Julien Greimas' Proppian *canonical narrative schema* (1966), Jean Mandler's *story schema* (1984), Jerome Bruner's notion of *narrative structures* (1987) or Edward Branigan's understanding of *narrative schemas* as recurring arrangements of knowledge in films (1992: 1–32). The following sketch (Figure 2.1), borrowed from our previous discussion of the process (Kiss 2015: 54), outlines the hierarchy between elementary formal schemas and higher-order story schemas, as well as the development from the former to the latter.

How can this embodied extension of cognitive theory be a useful approach in describing the effects of complex film narratives? If one's comprehension of various narrative forms and stimuli is based on a top-down governance of bodily rooted image schemas, then narrative complexity can be understood as a hindrance of this nexus. A strategic, formal-structural complexification can problematise one's reliance on image schemas as primary organisational

---

[7] For a detailed description of the correspondence between image schemas and narrative schemas, see Kiss 2015.

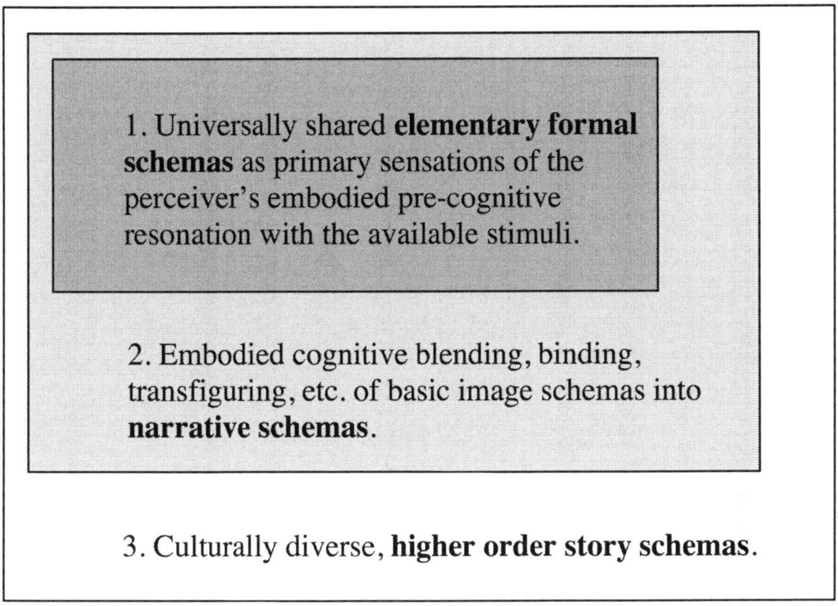

Figure 2.1

frames. If '[a]n image schema is a recurring dynamic pattern of our perceptual interactions and motor programs that gives coherence and structure to our experience' (Johnson 1990: xiv), then formally and structurally complex film narratives threaten this coherence by thwarting viewers' ingrained dependence on these deep-seated schemas. Radically complex story structures may not only interfere with our use of higher-order, memorised and conventionalised story schemas (level 3 in Figure 2.1), but can also problematise our reliance on more fundamental narrative building blocks (level 2) and habitualised patterns of elementary bodily experiences (level 1) on which these narrative schemas are modelled by origin. In this sense, narrative complexification can be achieved through, for example, formal or diegetic over-complication (testing our PART-WHOLE schema through shattered plot structures), in ontological ambiguation (challenging the CONTAINER schema by metaleptic structures transgressing the boundaries of stories within stories) or through narrative strategies that dismantle chronology or disrupt causality (which problematise our reliance on the SOURCE-PATH-GOAL schema, such as in non-linear or forking-path stories). As some of our earlier analyses argued, intensely embedded *and* metaleptic stories, like Christopher Nolan's *Inception*, can intensify and actually play with one's reliance on the CONTAINER schema (Kiss 2012); or confusingly warped causality, like in Christopher Smith's endlessly looped *Triangle*, may challenge the governing value of our SOURCE-PATH-GOAL schema

(Kiss 2013). This embodied-cognitive approach to narrative structures will be particularly useful at the end of Chapter 3 (section 3.5), where we describe the confusing effect of intense complexification as a deliberate disruption of our elementary schematic tools of sense-making.

In light of the theoretical insights of cognitive approaches, we will argue that complex films of one sort or another are better defined as varyingly difficult cinematic experiences. Different types of films can complicate the reliance on different cognitive faculties and skills. If *protocognitivist* film philosopher and psychologist Hugo Münsterberg was right in claiming that the cinematic 'photoplay' is 'designed to facilitate the exercise of our faculties' (Bordwell 2009: 357), then complex film narratives not only facilitate such exercises, but push them to their limits. As a result of their overt and salient formal-structural experimentations, complex films can be easily studied and subsequently classified as variations of playful textual constructions; yet in order to fully appreciate their core function we need to understand and describe the puzzling effects they exert on the experiences of engaged and active viewers. The embodied-cognitive approach does not only examine the processes underlying viewers' experience of puzzlement, but can also explain the coping and rationalising mechanisms by which viewers tolerate and handle such psychological confusion. This is particularly pertinent, as complex movies' perplexing mediated strategies play (and prey) precisely on perceptual capabilities and embodied-cognitive processing habits that viewers utilise in their general real-life meaning-making exploration, as well as on acquired and conventionalised interpretive viewing competences they pick up through their media socialisation. These embodied-cognitive and accultured dimensions are not in opposition, but exist on a continuum which allows for their interaction, as human experience is fundamentally shaped by the higher-order cognitive patterns through which we engage with the world. This view thus acknowledges that there are variable degrees of 'competence' in viewers: individual viewers possess various degrees of acculturation as well as different cognitive capacities to deal with a given story's complexity. As a result, fixed and 'objective' boundaries of complexity cannot be made: after all, whereas one viewer may experience a film to be highly complex, another might have the interpretive tools, literacy and experience to swiftly make meaning of the story. However, such variations of *handling* the experience do not imply that one cannot make useful generalisations as to how different storytelling experimentations can *challenge* viewers' sense-making. Focusing on the latter, the various categories that we propose below aim at corresponding to the various degrees to which contemporary complex films undermine traditional narrative film viewing and comprehension.

Lastly, the embodied-cognitive inquiry is advantageous not only in revealing the processes behind the viewing of complex films, but (as a consequence) also in reassessing the findings of more traditional formal-ist-structuralist analyses. In the following two sections, we invoke the embodied-cognitive method in order to catalogue different types of 'general' complexifying strategies that films use, and provide alternative, reconceptu-alised categories that will emerge by sorting out the different cognitive effects of various complexities. Thus, in the next section we move onto our *cognitively informed approach to complexity*, where complexity's measure is its effect on viewers' narrative sense- and meaning-making processes, which will lead us to a *reassessment of complex cinema's traditional categorisations* in section 2.3.

2.2 VARIOUS FORMS OF COMPLEXITY AND THEIR EFFECTS ON SENSE-MAKING

For a simple but clear conception of viewers' *meaning-making processes*, we follow David Bordwell's four-tier definition of cinematic meanings. In his book entitled *Making Meaning*, Bordwell (1991: 8–9) distinguishes four types of meaning: *referential* meanings stand for viewers' spatio-temporal world-constructions; *explicit* meanings are directly expressed 'points' of the story (Bordwell's example is Dorothy's famous line 'there is no place like home' at the end of Victor Fleming's 1939 *The Wizard of Oz*); *implicit* meanings can be associated with 'themes' or 'issues' that can be construed by viewers' indirect or symbolic readings (the book's example is Hitchcock's *Psycho*, in which one of the implicit meanings could be that 'sanity and madness cannot be easily distinguished' (1991: 9)); finally, *repressed* or *symptomatic* meanings are assigned by the viewer to the film beyond those that are supposed to be intended and expressed referentially, explicitly and/or implicitly ('*Psycho* as a worked-over version of a fantasy of Hitchcock's' (ibid.: 9)). While in traditional mainstream cinema's classical narration *referential* and *explicit* meanings tend to be concrete and unambiguous, and hence part of viewers' basic comprehension, *implicit*, and most of all *symptomatic* meanings are less exact or universally shared and thus prone to interpretive differences. These latter types of meanings are most sensitive to the specific individual and socio-cultural background and horizon of interpretations that a given viewer brings in. It is easy to agree with Brad Chisholm's conclusion, according to which viewers, in general, 'will largely agree about the referential meanings, will agree less about the explicit mean-ings, and so on' (Chisholm 1991: 395). However, he goes on to argue that '[i]n difficult texts . . . merely grasping the preferred referential meaning can be a struggle' (ibid.: 395). Chisholm's lucid reasoning further highlights the ambition of most of the contemporary puzzle films: these films often hinder meaning-making *already* on the lower, explicit and referential levels, while the function of Norman N. Holland's puzzling art movies is to provide ambiguities on the higher, implicit and symptomatic, levels of meaning. We will come back to this idea in Chapter 5, when we examine this distinction between contemporary complex and modernist art-cinema puzzles more closely.

As for playing with viewers' comprehension efforts already on the lower, explicit and referential levels of meaning, the following typology is an inventory of different formal strategies that are in use to create narrative complexity in contemporary cinema. To provide a backbone for our further investigation, we connect these to corresponding cognitive operations. As noted, we will understand 'complexity' as a reception effect that follows from a viewer's (temporary or ongoing) inability to coherently integrate the narrative information into a causal, chronologic and determinate structure of events and other explicit and referential meanings.

2.2.1 Problematising narrative linearity

First (and, in terms of prominence in narrative experimentation, perhaps also foremost), films may play with temporal structures to *suspend or problematise narrative linearity*. Whether occurring through a *dismantling of chronology* or a *disruption of causality*, such strategies will often require a heightened concentration from viewers, as well as retrospective reading and mental reorganisation to overcome their cognitive puzzlement.

Dismantled chronology concerns the arrangements of plot events in a non-chronological order. Whether deceptively integrated in the narration or more explicitly marked, this strategy calls for a conscious temporal rearrangement on behalf of the viewer. Manipulations of the time structure force viewers to piece together the film's narrative – as happens, for example, when viewing the seemingly randomly shuffled plot segments of Tarantino's *Pulp Fiction*. Of course, achronological story presentation is widely used in mainstream cinema, and will remain relatively unproblematic most of the time. Techniques like flashbacks and flash forwards feature regularly in classical narrative plots, as their temporal disruptions do not endanger viewers' cognitive and hermeneutic work; on the contrary, when clearly signposted, they may even support their efforts. After all, in classical narratives, chronology is often subordinated to narrative logic; what should be shown first for the sake of the story trumps the chronological order of events. The 'right order of time' is subservient to the 'right order of events'. As Mieke Bal puts it, '[p]laying with sequential ordering is not just a literary convention; it is also a means of drawing attention to certain things, to emphasise, to bring about aesthetic or psychological effects' (Bal 1997 [1985]: 82). Ecological cognitivist Joseph D. Anderson underlines Bal's hunch about achronology's psychological effect:

> If presenting material out of order makes it more difficult to recall, then why do we do it? Why are stories not always told in chronological order? The reason is, of course, that in some cases stories may create a *more dramatic effect, greater emotional impact* if rearranged. (Anderson 1998: 149 – our emphasis)

These effects range from the most minor and elementary plot manipulations, giving rise to basic changes in viewing attitudes – described by Meir Sternberg (1992) as *curiosity, surprise,* and *suspense* – to more complex narrative experiences. As much as flashbacks (and, less frequently, flash forwards) are common and unproblematic chronological manipulations, more radical dismantlings of the sequential order of events might have serious consequences on the narrative and aesthetic, as well as on the emotional experience. While *Memento's* inverse chronology, for instance, is motivated as providing viewer-identification with the film's anterograde amnesiac protagonist, thus exemplifying the heightened dramatic effect of the achronological narrative, the inversion in Gaspar Noé's *Irréversible* (*Irreversible*, 2002), reversing the temporal order between the film's emotionally loaded scenes, causes greater emotional impact (as seeing a happy couple's terrible future in advance puts their joyful relationship in a completely different emotional perspective).

More radical forms of non-linear temporality, however, can also distance the film experience from its viewer's everyday, ecologically grounded, real-life perception. While the *duration* of time might be a subjective and relative experience, temporal *direction* is universally perceived as a more or less straight and continuous flow on a linear timeline (although, on a more abstract, higher-order scale, cultural conceptions of time can of course also be cyclical or layered). As Torben Grodal points out, 'linearity is not a product of Western metaphysics but it is based on fundamental features of the world, action and consciousness. An experiential flow – unless totally unfocused – is a linear process in time' (Grodal 2009: 145). Temporal direction is a universal experience because it is based on humans' proprioceptive bodily existence and exteroceptive engagement with the surrounding environment. It relies on basic bodily rooted image schemas such as the SOURCE-PATH-GOAL schema (when moving from a source, through a path, to a goal), by which we tend to map plots as linear, chronological experiential paths with a certain continuity and teleology (from the beginning, through a middle, to an end). Whereas realism and its classical mimetic narration in film offers scenarios that imitate temporal linearity and thus maintain fundamental schemas of temporal progression and action, extreme achronology disrupts viewers' universal reliance on these intrinsic schemas, and heavily problematises such temporal ordering to hinder habitual comprehensive routines.

Disruption – or at least loosening the close adjacency – *of causality* in story logic is often a consequence of a non-linear chronology (as is the case, for example, in *Memento*). To reconstruct chronological and causal relations, viewers need an intensified reliance on basic cognitive competences such as recollection from memory and mental narrative rearrangement. Non-linearity's challenge to memory plays on the relation between story structure and causal comprehension. As Anderson, paraphrasing Jean M. Mandler (1984: 47), remarks,

> [e]xperimental research indicates, in fact, that as material is presented out of sequential order and one is asked to hold events or ideas in memory for longer periods of time before they are resolved or connected to other events or ideas, one's capacity for recall suffers. (Anderson 1998: 149)

Mental rearrangement is an important problem-solving skill in real-world cognition too, associated with spatial reasoning, cognitive mapping and situation-model updating (for example, Morrow et al. 1989; Zwaan and Madden 2004; Radvansky and Zacks 2011). An appropriation of such real-world competences to viewers' temporal and causal rearranging abilities in mediated experience results in 'mental narrative rearranging skills', which can be described as a mental reorganisation of chunks of story particles (scenes and sequences) on a chronological timeline or causal chain, involving such complex (mnemonic and creative) cognitive tasks as retroactive revision, mental rotation, displacement and restructuring.[8]

However, disrupted causality can also be the primary strategy to create non-linear narrative experiences in itself, as is exemplified by more experimental 'multiple-plot' films like Kar-wai Wong's 1994 *Chung Hing sam lam* (*Chungking Express*) or Tom Tykwer and the Wachowskis' 2012 *Cloud Atlas*. Causality is, after all, mostly a matter of inference-making; establishing causal connection between events is paramount to narrativity. Stories that leave uncertainty or ambiguity over causal connections between events may thus problematise viewers' narrative construction on a fundamental level, leaving them wondering, or attempting to infer, how the presented events might be connected. While Wong's film 'links' its disjointed plots through mere spatial contiguity, *Cloud Atlas* exchanges the traditional event-driven causality of a *single* story for a narrative unity created through thematic coherence and character continuity among *multiple* stories. As we will see in Chapter 5, loosening causality on the level of plot has been one of the key strategies of complexification in the tradition of art cinema (see also Bordwell 1979).

---

[8] On the application of cognitive mapping, situation models and mental rotation to literary and film narratives see, among others, Bjornson 1981; Ghislotti 2009; Kiss 2013; and Coëgnarts et al. 2016 (regarding the relation between real-life skills of orientation and navigation, and cinematic comprehension, section 6.2 will also provide more details).

2.2.2 Complicating narrative structures and ontologies

Somewhat similar to these techniques, which break the linearity of chronological and causal order, there are other strategies that can subvert one's
smooth experience of narrative progression. Modular forking paths (parallel
presentation of two or more separated events splitting from a single 'forking
point'), multiple drafts (subsequent presentation of two or more outcomes
from a single forking point) or a multiplicity of embedded plotlines may go
far in complicating narrative structure. Obfuscating the clarity of their intricate narrative organisations, films with complex story structures might reach
beyond viewers' comprehensive accommodation range. While early modular
forking-path films like Peter Howitt's 1998 *Sliding Doors* or trendsetter multiple-draft narratives such as Tom Tykwer's 1998 *Lola rennt* (*Run Lola Run*)
only carefully experimented with the option and did not really endanger comprehension (see Bordwell 2002a), contemporary complex versions of these
narrative structures became more convoluted, and therefore more cognitively
demanding – see, for example, Jaco van Dormael's 2009 *Mr. Nobody* or Doug
Liman's 2014 *Edge of Tomorrow*, which represent both the more alternative and
the mainstream end of the (post-)classical spectrum.

As for embedded plotlines, the hierarchical separation between 'telling'
and 'told' is as old as the act of storytelling itself. An intensified playfulness with the contained logic of embedded plotlines, however, can cause
unique and perplexingly intricate structures featuring complex, many-layered
hypodiegetic levels of stories within stories (Figure 2.2).[9] Examples can span
from more signposted and sequentially embedded (and thus cognitively
more manageable) structures, like John Brahm's 1946 flashback within a
flashback within a flashback *The Locket*, to less consistently nested (and hence
confusingly subtle) variations, such as Nolan's *The Prestige*.

Moving from strategies that relate to storytelling to complexities that can be
located on the level of the storyworld (that is, in the told), the disruption of a
singular ontological reality in narrative fiction forms another strategy by which
films can complicate viewers' sense-making. Some films present multiple
– interrelated, parallel or contradictory – worlds as different parts of their fictional universe. Building on Janet H. Murray's (1997) seminal work, Matthew
Campora highlights the ontological multiplicity of multiform narratives as a
mode of narrative complexity, which is different from the complications of
multi-strand narratives in storytelling (2014: 27–8). The parallel or conflicting

---

[9] The analytical distinction between embedded narrative levels comes from Gérard
Genette (1980 [1972]). However, the term 'hypodiegetic' was coined by Mieke Bal (1977: 24,
59–85) and was meant to replace Genette's confusingly loaded term of 'metadiegetic'.

EXTRADIEGETIC LEVEL

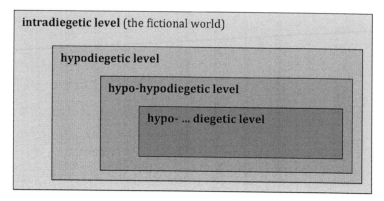

Figure 2.2

realities of multi-layered, multiform possible worlds require the viewer to keep track with two or more simultaneously existing diegetic universes. Such worlds put viewers' comprehension routines to the test not only by pushing the degree of their required working memory use, but also by challenging their habitual worldview, as parallel and malleable reality-scenarios corrupt one of our deepest ontological experiences – the notion of our shared reality's ontological singularity and spatial and chronological rigidity.

Time-travel stories often play with the possibility of *alternative* and *altering* universes. Focusing on their time travellers' subjective linear experiences, however, most of the time such fictions do not present storyworlds that actually *co-exist* (Kiss 2003). While traditional time-travel films – like Don Taylor's 1980 *The Final Countdown* or Robert Zemeckis' *Back to the Future* trilogy (1985; 1989; 1990) – remain within a narrative logic of linearity (and, in case of the latter, only pose a challenging paradox to the viewer by way of a cunning title), complex multi-levelled 'slipstream' fictions – such as John Maybury's 2005 *The Jacket*, Tony Scott's 2006 *Déjà Vu*, Duncan Jones's 2011 *Source Code* or Nolan's 2014 *Interstellar* – present multiple simultaneously existing (often incompatible) worlds within a single diegetic universe. The latter category provides a potentially more confusing experience, taxing both their viewers' mnemonic capacities and fundamental ontological notions about possible worlds.[10] Furthermore, beyond intensified versions of traditional flashbacks

---

[10] 'Slipstream fiction', a term coined by Bruce Sterling in his text for the fanzine *SF Eye* (1989), is more than magic realism, fantasy or science fiction. It is actually not a genre, but rather an effect triggered by our confrontation with a subtle *disruption of a singular ontology*. According to Warren Buckland, '[t]he key to slipstream fiction is that the fictional world is not unified but is formed from two or more incompatible realities, creating a sense of cognitive dissonance' (Buckland 2014b: 6).

or flash forwards' temporal disintegration, *flash sideways* represent an alternative strategy that combines temporal complexification with a diegetic disruption of viewers' default ontological notions of a single actual reality. The final, sixth, season of J. J. Abrams et al.'s television series *Lost* (2004–10) introduced such a narrative technique, presenting events as both alternative *and* co-existing, thereby suggesting two simultaneous timelines that not only run parallel, but also – through characters' mysterious sensations and other déjà vu-like experiences – subtly seep into each other.

Metalepsis is a special case that combines the last two categories of *complicated narrative structures* and *disrupted singular ontological reality* (and through that potentially accumulates the cognitive effects that characterises these). Metalepsis was defined by Gérard Genette as a contamination between embedded narrative levels; in his words 'any intrusion by the extradiegetic narrator or narratee into the diegetic universe (or by diegetic characters into a metadiegetic universe, etc.), or the inverse (as in Cortázar)' (1980: 234–5). One common metaleptic strategy, for instance, occurs when fictional readers or authors (who usually belong to distinct ontological levels) show up in their read or authored fictional storyworld (for the first option see, for example, Cortázar's *Continuity of Parks* – here referred to by Genette, and discussed in our preface). Two distinct types of such level-contaminations must be discerned. As Marie-Laure Ryan has noted, drawing from the work of John Pier, there are the unintended, covertly 'unnatural' level-contaminations that are '*rhetorical* metalepses' and there are deliberate, overtly playful transgressions that are '*ontological* metalepses' (Ryan 2006a: 247); 'the one based primarily in the (rhetorical) effects produced by representation through discourse or other semiotic means, the other in the problems of logical paradox encountered by modern science' (Pier 2011, section 11). Whereas the former relates mostly to an effect in the discourse of a literary narrator, the latter is an effect of the storyworld and can be found in several contemporary complex films (see also Kiss 2012: 36). Therefore, in this book, when we speak of metalepsis, we will be referring to the second, *ontological* kind.

Complex films, like Spike Jonze's 2002 *Adaptation* or Marc Forster's 2006 *Stranger Than Fiction*, feature ontological metalepses (writers appearing in their stories; characters appearing to their writers), and, by entangling the levels of the telling and the told, often run into the kind of logical paradox that John Pier is talking about. In the cases of *Adaptation* and *Stranger Than Fiction*, for example, metalepsis happens by employing characters that are both a writer or character *and* a protagonist of the very same story, which they create themselves, and which is the story that the viewer, in turn, actually witnesses. Presenting puzzling transgressions between conventionally isolated levels, metalepses conflate viewers' real-life categories, but also challenge ingrained experiential models. Metalepses specifically exploit viewers' reliance on their bodily determined CONTAINER schema – the *inside* and *outside* logic that emerges as an awareness of the build-up of their bodies, and regulates the boundary between the subordinated narrative layers in fiction (that is, determining what happens 'inside' or 'outside' a framed story). This elementary logic is challenged by metaleptic effects as a complexifying technique that upsets these boundaries.

Nolan's *Inception* represents a peculiar example within the specific case of metalepsis, as it adapts the narrative idea of level-contamination to its story-world's diegetic logic. The film actually does not offer a 'proper' example of metalepsis, because the transgressions between its levels are neither ontological nor rhetorical, but rather a motivated part of the fictional storyworld (and, in fact, illusory – see Kiss 2012). *Inception* presents a fantastic world in which people can transgress the private thresholds of each other's dreams – a storyworld logic that in fact fictionalises the storytelling logic of metalepsis.[11] This does not mean, however, that this film is not challenging; on the contrary, one could even argue that it is precisely *Inception*'s vague delineation of the nature of its illusory metalepsis that causes the film's ultimate ambiguity. More specifically, what can frustrate viewers' meaning-making efforts is the difficulty in overviewing the story-related consequences of how the film diegetises a narrative idea of metalepsis.[12] Altogether, *Inception* is a prime example of an 'unconventionally conventional' (Bordwell 2012) 'mainstream complexity' (Kiss 2012), with which label we argued for its calculated balance between challenging but cognitively manageable intricacies.

2.2.3 Understimulation and cognitive overload

Diegetic narrative under- and overstimulation can also lead to a variety of puzzling viewing experiences.

---

[11] Such extreme reciprocity between storytelling mode and represented story logic is a recurring drive behind Nolan's cinema. See, for example, his *Memento*, where the narrative inversion is motivated by the protagonist's anterograde amnesia, or *The Prestige*, where magicians' double-crossing rivalry gets mirrored in the film's unreliable and twist-laden storytelling.

[12] Actually, the case is not as simple as can be concluded from the above: 'While in *Inception* the fictionally (thus neither narratively nor ontologically) embedded dream-structure only imitates the metaleptic logic, an additional diegetic law is introduced, which necessarily qualifies the film as a "proper" metaleptic narrative. Both Nolan's, as well as, for example, Ruben's film [Joseph Ruben's 1984 *Dreamscape*] raise the dramatic stakes of the dream-invading idea by creating a rule, which establishes a bi-directional physical and thus body-related contamination among the embedded dream-layers. This simply means that as much as diegetic actions have consequences on the hypodiegetic levels of dreams, dreams also have consequences on the frame story of the diegetic reality' (Kiss 2012: 39).

Diegetic understimulation, on the one hand, is less of a concern for us here, as this storytelling strategy appears mostly in art-cinema narration, and does not lead to the same kind of cognitively complex experience on which we focus. In art films, the main function of understimulating or underdetermined narration is usually to divert the viewers' attention away from the minimal action that these films present and towards the psychological or philosophical registers that underlie the narrative. A quintessential example is Chantal Akerman's 1975 *Jeanne Dielman, 23, quai du Commerce, 1080 Bruxelles* (*Jeanne Dielman, 23 Commerce Quay, 1080 Brussels*). For over three hours, Akerman's film presents only a minimal amount of plot, and within that plot even omits the few key narrative moments. Instead, the film focuses on long stretches of 'temps mort', offering a moment-by-moment and often real-time examination of the life of a single mother and housewife in Brussels, without explicitly determining the salience or point of this narrative approach. Such diegetic understimulation is obviously not the same as the disorienting or deceptively constrained knowledge distribution of unreliable narratives: understimulation does not disorient or mislead viewers, but revokes access to essential story elements and provides an alternative to the traditional narrative experience that is driven by a dense cause-and-effect logic. For example, through slow action or obscured causality, narrative understimulation provides viewers with a different, more perceptual or attentional challenge than the kind of cognitive problem-solving type that characterises contemporary mainstream complex cinema. On this note, we have to disagree with William Brown's conclusion, according to which Nolan's *Inception* would be 'less complex' than Abbas Kiarostami's 2003 *Five Dedicated to Ozu* (Brown 2014). Beyond the fact that Brown's approach (as well as his somewhat fuzzy definition of complexity, borrowed from physics and mathematics) does not help in comparing the differently complex experiences that Nolan's and Kiarostami's cinema evoke, the main problem with his argument is that it mistakes elementary narrative comprehension for perceptual and interpretive domains: it confuses the cognitive effort of narrative comprehension (that is, the construction of referential and explicit narrative meaning) with the variety and richness of simple or complex perceptual and interpretive responses to these films (also involving more implicit and symptomatic meanings), and in conclusion labels *Inception* as a 'simple' and *Five* as a 'complex' film. One can of course argue for such a difference, but then the type of 'complexity' being discussed should be clearly distinguished (for example, narrative, interpretive, emotional or perceptual).

On the other hand, from Howard Hawks' famously entangled 1946 film noir *The Big Sleep*[13] to the gleefully overcomplicated psychedelic neo-noir plot

---

[13] In his book dedicated to the film, David Thomson recalls the curious case: 'at some

of Paul Thomas Anderson's 2014 *Inherent Vice*, movies have also challenged viewers' comprehension through *cognitive overload*. Such 'overstimulating' stories bombard viewers with too many events, too many plotlines, too many characters or too many relations between characters. In his *Screening Modernism*, András Bálint Kovács argues that one of the specificities of the film noir genre is that it has a transitional role between classical and modern art-cinema narration: 'it breaks up classical narrative logic while maintaining classical narrative structures' (Kovács 2007: 246). While modernist art-cinema narration challenges classical logic by decreasing its narratives' causes and effects, (neo-)noir does practically the same from the other extreme, overcomplicating classical cinema's dominant causality – think, for instance, of the intricate storylines in a script like Roman Polanski's 1974 *Chinatown*. Notwithstanding the abundance of examples, diegetic overstimulation is not limited to the noir genre, and can be found throughout platforms and genres. Through, for example, constantly opening up and extending plot trajectories – as in Mark Frost and David Lynch's 1990–1 television series *Twin Peaks* – or by endlessly complicating and exceedingly obscuring the web of character relationships – as is the case in Tomas Alfredson's 2011 *Tinker Tailor Soldier Spy* or Stephen Gaghan's 2005 'hyperlink movie' *Syriana* – overstimulation offers extreme information load in the form of 'overabundance of facts' (Chisholm 1991: 392), resulting in a compl(exif)ication mode that can put viewers' comprehension abilities to the test. Such 'detail overload' (ibid.: 392) can take up most of our available cognitive resources, as it calls for heightened attention and intensifies reliance on both short-term (or working) memory and long-term memory work (Figure 2.3).

Diegetic overstimulation is a technique that can encourage second (or more) viewings. As much as additional viewing may increase comprehension, however, excessive detail overload can also be the intended effect of a particular film that does *not* need to be tackled by multiple concentrated viewings. This can be the case with many art-cinema narratives, some classical film noirs (for instance, according to Roger Ebert, *The Big Sleep* 'is about the process of a criminal investigation, not its results' (Ebert 1997)) and some threshold (post-)classical cases like David Fincher's 2007 *Zodiac*, Anderson's

moment amid the mayhem of *The Big Sleep*, more to make conversation than in search for meaning, Bogart asked who had done one of the killings in the story. No one had the answer, not Hawks nor Jules Furthman, his favoured "on-set" writer. So they asked [screenplay writers] William Faulkner and Leigh Brackett – no dice. Then they called [Raymond] Chandler [the author of the novel] (never far from the production), and he didn't know either' (Thomson 2010: 34).

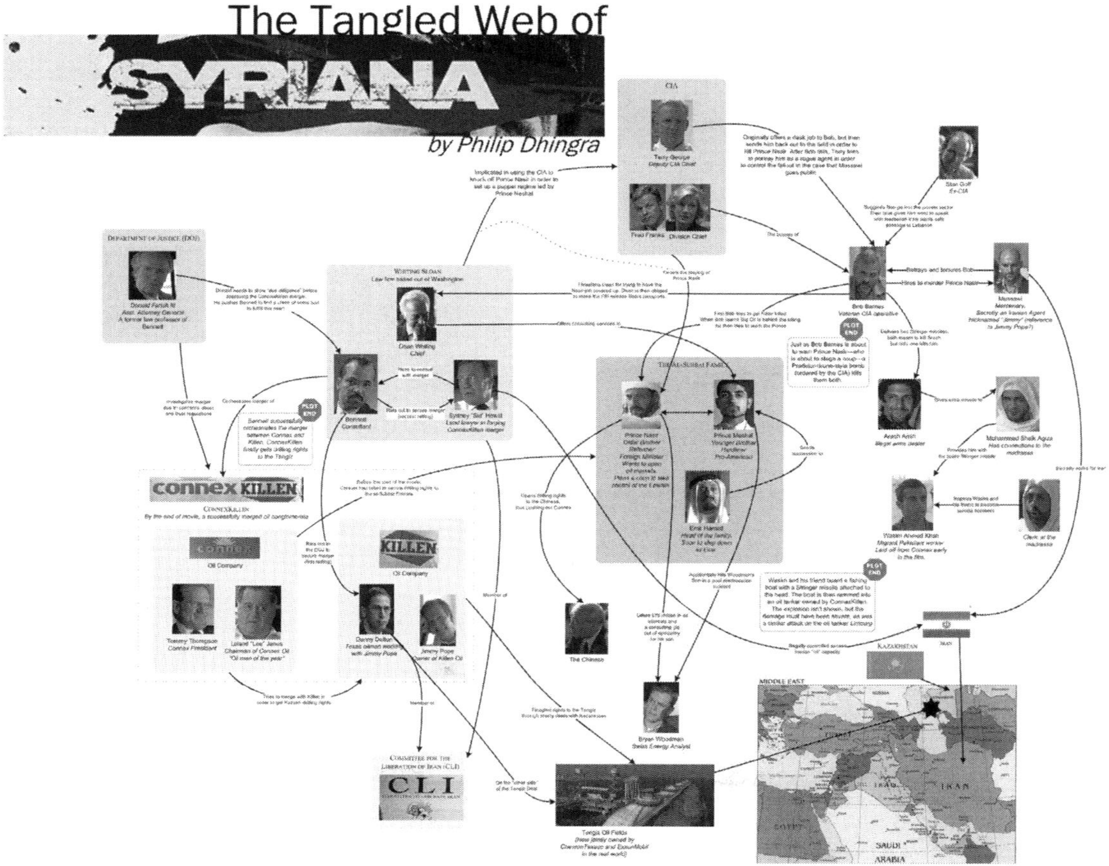
The Tangled Web of
SYRIANA
by Philip Dhingra
CIA
connex KILLEN
KILLEN
CLI
Bob Barnes
Veteran CIA operative
KAZAKHSTAN
MIDDLE EAST
IRAN
SAUDI
ARABIA

Figure 2.3

Inherent Vice or Gaghan's *Syriana*.[14] The latter, depicting the extremely complex (read 'deeply corrupt') case of oil-driven politics in the Middle East through an exceedingly entangled plot, refuses to offer simplified explications; on the contrary, in order to represent the misty intricacies of the global oil business, the film deliberately keeps its intertwined plot knotted. As a result, Gaghan does not only represent complexity, but also creates an experience of it. As Roger Ebert concluded,

> [t]he movie's plot is so complex we're not really supposed to follow it, we're supposed to be surrounded by it . . . I liked the way I experienced the film: I couldn't explain the story, but I never felt lost in it. I understood who, what, when, where and why, but not how they connected. (Ebert 2005)[15]

Pondering the question of how to represent, cope with and, ultimately, explain multi-faceted issues of our complex world, Ien Ang has pleaded for a kind of 'cultural intelligence' that could aim at 'sophisticated and sustainable responses to the world's complex problems' (Ang 2011: 779). If we agree with her on the point that an apt way of representing complexity needs to avoid simplistic solutions that are 'unsustainable or counter-productive' (ibid.: 779), then Gaghan's diegetic overstimulation can be seen as one good example of how to turn abstract ideas like 'complexity' into an uncompromisingly complex cinematic representation and experience.

2.2.4 Contradictions and unreliabilities

Contradictions in a story often form logical insolubilia or paradoxes. For philosopher Nicholas Rescher, a paradox 'arises when a set of individually *plausible* propositions is collectively inconsistent' (Rescher 2001: 6 – our emphasis).[16] Logical contradictions between 'individually plausible but collectively inconsistent' story elements can thus result in paradoxical scenarios, which, by their effect of cognitive dissonance, can block viewers' narrative construal (as it is the case with slipstream fiction's effect – see above). Logical

---

[14] As for the case of *Inherent Vice*, such recognition leads to the next logical question: 'Should Critics See Films More Than Once?' (Gilbey 2015).

[15] Roger Ebert called *Syriana* a hyperlink movie: '[t]he term describes movies in which the characters inhabit separate stories, but we gradually discover how those in one story are connected to those in another' (Ebert 2005).

[16] In her book about novel strategies in resolving paradoxes, Margaret Cuonzo offers an exhaustive overview of different definitions, according to which there are 'three ways of defining *paradox*, namely as (1) *a set of inconsistent statements, in which each statement seems true* (Rescher 2001), (2) *an argument with seemingly good assumptions, seemingly fine reasoning, but an obviously false conclusion* (Mackie 1973), and (3) *an unacceptable conclusion derived from seemingly good premises using seemingly good reasoning* (Sainsbury 2009)' (Cuonzo 2014: 17).

contradictions in narratives can entail confronting reflections for viewers on the habitual ease of their inferential reasoning, and may consequentially lead to a deautomatisation of narrative experience. Paradoxical contradictions in narrative fiction can also heighten the amount of cognitive labour required: paradoxes prompt viewers to revisit their gathered knowledge and, by re-evaluating the individual plausibility of mutually inconsistent propositions, to revise their primary hypotheses. Whereas, according to Bordwell, the primary aim of contradictory clues in art-cinema narration is 'to throw us off balance' (Bordwell 2008: 168 – his example is Agnès Varda's 1985 *Sans toit ni loi* (*Vagabond*)), conflicting information in contemporary mainstream complex cinema might have another, less radical impact in terms of narrative immersion. One of the primary aims of this book is to describe the diverse functions and cognitive effects of irreconcilably contradictory, conflicting, mutually exclusive and 'impossible' story elements (which we will discuss in more detail in Chapter 3), as well as the variety of coping strategies they evoke in different narrative modes (see Chapter 4).

Finally, unreliability – as a narratorial discourse strategy (Shen 2013) that plays with the veracity of the presented information or that cleverly ambiguates potential readings of the same story – can be a source of complex story experiences. Although there are different ways to achieve unreliability, or, more precisely, there are different methods to make one consider a narrative as unreliable, it must be noted that not all of these techniques lead to a complex – that is, cognitively challenging – experience. Two primary strategies of unreliability can be discerned. These are, first, providing an objective but restrictive (in terms of the narrative's *communicativeness*, see Bordwell 1985: 59) view on the events of the storyworld; or, second, offering seemingly highly communicative (apparently undiminished) access that is later revoked as having been a concealed-subjective, falsified or distorted view on the diegetic events.[17]

As for the first case, through cleverly controlled information distribution, movies like Jean-Pierre Melville's 1962 *Le doulos* or M. Night Shyamalan's 1999

---

[17] A third type of unreliability could be added here, namely unreliability concerning morals or ethics. This can occur when a narrating or focalising character misrepresents, distorts or justifies events or acts that the viewer would, from a different (or more objective) perspective, consider morally reprehensible. As Jan Alber has noted, 'it makes sense to discriminate between cinematic forms of *normative* unreliability on the one hand, and cinematic forms of *factual* unreliability on the other (see also Laass 2008: 30–2). In both cases, we are invited to see that the character-narrator's norms differ significantly from the norms of the film, and our hypotheses about intentions and motivations obviously play a crucial role' (Alber 2010: 172). Since the potential confusion that normative unreliability causes is usually of a moral-evaluative or normative kind (rather than being related to narrative comprehension), its discussion falls outside of the scope of our book.

The Sixth Sense put viewers on a wrong track. By presenting only restricted fragments of their storyworlds' objective reality, these films do not 'lie' to their viewers, but encourage them to set out on misguided inferences and draw erroneous conclusions from the presented information. Their challenge to meaning-making, if there is one at all, is often momentary and retroactive, concentrated in the moment of recognising the misguidance – the 'twist'.[18]

On the other hand, highly communicative narration can also host unreliability. Films like Alfred Hitchcock's 1950 *Stage Fright* or Ron Howard's 2001 *A Beautiful Mind* obscure the hierarchy between their narrative's diegetic reality and their narrator's subjective – disguised as objective – reality. Unreliability often hides behind 'subjectivity'; that is, these films often cue viewers to take the represented as an objective access to the diegetic world, which will later be revealed as only the subjective reality (that is, a lie, fantasy or hallucination) of one of the focalising characters' point of view. Throughout film history, subjective realist narration has been a rather popular storytelling strategy that deliberately blurs epistemological boundaries by 'disrupting the voyeuristic transparency of the classical style' (Campora 2014: 9). While subjective realism in art-cinema narration is an overt strategy that plays openly against objective and realistic representation (Bordwell 1979), in (post-)classical cinema it also takes the form of covert manipulation that regulates – and mostly maintains – viewers' false beliefs about the objectivity and thus the reliability of the presented information. By playing with the 'voyeuristic transparency' and ambiguating the border between subjective and objective representation, contemporary complex films may not only confuse viewers with regard to figuring out what is real and reliable and what is not, but can also work on a meta-level, reflecting on the functionality of such boundaries in narrative manipulation and comprehension (see also Panek 2006) (Figure 2.4).

As hinted at already, these narrative strategies do not necessarily always challenge viewers' meaning-making processes; they sometimes only mislead them. While cognitively challenging and disorienting unreliabilities often result in rationally incoherent and logically inconsistent scenarios (think about the puzzling effect of incoherencies in Lynch's *Mulholland Drive*, or the subtle but significant inconsistencies of Leonard's memories in Nolan's *Memento*), deceptive unreliability's concealing strategies exactly avoid such

---

[18] Covertly restricted information distribution in storytelling is always a question of degree; and as such one could wonder whether all narrative movies are partly unreliable, or perhaps none of them are at all, as playing games with the viewer through toying with the strings of communicativeness is just an intensified and highly strategic version of a traditional, elliptic mode of storytelling. Again, a cognitive take on unreliability, which considers the effects of narrative misguidance, will provide a more precise understanding of this storytelling strategy (see the next subsection).

Figure 2.4

confrontation with viewers and their habitual comprehensive logic (examples go back as early as Robert Wiene's insane narrator in his 1920 *Das Cabinet des Dr. Caligari* (*The Cabinet of Dr. Caligari*) or to the lying flashback in Hitchcock's *Stage Fright*). In the next section we come back to these categories when further detailing and exemplifying the crucial distinction between disorienting and deceptive unreliabilities, and relating their different aims, practices and effects to our cognitively informed concept of complexity.

In conclusion to this section, it must be noted that the strategies discerned above do not function as isolated modes of narrative manipulation. Intensely complex experiences happen exactly when these narrative tactics are combined, allowing their cognitive effects to accumulate. For instance, the combination of the disruption of unalterable reality with a diegetic achronology can result in somewhat logical yet highly complex scenarios, rendering viewers' coherent and causal meaning-making efforts practically impossible (as happens, for example, in Jack Heller's 2011 *Enter Nowhere*, in which viewers most likely face difficulties in fully grasping the plot, which presents three protagonists' dreams as flash forwards of their not-yet-lived futures). As an all-out version of such an amalgamation, Lynch's *Mulholland Drive* simultaneously features subjective unreliability, multiple ontological levels, contradictory and paradoxical elements, a non-linear progression *and* an overstimulating amount of information. The result is an experience that, undoubtedly, most movie viewers will label as complex. Hence, the strategies discerned above should be seen as the 'ingredients' that make up variously complex film narratives.

2.3 A COGNITIVE APPROACH TO CLASSIFYING COMPLEXITY

With the above taxonomy and cognitive approach in mind, we can reassess complex cinema's traditional categorisations. With this reconceptualisation, we aim to bring more specificity to often used, but generally under-defined labels like 'complex' or 'puzzle' films. First of all, we propose to detach the

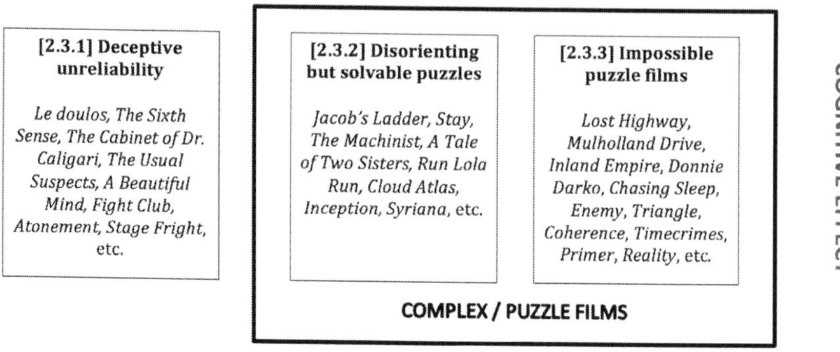

[2.3.1] Deceptive unreliability	[2.3.2] Disorienting but solvable puzzles	[2.3.3] Impossible puzzle films	
Le doulos, The Sixth Sense, The Cabinet of Dr. Caligari, The Usual Suspects, A Beautiful Mind, Fight Club, Atonement, Stage Fright, etc.	Jacob's Ladder, Stay, The Machinist, A Tale of Two Sisters, Run Lola Run, Cloud Atlas, Inception, Syriana, etc.	Lost Highway, Mulholland Drive, Inland Empire, Donnie Darko, Chasing Sleep, Enemy, Triangle, Coherence, Timecrimes, Primer, Reality, etc.	COGNITIVE EFFECT

COMPLEX / PUZZLE FILMS

Figure 2.5

term 'puzzle film' from its historical specificity (which would otherwise restrain the term to either modernist or contemporary trends). In the following we will use it to label the general overarching category of (post-)classical *complex cinema*, mainly because the cognitive consequences of narrative experimentations appear mostly as 'puzzles' to be deciphered. Within this main category of complex puzzle films, it is necessary to distinguish between two types of complex cinema. On the one hand (2.3.2), there are films that hinder viewers' narrative sense-making in some way, but which ultimately also offer (or at least allow the viewer to infer) satisfying resolutions to their temporarily 'puzzling' scenarios. We will call these *disorienting but solvable puzzle films*. On the other hand (2.3.3), there are films that do not grant such a way out, but rather evoke confusing effects more pervasively throughout their narration. We will call such permanently confusing movies *impossible puzzle films* (by which we do not mean that viewers cannot formulate interpretive solutions to these stories' 'impossibilities'). However, before introducing this twofold classification, we first need to address a problematic category in the traditional taxonomy of complexity, namely the case of the *deceptive unreliable film* (2.3.1). The chart in Figure 2.5 might be helpful in keeping track of these categories and their relation to the cognitively defined concept of cinematic complexity.

2.3.1 Deceptive unreliability and the twist film

As part of unpacking the differences between our main categories of (2.3.2) *complex but decipherable* and (2.3.3) *impossible and pervasive* puzzles, and in order to make our definitions perfectly clear, let us start with a perhaps somewhat surprising claim. If we define narrative complexity by its potential to evoke temporary or enduring cognitive puzzlement in the viewer, then many of the traditional unreliable twist movies – which normally occupy a prominent place in exemplifying the trend – should not be considered as part of the category of complex cinema. In one of the first studies that addressed the 'difficult viewing' experiences of complex narratives, Chisholm equally notes that

> [m]ysteries and narratives that trick viewers in the manner of *Stage Fright* (Hitchcock, 1950) or *House of Games* (Mamet, 1987) might seem models of difficulty, but they are not inherently so . . . [M]ost narratives that deceive viewers are designed to be readily understood in such a way that the eventual revelation of the deception will come as a complete surprise. (Chisholm 1991: 391)

Deceptive unreliable films, like Bryan Singer's 1995 *The Usual Suspects*, M. Night Shyamalan's 1999 *The Sixth Sense* or Ron Howard's 2001 *A Beautiful Mind*, do not really complexify the viewing experience. On the contrary, as the prototype of this kind of cinema, Hitchcock's *Stage Fright* proved as early as in 1950 that a smooth distribution of misleading information is actually a prerequisite for the operability of these films' unreliability. Chisholm argues for something similar when he states that the primary function of these films lies not in problematising the viewer's comprehension of a story, but in providing a temporarily deceived understanding, an unreliability which misinforms one's narrative comprehension up to the point when new information – the surprising 'twist' – offers a fresh hypothesis by which previous knowledge needs to be re-evaluated. Edward Branigan, who calls these films 'flip puzzles', writes similarly about a 'flipping' moment of recognition as a realisation of 'how enormous successions of small mistakes in judgments lead to fundamental miscalculations' (Branigan 2014: 248).

Daniel Barratt's article, which is ironically one of the highlights in Buckland's first *Puzzle Films* anthology, concentrates on the deceptive strategy of unreliability in *The Sixth Sense*. Barratt's main question is: 'How does Shyamalan make the first-time viewer "blind" to his film's narrative twist?' To sum up the film's story and narrative idea: the unreliability operates by presenting a forking point (Dr Malcolm Crowe (Bruce Willis) gets shot by a patient), from where the film highlights a likely option (he survives the gunshot and keeps practising as a child psychologist) and hides this option's alternative (the gunshot is fatal, the doctor dies and walks around as a ghost). The film's deceptive narration encourages the viewer to go for the first option; it is only upon its twist that the narration reveals that the latter option is in fact the actual diegetic reality, exposing how the film is actually a supernatural story. It is important to realise that even though throughout its narrative development the film maintains its deceptive unreliability by offering 'clues at two levels' (Currie 1995: 25), these two contradictory levels never confront each other (the doctor is never alive and dead at the same time). Establishing a 'surprise gap' (Sternberg 1978: 245) – which is the wide story-territory between the forking point and the revealing twist – deceptive unreliable films elicit a surprising effect, but not a perceived ambiguity or sensed puzzlement. Rather, in order to maximise the effect of the surprise, the primary strategy of such films is to keep their inherent ambiguity hidden. Consequently, there is no confusion in the 'online' viewing experience besides the single moment *during* the twist, when viewers are invited to switch between the two outcomes. Because up to the moment of the twist, misled 'viewers do not even know that there is some relevant thing they do not know' (Klecker 2013: 131), no one is supposed to have doubts about the reliability of the first option. Likewise, after the revealing twist, few people will have difficulty accepting the new alternative scenario.

According to Cornelia Klecker, Shyamalan's film, together with films like Fincher's *Fight Club*, make up a 'small genre' of *mind-tricking narratives*. Contrary to our view, Klecker claims that these films form a subtype within contemporary complex cinema. She argues that the narrative techniques of mind-tricking films 'deliberately play with the viewers' experiences, responses, and expectations *during* the viewing of a film and feature an utterly surprising outcome in the end' (Klecker 2013: 121 – our emphasis). Even though we tend to agree with Klecker's dissatisfaction with the vagueness of Buckland's complexity definition, the indiscriminate list of puzzle films and the category's misty description (ibid.: 128 – see also our discussion in section 1.3), we see a similar risk in her concept too. If the experience of mind-tricking plot-twist films is smooth, and the viewer's meaning-making practice remains unhindered, then why should one categorise them under the general label of *complex* cinema in the first place? Again, one has to wonder what the substantial criteria of 'complexity' are. Is it about formal-structural experimentation, and about (c)overt playfulness and surprising narrative punches? Or is complexity, as we aim to suggest, measured by films' capacity to evoke confusing sensations and to hinder straightforward comprehension? Although both *Fight Club* and *The Sixth Sense* undeniably pull off a brilliant plot twist (Ryan 2009), with the latter even deserving the title of 'best twist ever' according to some (Wheat et al. 2010: 39), we would argue that their overall viewing processes, as well as their moments of sudden, anagnoristic revelation, are ultimately experienced unproblematically. They are in any case not comparable to the steady narrative and mental confusion that films like, for example, *The Prestige* or *Primer* evoke and maintain throughout their entire plots. Returning to our emphasis in Klecker's definition, we agree that mind-tricking (that is, deceptively unreliable) plot-twist films do play with viewers' hypotheses and expectations during their unfolding misleading strategy, but, since they do so in a totally unmarked and covert manner (viewers are not

Cognitive Approach to Contemporary Complex Cinema   55

aware that these films are playing games with them), we do not think that deceptive unreliable films like *Stage Fright*, *Fight Club* or *The Sixth Sense* genuinely challenge viewers' sense-making processes. That is, they do not challenge the 'online' process of making sense of the narrative *during* the viewing, and therefore, in our cognitive definition, do not provide any complex, let alone confusing, experience beyond the surprise effect.

One could argue that the magnitude of the revealing turning point's effect in deceptive unreliable twist films might reach beyond a momentary psychological confusion. According to this claim, movies like *Fight Club* or *The Sixth Sense* may be considered complex insofar as their twists – by introducing a new causality to their plots – call for a complete retroactive rearrangement from memory that requires reasonably high cognitive effort. Adopting Sternberg's term, one could say that mind-tricking films represent 'an *extreme* case of a surprise gap' (Klecker 2013: 131). In Klecker's view, such extremity distinguishes mind-tricking cinema from similar strategies in more classical narratives. After the instantaneous punch of the revealing twist in *The Sixth Sense*, one needs to revisit one's memories about the details of the entire story and reinterpret previous clues and hidden possibilities in accordance with the just-revealed truth. As Erlend Lavik lucidly argues,

> *The Sixth Sense*'s fabula is certainly coherent up to the turning point, but with the introduction of the twist it is liable to break down, and it is not easy to immediately piece together a new one where everything adds up. There is simply too much previous syuzhet information that appears to contradict what we are now being asked to accept. (Lavik 2006: 55–6)

Relating this retrospective – or re-reconstructing (Klecker 2013: 139) – puzzlement to the definition we provide for the experience of complexity is, as a matter of fact, a reasonable assertion. Gregory Currie (1995), for instance, sees a direct proportionality between the amount of interpretive re-evaluation (between the misleading and true versions of an unreliable story) on the one hand, and the degree of experienced complexity on the other. Accordingly, he claims that the greater the surprise in the surprise gap, the more complex the experience.

True as these objections may be, we are not convinced by their implications, as these claims lead to linking film narratives with very different experiential qualities. Although 'the filling in of the surprise gap is likely to cause an intense shock' (Klecker 2013: 131), this shock, we believe, is only temporary. Usually, the new information will make immediate sense and lead to an instantly comprehensible new coherence among the narrative events. The narration often also instantly reinforces the acceptance of the new resolution by briefly revisiting earlier key moments in light of the new knowledge (as happens in *The Sixth Sense* through the flashbacks after Dr Malcolm's final realisation). This sudden psychological effect of a shock offers, in our view, a rather dissimilar viewing experience compared to the more enduring hindrances of problem-solving cognition.

All in all, if one determines complexity by its impeding effect on viewers' cognition and meaning-making, then it becomes apparent why one needs to distinguish between different types of narrative (created by a variety of formal narrative strategies). We believe that the effect of covert and momentary disorientation through deceptive knowledge distribution in traditional twist films (2.3.1) is dissimilar to the effect of overt and lengthy – and by that temporarily or permanently disorienting – complexification in complex puzzle (2.3.2), and impossible puzzle films (2.3.3).

2.3.2 Disorienting but solvable puzzle films

While deceptive unreliable plot-twist movies do not pose any problem to comprehension during their misleading narrative actions, disorienting complex narratives do problematise – and, in our view, truly complicate – the viewing experience by taking their audience through lasting moments of puzzlement. Therefore, *disorienting but solvable puzzle films* do not only purposefully delay, but also deliberately muddle meaning-making efforts throughout parts of their unfolding experience, and consequently do belong to the cognitively defined class of complex cinema. These films – through suspending or problematising narrative linearity and causality, complicating narrative structures, disrupting their dieateses' singular and unalterable reality, employing perplexing metalepses, providing under- and overstimulation of diegetic scenarios, presenting conflicting logical contradictions or disorienting unreliabilities – strategically hinder viewers' rational meaning-making efforts to complexify the experience. Disorienting puzzle films present *lasting* moments and situations of puzzlement by establishing and maintaining 'curiosity gaps' (Sternberg 1978: 244–5) throughout the viewing process. Curiosity gaps, in contrast to the camouflaged surprise gaps, are overt and therefore invite the viewer to bridge their clearly presented mysteries and other perplexing disturbances through continuously generating hypotheses. However, being puzzles with solutions, at the end of their perplexing ride these disorienting puzzle films will often close their curiosity gaps (in the form of a twist or other, less powerful, resolution), or will at least provide sufficient clues to allow the generated confusion to be resolved.

Many of the disorienting puzzle narratives elicit temporary confusion by obscuring their storyworld's reality status through an unmarked blending of the film's objective realm and its characters' subjective realities. These focalised stories of psychologically fallible and sometimes morally dubious protagonists – for instance, the disturbed Jacob (Tim Robbins) in Adrian Lyne's unreliable *Jacob's Ladder*, the inventively hallucinating Henry Letham (Ryan Gosling) in Marc Forster's *Stay* or the troubled Su-Mi (Su-jeong Lim) in Jee-woon Kim's staggeringly intricate *A Tale of Two Sisters* – can disorient viewers by confronting them with conflicting truths, paradoxical scenarios and other apparent narrative impossibilities during the viewing process. As the viewer's access into these films' diegetic worlds is restricted by an untrustworthy character's mind's eye, the resulting focalised reality will often be distorted to a great extent. Prior to a certain moment in the narrative development, the viewer of these films will usually encounter difficulties in making coherent sense of the presented world. Up to that 'flipping' point, the contradictions and other strange and unnatural elements in the narrative ask for conscious inferences and hypotheses from the disoriented viewer – like inferring a fallible narrator, or assuming an incoherent or illogically organised storyworld (more on such strategies will follow in Chapter 4) – anything, in fact, that can help the viewer come to terms with the experienced oddities and incomprehensibilities. Often, as for example in Kim's *A Tale of Two Sisters* or Brad Anderson's 2004 *The Machinist*, the mentally unstable focaliser ultimately breaks down under the psychological weight of the presented lie, or collapses due to the intolerable repercussions of an illness. As the character's subjective reality crumbles, the process culminates in apparently nonsensical, inconsistent or irrational scenarios that ultimately debunk the representation's subjective nature. Note, that Lyne's, Forster's, Kim's and Anderson's mentioned films all provide a perfect inside-out version of the aforementioned category of misleadingly unreliable deceptive plot-twist narratives: the main function of their twists is not to deliver a surprising revelation, but mainly to fix an otherwise irrational and incoherent story into which the plot got gradually tangled up when presenting a subjective realist view of some untrustworthy, hallucinating, mad or simply fallible character.[19] In these films, in contrast to Singer's or Shyamalan's deceptive unreliability, the narrative twist is not a sudden switch between two plausible scenarios, but a revealing moment that closes the film's curiosity gap, restores rationality and coherence, and discloses the focalising character's irrational story as the result of a mental breakdown, hallucination, lie or dream. If, following Aristotle's traditional definition, complication 'extends

---

[19] On the different narrative strategies, textual and audiovisual markers, and experiential outcomes regarding untrustworthy, mad, fallible and other unreliable characters see, among others, Yacobi 1981; Currie 1995 and 2004 (Chapter 7); Nünning 1997 and 2005; Olson 2003; Hansen 2007; and Barratt 2009.

from the beginning of the action to the part which marks the turning-point' (Aristotle 1902: 65), then the primary role of the resolution in deceptive unreliable plot-twist narratives is to *surprise* the viewer about the misleading truthfulness of the narration. For disorienting complex stories, on the other hand, the resolution's function is to *unravel* the untenable confusion that followed from the narrative's disorienting action.

In order to maintain the category of 'mind-tricking films', Cornelia Klecker downplays the dissimilarity between the above cognitive effects – that is, between those triggered by 'surprise gaps' and those that are formed through 'curiosity gaps'. Moreover, instead of disclosing the distinctive impacts that surprise and curiosity gaps evoke, she introduces Meir Sternberg's third possibility of 'mixed gaps' (Sternberg 1978: 244), and presents Nolan's *The Prestige* as a film that combines deceptive and disorienting strategies. Although we agree that such a combination can be accountable for eliciting a highly perplexing experience, we would also argue that in such combinations it is not the surprising shock of a revealed deception, but rather the narrative's continuous and overtly disorienting design that maintains viewers' puzzled curiosity. Therefore, we would identify this puzzlement as the key ingredient of the narrative's complexity.

We would like to stress that disorienting unreliability is just one of many complexifying techniques, which should not be given the privileged status it has often received in previous conceptualisations of cinematic narrative complexity. Technically, it does not matter which formal-structural strategy and experiential path leads to viewers' cognitive puzzlement. Once again, what we aim to explore in our book is the general experience of temporary or pervasive confusion: in many cases unreliability is only a viewer inference following perceived complexity, rather than a device that actually creates complexity. Moreover, there are plenty of disorienting but solvable puzzles that provide cognitively challenging experiences without employing any of the storytelling strategies connected to unreliability. In many complex narratives there are no curiosity gaps that could be closed by a revealing twist, or that would otherwise be exposed as a misleading or subjective realist scenario. These films' playfulness is not about a misleading or lying narrative communicativeness; instead, their appeal is based on a deliberate, consistent and narratively motivated complex story logic. *Inception*'s multiple-embedded narrative structure, for instance, or the subtly interwoven hierarchy among the six stories of *Cloud Atlas*, are not part of any unreliable agenda, but examples of complex forms and structures that are motivated by the stories and storyworld concepts they envelop: while *Inception*'s hypo-hypo-. . .-diegetic Russian doll structure is motivated as a narrative rendition of the film's fantastic option of descending into characters' embedded dreams, *Cloud Atlas*'s highly entangled but delicately connected plot trajectories give rise to the film's ambitious overarching concept concerning the cyclical nature of life (the 'universal and everlasting kindness, through which we are all connected, and which ripples across ages, genders and centuries').

Looking beyond the above examples, one might wonder if there are any kind of puzzle or mind-tricking mainstream narrative films that evoke serious forms of confusion in the viewer, but do not provide a resolution through any kind of gap-closing conclusion (surprising or not) or by any other story-related or explicit conceptual motivation. Usually, movies that set up a puzzle without providing a diegetic closure or other motivational solution are considered to be examples of art-cinema narration. András Bálint Kovács discerns two major strategies with which art-cinema narration compensates for its lack of solutions: '[w]hat makes a modern investigation film different from a classical one is the lack of focus on finding the solution to the initial problem. This occurs either because no solution exists, or because other equally or more important problems arise' (Kovács 2007: 99). Kovács's examples are Bernardo Bertolucci's 1962 *La commare secca* (*The Grim Reaper*) and Michelangelo Antonioni's 1960 *L'Avventura*, respectively. On the other hand – and this is one of the central claims of this book – next to art cinema and its deliberately open-ended 'solutions', there is another set of (post-)classical films that do plant, play with and ultimately refuse to fully close complicated curiosity gaps. These films, through their complex stories and storytelling modes, frustrate referential and explicit meaning attributions without explicitly providing any reassuring resolution. In the next section we introduce this distinct sub-category and argue for its complexity as operating somewhere between art-cinema and classical narrative modes.

2.3.3 Impossible puzzle films

Our approach, which defines and evaluates narrative complexity through its capacity to evoke variously demanding cognitive effects, marks out another option beyond disorienting but decipherable puzzles. Even though we agree with Bordwell, Staiger and Thompson's claim that 'if temporality and causality did not cooperate . . . the spectator could not construct a coherent story out of the narration' (Bordwell et al. 1985: 44), we do not think that this stipulation is an exclusive rule for all manifestations of (post-)classical, even 'mainstream' modes of narration. Complex narratives that do deny coherent story-construction – and thereby create not only lengthy, but even permanent confusion through seemingly irresolvable puzzles – can form a distinct class of films within the (post-)classical narrative paradigm.

This group of films – and the argument for their distinct category of viewing experiences – will be the primary focus of this book. *Impossible puzzle films* are movies that never fully close their curiosity gaps, but still aim to sustain viewers' narrative concern. Although these films deliberately maintain a constant sense of narrative disorientation, they still keep viewers hooked and encourage their attempts at making sense of the puzzling scenarios.

In our choice of term, we follow Edward Branigan's (2014) classification and apply his 'impossible puzzle' label to cinema that seems to occupy a specific niche within contemporary complex films. Branigan's term provides an instantly clear idea about the topic of our book, as well as an interesting starting point for a definition. '"[I]mpossible" puzzles,' Branigan notes, are picture puzzles and films that 'appear perfectly correct but whose largest perspectival representation proves impossible' (ibid.: 234). In his choice of examples, Branigan apparently does not distinguish between (post-)classical and art-cinematic modes of narration: he includes David Lynch's *Lost Highway* and *Inland Empire*, Emmanuel Carrère's *La moustache*, but also Carlos Reygadas' *Post Tenebras Lux* or Alain Resnais' *Last Year at Marienbad*. In our discussion, however, we will argue for the significance of such a distinction as part of our attempt to define the specificity of the impossible puzzle film category (see particularly Chapter 5).[20]

Impossible puzzle films tend to evoke enduring states of confusion, ensured by their persistent ambiguities, paradoxes, irreducible uncertainties, counterintuitive events, character multiplications or others features of complex storytelling. Impossible puzzles differ from other disorienting but

---

[20] Specifying his definition of impossible puzzles, Branigan further argues, 'this type [of picture puzzles and cinema] includes puzzles in which the parts are impossible, but new possibilities emerge in the whole' (Branigan 2014: 234). In this respect, impossible puzzle films seem to comply with the criteria that complex systems theory postulates on a complex experience, which is beyond mere complication. While a simple system (and a simple film narrative) offers a close and transparent relation among its constituting (story) elements, the complication of such a system creates distanced but still lucid connections. However, complex systems (and, accordingly, complex film narratives) present (story) elements that are all part of the same (narrative) agglomeration, but the aggregate of which is more than the sum of their parts. Whereas chaotic systems do not form any connection among constituents, in a complex (narrative) system elements do relate to each other, respond and interact, but do not allow for a coherent and lucid overview to their perspectival complexity. Complex (narrative) systems are open ended to the extent that they evolve and function without any comprehensive equilibrium or endpoint. While we do not follow this explanatory model, for a comprehensive application of complex systems theory to complex cinema, see Maria Poulaki's 2011 dissertation, *Before or Beyond Narrative? Towards a Complex Systems Theory of Contemporary Films*. For Poulaki 'complex films do not reflect complex systems, but function themselves as such' (19).

resolvable complicating cinematic puzzles in terms of their genuine breach with the 'cooperation of causality and chronology', which – although experimented with and played upon in many contemporary complex films – still characterises classical and post-classical cinema (as Bordwell also maintains). Returning to our earlier example, if Shyamalan's deceptively unreliable *The Sixth Sense* works with 'clues at two levels', which are never contradicted in the film (the doctor is never alive *and* dead at the same time) and which are clearly resolved after the twist, then impossible puzzle films do the exact opposite: not only do they play games with explicitly contradicting clues, but also they do not offer (at least not explicitly) any relieving resolution to their created incongruities. Michael Walker's *Chasing Sleep*, Emmanuel Carrère's *La moustache*, Lynch's 'Los Angeles trilogy' of *Lost Highway*, *Mulholland Drive* and *Inland Empire*, Richard Kelly's *Donnie Darko*, Csaba Bollók's *Miraq*, Shane Carruth's *Primer*, Duncan Jones's *Source Code*, Jack Heller's *Enter Nowhere*, Denis Villeneuve's *Enemy*, Quentin Dupieux's *Reality*, Christopher Smith's *Triangle*, Nacho Vigalondo's *Timecrimes*, Isti Madarász's *Loop*, Thomas Jane's *Dark Country*, Michael and Peter Spierig's *Predestination* and James Ward Byrkit's *Coherence* are all examples of impossible cinematic puzzles that give up on (post-)classical narration's trusted cooperation of causality and chronology. In terms of the strength of their posed cognitive challenges, these films go beyond both the disputed complexity of deceptive unreliabilities and the relatively 'simple complexity' of the majority of the contemporary popular puzzle films. Particularly good examples of impossible puzzle films are loop narratives such as *Timecrimes*, *Triangle*, *Loop*, *Dark Country* and *Predestination*, which all present paradoxical scenarios and overtly play with formal composition and classical narrative norms. Through these open-ended games, impossible puzzle films represent a niche sub-category of complex cinema, within which films strategically plant disorienting curiosity gaps in their narrative structures that they do not close. In his DVD commentary of *Triangle*, director Christopher Smith defines the distinction between puzzle and impossible puzzle films in plain and simple terms: 'I didn't want this movie to be a movie that ends with one twist. I wanted it to be a movie that ends like a riddle.'

Both disorienting but solvable puzzles and impossible puzzle films play 'mind games', but they offer different mental experiences. A puzzle, in general, is 'a game, etc. that you have to think about carefully in order to answer it' (*Oxford Advanced Learner's Dictionary* 2000: 1076). A puzzle game creates momentary cognitive perplexity and excitement by exhibiting elements that seemingly do not make sense. Puzzles earn ultimate appreciation, however, by restoring coherency through presenting a solution (or a clear possibility of a solution) to their enigma. In cinema, this can take the form of a surprising twist, an awe-inspiring and cognitively manageable answer that no one could have been able to figure out or, if nothing else, a strong hint pointing towards a logical solution that should enable a viewer to crack the puzzle (Leiendecker 2013).[21] While puzzles grant players (and viewers) a way out of their mazes, impossible puzzles seem to function like riddles that exhibit 'mysterious event[s] or situation[s] that you cannot explain' (*Oxford Advanced Learner's Dictionary* 2000: 1144).[22] Impossible puzzle films generally evoke enduring conflicts within their diegetic storyworlds, their narrative structures and, ultimately, also in the viewing experience they offer. For example, narratives like *Timecrimes* or *Triangle* contain tricky loops both in the storyworld and in the storytelling. This double-complexification, in turn, causes a pervasive sense of confusion and puzzlement for the viewers who finds themselves confronted with strong paradoxes.

It must be noted that by labelling these films 'impossible puzzles', we do not intend to claim that it is impossible for viewers to attain any interpretation of these films. After all, one can find plenty of viewers on message boards and other social media platforms who feel that they have more or less cracked the underlying puzzles of films like *Mulholland Drive*, *Donnie Darko* and *Primer*. We do not mean to argue that such efforts would be misguided, and that these puzzles are 'objectively impossible' to solve. Rather, our claim is to point out that on the level of narration and narrative structure, these films contain permanent gaps, ambiguities and contradictions, and, as such, they partially undermine their own narrative coherence and congruity. Their puzzles are 'impossible' in the sense that they are narratively contradictory or logically incongruent, and that no explicit resolution for this incongruence is being offered. This means that much of the work needed to achieve some form of narrative closure or conclusive interpretation is left

---

[21] Filmmaker David Fincher's take on the perfect twist is somewhat tongue-in-cheek (or perhaps plainly sceptical). According to him '[w]hat people want from movies is to be able to say, I knew it and it's not my fault' (Smith 1999: 62) – as if viewers would prefer to pretend to be upset because they knew what would happen, rather than being completely misled by a film (see the outcry of disappointed viewers of Hitchcock's 1950 *Stage Fright*).

[22] Following this distinction, in our earlier attempts at defining impossible puzzles we used the term 'riddle film' (Kiss 2013). This name was found to be problematic, primarily because riddles by their definition overlap with puzzles, implying a solution to their conundrum (which is exactly the opposite of the definition we are aiming for). This definitional complication has led to another problem, according to which the term 'riddle film' cannot express a specific quality and therefore it is unable to mark a distinct field of study in relation to the widely discussed domain of 'puzzle film'. We have therefore decided to proceed from Edward Branigan's classification and use his 'impossible puzzle films' label, as it covers our interest and provides an instantly clear idea about the topic of our book. For a more nuanced and detailed explanation about the distinction between puzzle and riddle (that is impossible puzzle) films, see our article (Kiss 2013).

up to viewers' own analytic and interpretive skills (and willingness, for that matter). Extensive interpretation can allow viewers to (re)connect the pieces of information and (re)purpose the narrative events, and thereby support or disprove interpretive hypotheses. The 'impossibility' of these films should thus be located on the explicit, referential level of their narration, and not necessarily in the interpretive realm. However, as we will later see, the narrative impossibilities and incongruities of impossible puzzle films often also tend to function as continuous 'hermeneutic bait' on the level of interpretation: a key effect of many impossible puzzle films lies exactly in that they keep the game of interpretive work open, making it difficult for viewers to settle on one single, unambiguous reading of their conundrum.

Exceeding puzzle films' relatively simple and decipherable complexity, impossible puzzles thus offer narrative scenarios that point beyond one's everyday experiences and habitual strategies for fictional and real-world sense-making. Their narrative modes are designed in such a way that they encourage, but do not allow, instant and easy constructions of a coherent and logical storyworld or event sequence. Engaging in multiple viewings, delving into extensive investigations and close readings, or yielding to an (online) urge of sharing interpretations with other bewildered viewers can be the results of (and compensation for) this inability to make instant and stable sense of these films. Acknowledging the intense negotiation between an impossible analytical effort and creative interpretive work, one has to admit that the boundaries of the impossible puzzle film category are often loose. Some films may appear to certain viewers to be puzzles that are disorienting but ultimately coherent, whereas the same film may seem completely impossible or incoherent to others. Some movies in particular divide audiences in this respect: for example, Lynch's *Mulholland Drive*, Kelly's *Donnie Darko* and Walker's *Chasing Sleep* represent those curious cases which could be placed in the intersection between impossible and disorienting but solvable puzzles. For another share of viewers, these films might even be completely excluded from either of these categories, considered as examples of art-cinema narration or even instances of experimental filmmaking that abandon narrative coherence altogether. Indeed, impossible puzzle films share some similarities with (and arguably take inspiration from) the art-cinema tradition in keeping their formal, narrative and interpretive games open. Although typical mainstream puzzle films – or, in Allan Cameron's terminology, *modular-narrative films* – generally display complexity that does not achieve the disorienting effect of a Robbe-Grillet novel (Cameron 2008: 6), impossible puzzle films, on the other hand, do aim to achieve such destabilising experiences, but, for most viewers, remain within the (post-)classical narrative paradigm of cinematic storytelling and film viewing. We will argue that there are distinct features that do seem to separate impossible puzzle films from the tradition of art cinema – a comparison we will examine in more detail in Chapter 5.

To conclude, it should be noted that, from a cognitive point of view, puzzlement and confusion are mental states which one would normally, under most circumstances, consider to be unpleasant or troublesome. Meanwhile, as the recent trend has shown, narrative complexity in contemporary cinema seems to be appealing to a growing audience. Back in 1963 Norman N. Holland was bothered by a similar discrepancy when he formulated his questions: 'But why do they [the puzzling movies] appeal to anybody? . . . Why should that feeling of puzzlement give us pleasure?' (Holland 1963: 18). In line with Holland's early inquiry, one of the aims of this book is to explain what makes narrative complexity, and its subsequent challenge to reason and comprehension, an attractive effect in cinema. The category of impossible puzzle films is particularly interesting in this respect, as it enables us to re-posit Holland's original questions in the post-classical context: why, after all, would viewers be attracted to stories that resist sense-making? Why would they eschew the gratification of a (surprising) resolution and embrace the sensation of pervasively and permanently confusing stories?

While so far we have introduced the general trend of cinematic complexity, established and justified our choice for the (embodied-)cognitive approach, redrawn boundaries in narrative taxonomies and defined the niche of impossible puzzle films, the rest of this book will focus on questions such as these. How do impossible puzzle films create impossible and 'non-natural' story structures? How do these movies keep their viewers hooked on their excessive complexities? What can viewers do to make sense of such narratives? And what may be pleasurable about this experience? The ultimate aim of this book is to study the kind of 'non-rational but meaningful energy' (Buckland 2009c: 57) that surrounds these films, and to explore the cognitive substrate of the *attractive struggle* that governs one's meaning-making processes in response to impossible puzzle films' confusingly complex film narratives.

CHAPTER 3

Narrative Complexity and Dissonant Cognitions

> If you want to express something impossible, you must keep to certain rules. The element of mystery to which you want to draw attention should be surrounded and veiled by a quite obvious, readily recognisable commonness.
>
> Maurits Cornelis Escher: *The Impossible*

On a beautiful sunny morning Jess (Melissa George), a single mother of an autistic son Tommy (Joshua McIvor), joins a group of friends to go sailing. She plans to go on the trip with Tommy, but shows up at the harbour alone and distressed. Jess's anxiety appears justified when the yacht is caught in a violent electrical storm and capsizes. When the weather clears, the survivors, including Jess, climb onto the upturned boat and spot a huge ocean liner heading towards them. They yell for help as they believe they have spotted someone on the deck, but, after they manage to climb onboard the ship, they find no one there. Yet it turns out they are not alone: a mysterious figure in a burlap mask starts hunting them down one by one with a shotgun. Jess, the last survivor, confronts, then overcomes, the murderer, who falls from the deck into a watery grave. A sound of distant shouting pulls Jess out of her shock. What she sees is beyond reason: she and her friends standing on an upturned boat and yelling for help. Jess quickly steps back before they see her. Or have they already? . . . Stunned – but not paralysed – by the impossibility of the situation, she tries to break out of the never-ending loop. Notwithstanding her various interventions, the fateful events repeat over and over, and the loop hits a reset each time everyone is killed. Finally, setting herself up as the masked killer, she takes over the role of the hunter, only to ultimately be defeated by 'the latest' version of Jess/herself. Thrown overboard, she wakes up washed ashore. Arriving home, she encounters another version of herself ill-treating her son Tommy. The 'survivor Jess' we have been following kills the 'bad mother Jess'. Driving away with her son, they have a serious car accident that leaves Tommy dead. Jess, alone and distressed, takes a cab and goes to the harbour. On a beautiful sunny morning, ready to have another try at outmanoeuvring her excruciating fate, the distressed single mother Jess decides to join her friends and go sailing . . .

In the DVD commentary to *Triangle*, as quoted in the previous chapter, director Christopher Smith reveals his film's primary intentions: 'I didn't want this movie to be a movie that ends with one twist. I wanted it to be a movie that ends like a riddle, and that you can't quite see where the movie ends and begins.' And indeed, in line with the perplexing twist of Cortázar's *Continuity of Parks*, *Triangle* allows the potential of a *character-multiplying loop* story to fully unfold. Smith's film combines the familiarity of the classical horror genre with a bold narrative move of interlocking transgressing story paths. The result is a rather mind-bending puzzle, a challenging story that problematises many of the fundamental features of a coherent narrative like chronology, development, causality and character unity. These features make *Triangle* a perfect illustration of the type of movies we labelled 'impossible puzzle films'. But how exactly do the film's narrative manipulations lead us to construct an impossible, but otherwise perfectly inhabitable and immersive 'beautiful and sunny' diegetic world? How does the paradoxical co-existence of the differ-ent *and* simultaneous versions of the same events problematise our narrative comprehension? And, ultimately, how can we understand and describe the powerful and pervasive effect of such narrative impossibilities?

In the previous chapter we identified the distinct category of impossible puzzle films within contemporary complex cinema, characterising them as a set of films that feature narrative difficulties and irresolvable paradoxes that resist cognitive resolution. The next step is to describe in more detail the viewing experiences that these films elicit and thus substantiate the defini-tion of impossible puzzle films. We do this by examining the *cognitive effects* of these films' narrative strategies, which we will relate to the notion of *dis-sonant cognitions*. To achieve this, the current chapter will first introduce and revise the traditional concept of *cognitive dissonance* to understand and describe the impact of impossible puzzle films on viewers' sense-making processes. We put forward the thesis that impossible puzzle films achieve complex effects by evoking 'cognitions' (elements of narrative or real-world knowl-edge) that are in irresolvable conflict. This brings about mentally dissonant experiences that exert a certain pressure on viewers to resolve the conflict through cognitive and interpretive means. But before analysing the kind of cognitive dissonance that impossible puzzle films evoke, we first need to dedicate some space to an explication of our specific use of the term.

3.1 THE CONCEPT OF COGNITIVE DISSONANCE

Cognitive dissonance is one of the most widely discussed concepts in psy-chology, and has been particularly prominent in social psychology. With regard to the latter, it usually refers to the effect of inconsistencies in behav-iours and attitudes of real-world individuals (see, for example, Cooper and Fazio 1984; Steele et al. 1993; Stone 1999) or mediated fictional characters (for example, Caracciolo 2013; van der Pol 2013). Our use of the concept, however, will be different from this customary social and behavioural understanding of the notion. We are interested only in the *cognitive core* of cognitive dissonance theory, which we will connect to cognitive approaches to film and narrative in order to explain puzzling conflicts in narrative comprehension. We argue that one of the key characteristics by which impossible puzzle films achieve their distinct effects is their strategy of confronting viewers with *cognitions that are dissonant*. This understanding does not necessarily define the sensation of discomfort traditionally associated with 'cognitive dissonance', but it does rely on related concepts and psychological patterns.

The original notion of *cognitive dissonance* was first theorised in the mid-1950s by the American social psychologist Leon Festinger (1956; 1957). In *A Theory of Cognitive Dissonance*, Festinger summarised the basis of the concept as follows:

> The core of the theory of dissonance ... is rather simple. It holds that:
> 1. There may exist dissonant or 'nonfitting' relations among cognitive elements ... To state it a bit more formally, x and y are dissonant if not-x follows from y. (Festinger 1957: 31, 13)

Psychologist Joel Cooper's formulation is even more general: 'If a person holds cognitions A and B such that A follows from the opposite of B, then A and B are dissonant' (Cooper 2007: 6).

These cognitive elements, or *cognitions*, can take many forms. They can be perceptions, knowledge, beliefs and so on. In short, 'anything that can be thought about is grist for the dissonance mill' (ibid.: 6). When offering the first account of the idea, Festinger saw three possible relations between cognitions: '[p]airs of elements can exist in irrelevant, consonant, or dissonant relations' (Festinger 1957: 260). Regarding *irrelevant* relations, '[m]ost cognitions coexist peacefully in our minds, sharing nothing in common (e.g., my knowledge of my hunger and my knowledge of last year's Super Bowl winner)' (Cooper 2007: 6). Arguably, irrelevant relations are by definition also irrelevant with regard to narrative experiences, since narrativisation, by its very nature, exactly comprises the establishing of relevance between cognitive elements (whether causally, spatio-temporally, teleologically, rhetorically or thematically). As for *relevant* relations between cognitive elements, one can talk about *consistency* and *inconsistency*. Festinger argued that consistent cognitions lead to a feeling of *consonance*, whereas inconsistency or contradiction between two cognitions is responsible for eliciting *cognitive dissonance*. The theory assumes that the human disposition is to always strive for consistency and congruity between relevant cognitions. This entails not just a preference for consonance, but also a pressing psychological necessity to *resolve dissonance*. The occurrence of cognitive dissonance therefore elicits a psychological discomfort, a *drive* in the form of an unpleasant mental or emotional state that demands a resolution from the experiencing individual.

Festinger observed that cognitive dissonance gives rise to pressures to resolve or reduce the conflict through what he called *dissonance-reduction* strategies. Since in our mental reality dissonance is a fairly common phenomenon (dissonance that is present in only a small amount and/or is contextually irrelevant will often not exert any psychological pressure), it is important to consider a given dissonance's *magnitude*. The magnitude of the conflict is its significance relative to its content and context and 'is an important variable in determining the pressure to reduce dissonance' (Festinger 1957: 17). In general, the strength of the pressure of reducing dissonance is approximately proportionate to the magnitude of the dissonance. There are generally three options for dissonance reduction, which serve to either create consonance or reduce the magnitude of the dissonance. When two cognitions are in conflict, one may alter one (or more) of the relevant cognitions; one may integrate or acquire new information relevant to the conflict to change the situation; or one can reduce the importance attributed to one (or more) of the relevant cognitions. In all these situations, either the cognitions themselves or one's attitude towards them are altered to create a (more) consonant and therefore more mentally manageable and sustainable situation.

3.2 Cognitions in dissonance: from social psychology to narrative engagement

In his article about the effect of cognitive dissonance when watching Krzysztof Kieślowski's *Amator* (*Camera Buff*, 1979), Gerwin van der Pol has aptly pointed out that throughout its scientific evolution, 'cognitive dissonance theory moved from a strictly cognitive problem to a social/moral problem' (van der Pol 2013: 358). Indeed, in the years after its publication, Festinger's theory caused a stir in social psychology. By virtue of its elegant simplicity, the theory proved able to predict (otherwise rather unexpected) patterns in behaviour and attitudes in people who were confronted with situations that induced some kind of dissonance in them. Further developments of Festinger's theory focused on experimental settings enabling various behavioural observations, as well as on the exact empirical circumstances under which cognitive dissonance would become manifest as a drive. These studies led to various observations of dissonance-reduction operations in individuals in empirical settings (for an overview, see Cooper 2007).[1] The intention of this book, however, is

---

[1] This social-behavioural research on cognitive dissonance included studies on *belief-confirmation* (for example, Festinger's own work on the dissonance reduction strategies of

not to conform to and work with these behavioural findings. There are at least two reasons for this.

First of all, social and behavioural inquiry into cognitive dissonance has focused on mainly real-life interpersonal situations in which there is always some action to be performed by an individual, and in which this individual has a high degree of free choice. In short, the social-psychological theory deals with '[b]ehaviour that is at variance with attitudes [causing] dissonance, but only under conditions of high-decision freedom' (Cooper 2007: 35). In such situations, a perceived dissonance between one's actions and one's attitudes has been found to lead to an arousal of negative emotions in the individual, resulting in empirically observable changes in behaviour. However, film, as a mediated and pre-structured form of communication, displays different features and allows only limited affordances for dissonance reduction compared to real-life options. Fictional scenarios in film (as we know the medium *anno* 2016) are characterised by the absence of the social components of (inter-) action and free choice. Viewers cannot alter the film's fixed flow of representation; they only have choices in terms of interpretations and attitudes taken towards the cinematic experience in question and not in terms of actions and behavioural changes. Interpreting fiction is also arguably not an interpersonal affair (at least not under most circumstances in which we engage with fictional stories), and decisions we make with regard to interpretation generally do not carry significant or direct consequences for our everyday lives, concrete actions or social relations. In short, in Festinger's terms, the magnitude of cognitive dissonance in fiction is likely to be relatively small, and with that, so are the observable psychological discomfort, the strength of negative emotions and the need for behavioural changes.

Second, our take on cognitive dissonance is fundamentally different from the social-psychological approach to which Festinger's original idea has been extended. We not only deal with *fictional narrative* situations in film, but, within this, we also aim to understand underlying cognitive processes of *comprehension and sense-making*. As Festinger worked within the behaviourist paradigm of psychology, his theorising had to abstain from making claims about the cognitive 'inner mechanisms' that underlie dissonance. After all, behaviourism approached the mind as an impenetrable 'black box', the workings of which

cult members who faced the disconfirmation of their strong beliefs), on *induced-compliance* experiments (people's justification of their performance of actions that are not in line with their beliefs or their own attitude), on *free-choice* situations (in which positive attitudes towards the non-chosen alternative are downplayed to achieve consonance with regards to the choice made) and on the notion of *effort justification* (the increased positive post-hoc appraisal of achieved goals that required unpleasant or dissonant experiences, to which we will return in section 6.4).

could only be accessed, explored and described in terms of its output – that is, through studying behavioural patterns. This approach therefore emphasised observations made in experimental settings, while downplaying aspects of mental interiority and sub- or pre-conscious operations.

In short, the domain within which we discuss dissonance is not the social-psychological one that aims at understanding human behaviour, but a narrative and cognitive kind that aspires to film-textual comprehension. Therefore, we hark back to and unpack the cognitive core of the original notion of cognitive dissonance, inherent in Festinger's initial theory, and apply it to viewer responses to incongruities among narrative elements. We thereby aim to complement narrative study with cognitive analysis: our eventual goal is not only to shed light on formal-structural dissonance in impossible puzzle films, but also to apprehend viewers' understanding of and responses to these films' dissonant narrative scenarios. In sum, we argue that impossible puzzle films are highly prone to evoking what we call *cognitions in dissonance* – elements of sense-making that are contradictory, conflicting or that form a paradox. Their narrative fictional situations call for consonance; they exert a certain pressure on viewers to resolve or deal with the dissonance, meaning that they tend to demand cognitive solutions, interpretive strategies or attitude changes from those viewers. This, in turn, we hypothesise, can form an engaging, if not attractive, experience in one's encounters with puzzling and confusing narratives. One of the key advantages of conceptualising confusingly puzzling narrative moments as dissonances – rather than, for instance, as strictly 'logical impossibilities' or structural conflicts – is that this approach includes the acknowledgement that such formal strategies have an instant effect on viewers and their narrativising activity, and that they are likely to inspire in viewers certain interpretive and cognitive 'dissonance-reduction' strategies. We will explore these urges – to construct meaning and to do something about the dissonance – in more detail in Chapter 4. In conclusion, our relation to Festinger's theory could be described as what narratologist Marie-Laure Ryan called a *convergence method* of connecting cognitive and narratological models. According to Ryan, '[t]his method consists of quoting scientific research in support of more or less independently developed theses concerning the reading [or viewing] process' (Ryan 2010a: 487). Indeed, our hypotheses here will be developed independently and with primary regard to our object of study and observations we make about the experiences these films bring about. We nevertheless strive to make them at least consistent with the general paradigm of cognitive sciences and the particular notion of cognitive dissonance. The first step in developing this approach is to outline when cognitions become dissonant in fictional situations, and in which ways such films give rise to cognitively dissonant experiences.

3.3 Types of dissonance in narrative comprehension

We discern three types of dissonant relations between cognitions that can occur in narrative comprehension. Two of these are particularly prominent in impossible puzzle films. First, two or more elements of a story can be in a dissonant relation with each other in an intratextual conflict ('text' is shorthand for 'the film' and all of the information presented in it, whether narrated or diegetic, visual or auditory). In such cases, when textual elements are perceived to be conflicting, we will speak of *incongruities*. Second, there are situations when an element of the narrative is at dissonance *with cognitions held by the viewer*. Within this, we might discern narrative elements that are in conflict with elementary cognitions and frames that characterise our elementary real-world and fictional logic, knowledge and sense-making, in which case we speak of *impossibilities*. These should be distinguished from a third, more individually determined type of cognitive dissonance that we could call *belief conflicts*. The latter category occurs when elements of a narrative give rise to cognitions in viewers that are at odds with their acquired idiosyncratic cognitions, such as subjective beliefs, specific cultural norms or personal attitudes. Belief conflicts are closest to cognitive dissonance in the traditional social-psychological sense, and will be left outside of the scope of this book. The primary reason for this is that this type of dissonance usually does not relate to formal-structural complexity or to cognitive conflicts regarding such narrative complexity. This does not mean that belief conflicts cannot give rise to powerful aesthetic or emotional effects. On the contrary, in situations where, for instance, a narrative makes us identify with a narrator who – as notoriously occurs in Vladimir Nabokov's 1955 novel *Lolita* – turns out to be a murderer and a paedophile, this experience may be psychologically unsettling because the artwork can evoke in readers a cognition (such as 'this narrator is a charming and eloquent man') that is dissonant with other cognitions like personally held beliefs, attitudes or values (for example, 'this man engages in activities I find morally reprehensible'). Although such conflicts may be upsetting (or, contrarily, artistically thought-provoking), in terms of comprehending the narrative, we can easily overcome, suspend or expand our own beliefs to make sense of the story (see Caracciolo 2013). We reflect on the experience by telling ourselves that we do not have to agree with the narrator, that he has shortcomings, but that he may be a victim of circumstances, that the (implied) author is posing us an ethical challenge or that the character will be punished for his crimes, and so on.[2] In short, belief

---

[2] Cognitive dissonances in terms of beliefs, values or stances may pressurise viewers to change their attitude towards characters, narrators or the work's (implied) author. Liesbeth

conflicts tend to concern narrative interpretation and thematics, and generally do not affect – let alone threaten – processes of narrative comprehension per se. Therefore, in the following section, we will focus on narrative *incongruities* (3.3.1) and *impossibilities* (3.3.2), which represent the types of dissonance that seem to characterise the experience that impossible puzzle films evoke.

3.3.1 Narrative incongruities

We put forward the thesis that narrative *incongruities* and *impossibilities*, often functioning in overlap, make up the primary effects that characterise impossible puzzle films. However, it must be noted that incongruities and impossibilities are not exclusive features to these films, as both occur in various kinds of fictional narratives. Textual conflicts that cause incongruities, first, can, in their most common appearances, surprise viewers, or prompt them to form new hypotheses about the narrative in question. Such incongruities are often not permanent and will allow their dissonance effect to be resolved. For example, in Otto Preminger's classic film noir *Laura* (1944) we learn at the beginning of the film that a woman named Laura (Gene Tierney) has been murdered. Halfway through the film, when detective McPherson (Dana Andrews) is in the middle of investigating her case and is interviewing possible suspects, Laura suddenly appears, alive and well. Such basic narrative incongruities can form twists that create an element of surprise (one of the three key effects of narrative according to Meir Sternberg; see also Chapter 2). They can also cue viewers to engage in interpretation, as the new incongruent information requires them to revise their initial hypotheses and recalibrate their conventional 'whodunit' question to pose more specific ones ('Is Laura still alive? Did someone else die? Is McPherson, in his obsession with the murder victim, imagining all this?'), or to even bring their inquiry to meta-level ('Have we been misled?').

Such common narrative incongruities and their cognitive effects tend to be temporary. The dissonance they invoke will usually be resolved by the narration itself, which may for instance reveal previous information to have been false. In cases where incongruities are *not* explicitly resolved, there is often still an implicit hierarchy of reliability involved, in which one of the conflicting cognitions is given precedence over the other. Viewers may for instance consider the incongruities to be epistemological corrections: new information has become available and since it contradicts the previous knowledge, the

---

Korthals Altes has related such interpretive operations to the notion of 'ethos attributions', which, according to her, are fundamentally implicated in the interpretation and evaluation of narrative fiction (see Korthals Altes 2014).

earlier information is considered to be false. This corresponds to a cognitive bias in temporal order that has been described as the *recency effect*, by which precedence is given to the most recently revealed information. As Bordwell, building on Sternberg (1990, 1992), puts it, '[w]hat comes later modifies our understanding of what went before' (Bordwell 2002a: 98).[3] Such basic, limited, local and, most of all, temporary incongruities generally do not cause prolonged cognitive dissonance in viewers, and will consequently not pose radical challenges to one's comprehension.

In literary fiction, Brian Richardson has discerned another, potentially more troubling kind of incongruity that he has labelled *denarration*. Denarration is 'an intriguing and paradoxical narrative strategy that appears in a number of late modern and postmodern texts' (Richardson 2001: 168). Richardson coined the term for cases in which the narrator of a story 'denies significant aspects of the narrative that had earlier been presented as given. The simplest example of this might be something like, "Yesterday it was raining. Yesterday it was not raining"' (ibid.: 168).[4] This strategy can be used to different effects, ranging from local, relatively unobtrusive rhetorical instances to more global, disconcerting and destabilising incongruities. Local instances of denarration can often be naturalised epistemologically – as the result of a shift in perspective, or a narrator who is revising his or her previous story (ibid.: 169). However, particularly in late- and postmodernist fiction, narrators like the one in Samuel Beckett's 1951 *Molloy* may persistently contradict themselves and consistently erase the story they have been narrating, which can be particularly problematic for the reader in his or her attempt to construct a stable

[3] By uncritically accepting the impact of the recency effect and generally applying its psychological predisposition to contemporary complex cinema (his examples include *Run Lola Run* and *Blind Chance*, movies that indeed privilege the last version of their multiple-draft plot), Bordwell downplays complex films' rich potential in playing with viewers' cognitive biases. As Nitzan Ben Shaul points out, Bordwell's generalisation implies that these films 'eliminate . . . the potential for optional thinking' (Ben Shaul 2012: 129), which is, for him, one of the key characteristics of general meaning-making in cinema that contemporary complex films play upon. Although we agree with Ben Shaul in questioning Bordwell's generalisation, we hesitate to fully accept his argument with regard to the case of *Run Lola Run*, as it is hard to see each narrative track in Tykwer's film as equally viable options for viewers to consider (in this film we tend to evaluate the final draft as the one that overwrites the one previously seen, and by which Lola is finally 'rewarded' (the director himself hints at such development too – see Tykwer 1999: 134)). In actually substantiating Ben Shaul's criticism, one could better list – impossible – puzzle films that not only maintain (for example, *La moustache*), but also thematise optional thinking (such as *Mr. Nobody*).

[4] 'The term "denarration" is currently used in two distinct senses: "ontological" denarration is the unresolvable denial of previously established story events, and "existential" denarration denotes the loss of identity in postmodern culture and society' (Richardson 2005: 100). The study of impossible puzzle films concerns cases of ontological denarration.

storyworld. Comparable examples of denarration, or *disnarration* (Warhol 2005), even *unprojection* (Ghosal 2015), can be found in film too – both on the local and global narrative level.

In film, local occurrences of the technique often function as rhetorical devices comparable to literary examples. They may for instance provide us brief moments of insight into a protagonist's mental state. This may happen when a film presents us with events in a seemingly objective manner, but shortly afterwards contradicts or corrects these as having been a lie or fantasy. One can think here for example of 'daydream sequences' such as in *High Fidelity* (Stephen Frears 2000), when the protagonist and narrator (John Cusack) encounters his ex-girlfriend's new boyfriend Ian (Tim Robbins), a confrontation of which we see several incongruent versions representing different fantasised outcomes, followed by a final, supposedly 'real' version in which the narrator's cowardly restraint stands in comical contrast to the previous ones; or in Ben Stiller's 2013 cinematic adaptation of James Thurber's 1939 short story *The Secret Life of Walter Mitty*, in which multiple scenes are corrected by the scenes that follow them, revealing the earlier presented events to have been daydreams of the absent-minded protagonist (interestingly, by comparison, Norman Z. McLeod's 1947 adaptation avoids this provisional confusion, marking its transitions from objective reality to daydreams rather clearly). However, as Robyn R. Warhol argues, such realist representations of subjectivity are actually part of the film's ordinary narration (and thereby do not qualify as examples of disnarration):

> the film tells that the character is having this fantasy or this dream, and the film signals (by the character's suddenly jolting awake, for instance) that the sequence is not to be taken as an authoritative set of actions within the diegesis. (Warhol 2005: 229)

A provocatively bold local example that does restore the denarrated action's authority within the diegesis appears in Michael Haneke's sinister hostage drama *Funny Games*.[5] In a particular scene, far into the otherwise perfectly realist plot, hostage Ann (Naomi Watts) suddenly grabs a rifle lying on a table and shoots Peter, one of her captors (Brady Corbet). Paul, the other captor (Michael Pitt), quickly takes a TV remote control, and by pressing the rewind button, reverses the story up to the point when Ann took the gun. Then, this time knowing Ann's intention, he acts faster and prevents Ann killing Peter. Paul's action does not only violate the classical rules of a fictional story, but also

---

[5] The ominous example appears in both Haneke's 1997 and 2007 version of the film (even though the US remake is a shot-for-shot version of the original, in order to avoid confusion with diegetic and real names of characters, actors and actresses, we describe the scene with reference to the 2007 variant).

imports the theoretical concept of denarration into the film's diegetic reality (and, through the use of the TV remote, does so in a seemingly self-reflective reference to the medium – an effect that is comparable to some of the modernist literary examples). Even though both of the contrasted events are part of the story, the incongruity of the scenes arguably does not evoke long-lasting confusion beyond a certainly shocking but only momentary surprise.[6]

Global instances of denarration, by which substantial elements start to contradict earlier presented parts of the story, can occur in film too. On the one hand, this strategy may serve unreliable stories or modular storytelling techniques. As for unreliability, the ultimate example is *Stage Fright*'s famous thirteen-minute-long 'lying flashback' at the beginning of the film, and the consequent negation of this extensive scene by the revelation of the truth towards the end. Also, erasure is often utilised in exposing subjective realist representations, as happens in, for example, Adrian Lyne's *Jacob's Ladder* or Marc Forster's *Stay* (in both films the disturbing reality turns out to be mere hallucinatory visions of a dying character). Global denarration can be a storytelling feature too. Here, presented variances are used to facilitate multiple-draft and other modular techniques. For instance, Tom Tykwer's trendsetting *Run Lola Run* presents three attempts (or runs) that Lola (Franka Potente) makes to save her boyfriend Manni's (Moritz Bleibtreu) life. However, it must be noted that in trying and retrying, Lola lives through, is aware of and learns from her previous attempts. Such narrative playfulness can therefore not be taken as a 'genuine' instance of denarration in the strict sense: there is no confronting erasure, only continuous overwriting of earlier attempts – from which, by reason of the recency effect, usually 'the last one taken, or completed, is the least hypothetical one' (Bordwell 2002a: 100).

In general, these mentioned variants of global denarration – whether they are used to set up unreliability, hide subjective realism or function as a non-linear storytelling device – do not pose serious challenges to the viewer. Their erasures do not create contradictory paradoxes within the diegetic world, but, on the contrary, resolve discrepancies by debunking false realities, or merely experiment with storytelling beyond the chronology-bound classical norm.

Global cases of 'proper' denarration that do act within the diegesis, however, can cause highly disorienting effects. Even though such more radical examples of contrasting incongruent elements are mainly reserved for art-cinema narratives' less realism-bound scenarios (remember the narrator's

---

[6] Ann's succeeded and failed attempts are both part of the film's story. Following the reversal and the prevention of Ann's action, Paul (being in full control of Haneke's game) looks back and reflects on the first version: 'You shouldn't have done that Ann! You are not allowed to break the rules!'

erratic retractions in *Last Year at Marienbad*), there are a few truly complex cases among (post-)classical narratives too. Alejandro Amenábar's mystery-drama *Open Your Eyes* is one among these, presenting a pervasive dissonance by maintaining two contradictory eventualities throughout the course of its story. After a car accident, in one of these states César's (Eduardo Noriega) face is left horribly disfigured, while in other moments he seems to be fully healed. This film exhibits a 'genuine' case of denarration, as its back-and-forth oscillation between contradictory states presents a paradox that is not just someone's subjective realism, but also part of this protagonist's actual diegetic reality. Viewers learn that César's healed moments are not fantasies or lies in an unreliable narrative, but glimpses of his 'artificial perception', created by a 'Life Extension' company for the time of keeping the protagonist's body in cryonic suspension. In this case the denarration is a global one, as the oscillation between César's contradictory perceptions takes about the half of the film's running time (around 55 out of the film's 117 minutes), before the resolving conclusion is revealed.[7] Alejandro González Iñárritu's *Birdman* (2014) offers a similar example of such diegetisation, in which case our protagonist's seemingly subjective realism turns into a part of the film's supernatural but seemingly objective storyworld. As Torsa Ghosal notes, '*Birdman* projects some fantastic scenes – logically impossible within the framing storyworld – as the protagonist Riggan's [Michael Keaton] hallucinations. However, in the final scene this impossible space is shown to be available to Riggan's daughter [Emma Stone]', collapsing the divide between the subjective and objective storyworld (Ghosal 2015).

Nevertheless, however ontologically unstable the presented storyworld can become as a result of denarration, disnarration or unprojection, we would argue that in these first-person (or focalised) narratives readers and viewers usually assess narrative instabilities as being epistemological problems. That is, they easily assign unreliability or fallibility to the person who narrates (or focalises) the incongruent story; such narrators are, after all, more susceptible to unreliability. This suspicion on behalf of the viewer may be the key in defusing the tensions in the incongruities: one can deem an incongruent narrator to be misleading, troubled, insane or even the subject of a meta-cognitive thematisation of the fundamental fallibility of memory and recall. In all cases, such inferences explain the textual incongruity and reduce the dissonance by naturalising it within the diegetic fiction (more on these naturalising strategies will follow in section 4.2).

---

[7] As a rather faithful remake, Cameron Crowe's *Vanilla Sky* (2001) closely follows Amenábar's story, but makes some significant changes regarding this resolving conclusion of the original.

Similar conflicts in narration, however, can become more troubling when occurring in instances of non-focalised or third-person narration, which, by convention, usually do not afford the possibility of inferring an unreliable or fallible character-narrator. Expounding on denarration's literary utilisation, Brian McHale has noted how particularly mid-twentieth-century postmodern novels have used the strategy of presenting contradictory events that are not resolved by the narrative, and are also not framed in any clear epistemological or ontological hierarchy (McHale 1984: 101–11). In these cases, the incongruity – or '[n]arrative self-erasure' (ibid.: 101) – is thus not 'framed as mental anticipations, wishes, or recollections of the characters, rather than left as an irresolvable paradox of the world *outside* the characters' minds' (ibid.: 101). Examples include Robert Coover's 1969 *The Babysitter* or Alain Robbe-Grillet's 1957 *La Jalousie (Jealousy)* as well as other novels from the nouveau roman tradition such as Robbe-Grillet's *Dans le labyrinthe (In the Labyrinth*, 1959) and *Projet pour une révolution à New York (Project for a Revolution in New York*, 1970). In such textual strategies of the nouveau roman and the postmodern novel, McHale observes, 'self-erasure may remain implicit, as when two or more – often many more – mutually exclusive states of affairs are projected by the same text, without any of these competing states of affairs being explicitly placed *sous rature*' (ibid.: 101).[8] The instabilities found in the nouveau roman and postmodern fiction thus become ontological (that is, an aspect of the storyworld) rather than epistemological (that is, tied to character subjectivity). According to McHale's analysis, literary modernism was focused on the epistemological conditions of subjective experience, while postmodernist literary experiments are characterised by these types of ontological destabilisation.

In film the same effect can occur when narration that seems omniscient (or at least not unambiguously focalised through a character) presents persisting incongruities. Probably the most famous cinematic example is Alain Resnais' 1961 film adaptation of Robbe-Grillet's screenplay *Last Year at Marienbad*. Resnais' film offers multiple mutually exclusive versions of events,

---

[8] Originating in the works of Martin Heidegger, but brought to extensive philosophical discussion by Jacques Derrida, *sous rature* (under erasure) is a philosophical technique that signals – usually by crossing out a word – the indispensable necessity but illegitimate inadequacy of language in signifying reality. McHale's take on the strategy, however, is less philosophically oriented, but primarily narrative: 'postmodernist fictions such as *Reflex and Bone Structure* [Clarence Major, 1975] place under erasure not signifiers of concepts in a philosophical discourse, but presented objects in a projected world; and their purpose is not, as with Derrida, that of laying bare the *aporias* of western metaphysics, but rather that of laying bare the processes by which readers, in collaboration with texts, construct fictional objects and worlds' (McHale 1984: 100).

the global structure of which remains in contradiction. Viewers are given no way of knowing which of the projected events are supposed to be more reliable or truthful. These incongruities thus create ontological conflicts, as they seem to form an aspect of the presented storyworld. Yet, it must be noted, this does not mean that these incongruities cannot be interpreted as subjective projections of the narrator X (Giorgio Albertazzi), or extratextual intentions of the authors (Robbe-Grillet and Resnais). After extensive interpretive attempts, one may agree with Susan Sontag, who, in her famous essay 'Against Interpretation', argued that 'Resnais and Robbe-Grillet consciously designed *Last Year at Marienbad* to accommodate a *multiplicity of equally plausible* interpretations' (Sontag 1967: 9 – our emphasis).

It is such ontological incongruities that permeate impossible puzzle films. Impossible puzzle films frequently project stories and storyworlds in which specific elements or global patterns stand in unresolvable contradiction, creating challenging cognitive dissonances. In some of these films, like in Abbas Kiarostami's playfully anomalous *Copie conforme* (*Certified Copy*, 2010), Christoffer Boe's intriguingly ambiguous *Reconstruction* (2003) or Emmanuel Carrère's *La moustache* (2005), ontological denarration is the core strategy of complexification. *La moustache*, for instance, plants a seemingly insignificant incongruity at the heart of its complication – a nuance that gradually grows into an overall puzzling anomaly. At the start of the film, we see protagonist Marc (Vincent Lindon) asking his wife whether she thinks it would be a good idea if he shaved off his moustache – a moustache that, so we learn, he has been sporting for all of his adult life. When Marc decides to shave the moustache, his environment, to his surprise, does not react to the change at all. His wife and friends tell him they have no idea what he is talking about, since he has *never* had a moustache. What we viewers have learned, and seen with our own eyes, is thus persistently contradicted from this point on. This incongruity (Marc had a moustache, as we have seen and he himself also believes/Marc never had a moustache, as everyone else around him asserts) becomes the first of a series of discrepancies in Marc's life, in which events and states give rise to ever more concerning – and, for the viewer, highly puzzling – contradictions. It is important to note here that the dissonance experienced by Marc is kept equally dissonant for viewers. What started as a seeming absurdity becomes the source of an insoluble ontological incongruity that pervades and propels the narrative.

Whereas *La moustache* still constructs a relatively basic narrative structure (apart from these absurd global contradictions, that is), other impossible puzzle films couple similar incongruities to more convoluted narrative structures. David Lynch's *Lost Highway* (1997) is a film often cited to illustrate more globally affecting incongruities. It opens with a scene in which we witness Fred Madison (Bill Pullman) in his apartment. Someone buzzes the intercom and tells him: 'Dick Laurent is dead'. Following a series of mysterious events, at the end of the film we follow Fred driving up to his own house. He buzzes *himself* to report: 'Dick Laurent is dead'. This suggests that, at the same point in the story, he was both the person ringing from outside and answering the buzzer from inside his house. Another, more local incongruity appears elsewhere in the film: the scene when the Mystery Man dials Fred's home and takes his own call at the other end of the line. Yet what is really confusing in the first example (and goes beyond the confined weirdness of the second) is that two fully-fledged global storylines collide spatio-temporally in an unresolvable manner. *Lost Highway* is riddled with such complexifying narrative moments and patterns. In the words of Murray Smith, in *Lost Highway* 'appearance and reality are dislocated; motivations are obscure, *cognitive dissonance* disturbs the very foundations of narrative coherence; temporal and causal sequences become paradoxical' (Smith 2003: 159 – our emphasis).

In short, more radically than in *La moustache*, dissonance occurs within many of *Lost Highway*'s narrative parameters (space, time, causality, character unity). Like most of Lynch's intricate stories, impossible puzzle films generally do not offer ways of establishing an ontological hierarchy among conflicting narrative elements. They do not clearly embed one set of narrative clues in another – for instance by unambiguously cueing viewers that a particular part of the narrative is in fact the fantasy, dream or mental projection of a character in another part of the narrative. In fact, the narratives of impossible puzzle films are rarely presented as unambiguously subjective and focalised; as we will later see, retaining uncertainty regarding the subjective or objective status of their narration can be a strategy to heighten ambiguous and dissonant effects. Such strategies make their incongruities generally not readily reducible to a matter of mere unreliability or character subjectivity (an interpretive strategy that we will discuss in more detail in Chapter 4). As no direct pathways of resolution are handed to the viewer, the conflicting story elements thus hold sway and tend to cause puzzling cognitive dissonances, comparable to the kind that postmodernist literary fiction poses.

Another complexifying device found in both many impossible puzzle films and postmodern literary fiction is that of the narrative loop. As McHale notes, a narrative

> can also '*bend*' a sequence back upon itself to form a *loop*, in which one and the same event figures as both antecedent and sequel of some other event. The presence of the same event at two different points in the sequence leaves the reader hesitating between two alternative reconstructions of the 'true' sequence, in one of which event A precedes event B, while in the other event A follows event B. (McHale 1984: 108)

Undeniably, narrative loops can also be radically destabilising, as they upset basic spatio-temporal relations and potentially undermine the clear hierarchy between narrative elements. In the impossible puzzle film *Triangle*, for instance, multiple (at least four) versions of the same temporal loop occur simultaneously within a single spatial setting, making many of the protagonist's actions concurrently the plot's cause *and* effect. Moreover, all these versions of the loop seem to be equally valid in terms of their ontological status (that is, none is the 'true' sequence referred to in McHale's definition), by which the loop remains fundamentally paradoxical. In James Ward Byrkit's *Coherence*, likewise, characters seem to have many concurrent incarnations, densely populating the overlapping and looping events that both preclude and exclude each other. Such entwining narrative structures cause strong cognitive dissonances by creating paradoxical and incongruous relations among looping diegetic elements (for example, among multiple existing versions of characters populating the same level and moments in the storyworld; or among events that function as both each other's cause and effect). However, in these more radical instances, narrative incongruities also overlap with the second (in some ways neighbouring) type of dissonance we discerned – that is, with narrative impossibilities.

3.3.2 Narrative impossibilities

Cognitive dissonance in narrative comprehension may occur not only when narrative elements are dissonant with regard to each other, but also when diegetic elements are at odds with the cognitions that make up viewers' real-life and fictional frames of sense-making. We call the latter cases impossibilities. Although we distinguish between these two types of dissonance, the difference between them may get blurred: after all, radical, unresolvable types of ontological narrative incongruities also tend to create impossible situations and scenarios, as they do not correspond to any real-world logic, story logic or other cognitive frames that most viewers hold. We argue that impossible puzzle films often rely on this specific combination of narrative strategies, creating 'impossible incongruities' that lead to complex, puzzling experiences.

Yet the two types do refer to different effects of narrative. The origin of dissonance in fiction may, for instance, depend on the established rules of a given storyworld: a fully developed loop narrative may be internally rational, congruent and coherent, yet may still give rise to oddities that are dissonant with our sense-making strategies trained in real-world experience (such as conflicting character duplications or spatio-temporal warps). As a result, such a story is likely to be experienced as 'impossible'. An example of this internally rationalised yet impossible scenario is offered by Nacho

Vigalondo's 2007 *Timecrimes*. Whereas in *Triangle* there is neither any clearly communicated reason behind the loop in the story (even though one could read the film's title as an allusion to the Bermuda Triangle – popular culture's go-to reference for paranormal activities happening in open waters), nor any explicit reset point that could structure the looping narrative sequences, *Timecrimes* does present a 'scientific' motivation for its impossible structure. It employs a time machine to 'rationalise' the overlapping loops, and, within its consistently presented storyworld, establishes and adheres to a set of more or less coherent internal laws. The following plot map of *Timecrimes* (Figure 3.1) exposes this inner congruent logic of the impossible looping story, revealing a rather simple narrative structure behind the otherwise complex viewing experience (the protagonist repeatedly travels approximately one hour back in time, but, when doing so, is actually being duplicated, and, as a consequence, keeps meeting his previous selves who continue to exist in their original times). What is difficult in *Timecrimes* is not getting Vigalondo's fairly simple idea (travelling in time causes character multiplication) or following this idea's inner logic (which Figure 3.1 reveals), but placing the looping and intertwined actions on a chronological timeline that is compatible with viewers' real-life time experience. Viewers may also have problems making rational or logical sense of the looping structure's fundamental paradoxes, such as the question of pinpointing the start of the first loop (a paradox that ensnarls basically all loop narratives).

It must however be noted that, when taken in the broadest sense, impossibilities are very common in fictional narratives. Film and literary history has been populated with an abundance of monsters, ghosts, demons, spaceships,

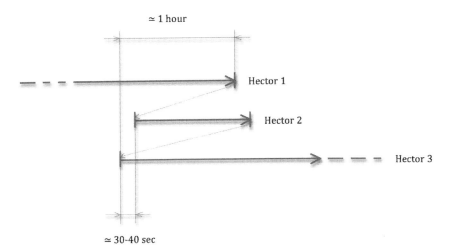

Figure 3.1

talking animals or people with superhuman powers that are all examples of narrative elements that transgress real-world experience. Nevertheless, the presence of a flying carpet in a fairy tale generally does not thwart our comprehension, nor does it leave us in bafflement with any pressing cognitive dissonance. Impossibilities seem to come in many forms, and the difference between them needs to be conceptualised here first.

In literary theory, special attention has been given to narrative impossibilities under the label of 'unnatural narratology'. Although various definitions of unnatural narratives have been provided, we will follow Jan Alber, who 'restricts the use of the term to narratives which represent storyworlds that contain physically, logically, or humanly impossible scenarios or events' (Alber 2013a: 69). As a research programme, unnatural narratology thus 'involves the systematic study of the various ways in which fictional narratives deviate from "natural" cognitive frames, i.e. our real-world understanding of time, space, and other human beings' (ibid.: 69). In his 2009 article 'Impossible Storyworlds – and What to Do With Them', Alber discusses how readers make sense of unnatural scenarios and impossible storyworlds that deviate strongly from everyday experience. He argues that while all narrative impossibilities have some defamiliarising effect, an important distinction can be made between elements in a story that are *physically impossible* (Alber's example is 'a speaking corkscrew') and aspects of a narrative that are *logically impossible* (his example is the presentation of 'mutually incompatible events', like the kind of ontological incongruities we have been discussing). With this distinction in mind, the difference between a fairy tale and a postmodern novel becomes apparent. Whereas many forms of narrative may contain physically impossible elements (again: talking animals, flying carpets, and so on), scenarios that are logically unreasonable (such as loops, character duplications or conflicting storylines) seem to be more characteristic of narratives that deliberately complexify the experience by hindering viewers' sense-making efforts. Indeed, as Alber also reasons – in line with our hypothesis on the approximate proportionality between cognitive effort and sensed complexity – 'the logically impossible is even stranger and more disconcerting than the physically impossible, and we have to engage in even more extensive cognitive processing to make sense of it' (Alber 2009: 80).

In fact, in the appropriation of the *possible worlds* theory for the understanding of fictional worlds, as developed in the work of Lubomír Doležel (1976, 1988, 1998), Umberto Eco (1979), Marie-Laure Ryan (1991, 1992, 2013) and Ruth Ronen (1994, 1996), logically unreasonable storyworlds are considered to be the only truly 'impossible' storyworlds. Derived from modal logic, in this understanding of fictional worlds as possible worlds, a (story)world is considered 'possible' if it represents a situation that can follow from the logical laws, options and constraints of an actual world (a connection known as the 'accessibility relation', originally defined by Saul A. Kripke). In respect of this delineation of possible worlds, Marie-Laure Ryan defines impossible worlds in the following way:

> By impossible worlds, I do not mean simply worlds where things happen that do not or could not happen in the real world, such as animals being able to talk, princes being turned into frogs, or people being kidnapped by space aliens. These are merely unnatural, or fantastic worlds; an important form of experimental literature creates worlds that cannot satisfy even the most liberal interpretation of possibility because they transgress the basic laws of logic: non-contradiction (you cannot have p and ~p) and excluded middle (you must have either p or ~p). (Ryan 2013: 131)

Storyworlds may thus allow all kinds of deviations in terms of physical properties, but remain 'possible' as long as they keep intact a basic logical structure underlying that world. 'The most common interpretation associates possibility with logical laws; every world that respects the principle of non-contradiction and excluded middle is a P[ossible]W[orld]' (Ryan 2005: 446). By consequence, impossibility is associated with contradictions within storyworlds, similar to what we earlier defined as ontological incongruities. Umberto Eco has argued that worlds that feature such logical incongruities can never really be 'worlds', noting that the term 'impossible worlds' is in fact an oxymoron. According to Eco, impossible – and, in their extreme instances, inconceivable – worlds can be mentioned, but never really conceived or constructed 'because their alleged individuals or properties violate our logical or epistemological habits' (Eco 1994: 76). On the other hand, as Ryan notes, a significant literary corpus of texts does feature such worlds. Literary works have contained impossibilities in the form of metaleptic transgressions of ontologically separate worlds (Ryan 2013: 133), impossible spaces (ibid.: 134) or impossible time (ibid.: 136), or have even invented other impossible texts (ibid.: 138) such as the fictive boundless texts described in some of the short stories of Jorge Luis Borges.

The corpus of impossible puzzle films is also characterised by a profusion of such logically unreasonable events, including ontological incongruities, temporal loops, character multiplications and other paradoxical features of fictional worlds. The principle of non-contradiction is strategically violated in these films to create dissonant cognitions in viewers. Eco has argued that the only pleasure we could draw from such worlds 'is the pleasure of our logical and perceptual defeat – or the pleasure of a "self-disclosing" text which speaks of its own inability to describe *impossibilia*' (Eco 1990: 77). Yet this does not seem to be entirely the case for all impossible puzzle films; over the course of this book we argue that even though these films may indeed turn out to be logically and perceptually defeating, and thereby somewhat inconceivable, this particular sense of cognitive failure is not the only appeal they have. On the contrary, impossible puzzle films often *do* encourage viewers to engage in various sense-making operations, whether these efforts prove fruitless or not, and lure them into pushing (and sometimes even questioning) their habitual comprehensive routines. Moreover, the dissonant element in impossible puzzle films can also not always be seen as a feature of their particular diegetic world only. These films also play extensively with convoluted storytelling and complexified story structures, which viewers can also hold accountable for the presented contradictions. Viewers may for instance be under the impression that there is logic to a given impossible puzzle film's storyworld, but that it is the complexity of the narration that does not give them proper access to this logic, and that this logic is exactly what needs deciphering – like a mystery at the heart of a film, comparable to an actual riddle. Nevertheless, underlying all these effects is a pervading sense of dissonance inciting readers and viewers to do something to resolve this sensation.

Returning to Jan Alber's distinction, one may wonder why it is that logically impossible stories create notable effects of dissonance, particularly when compared to physically impossible narrative elements. Or, more concretely, why do logically troubling impossible puzzle science-fiction films like *Donnie Darko*, *Triangle* or *Timecrimes* seem to demand more cognitive effort than an impossibility-loaded but otherwise highly classical and canonical narrative like *Star Wars* (George Lucas 1977) does? There are several ways of addressing this question.

One potentially viable approach is to distinguish fictional worlds from possible worlds. Fictional worlds and possible worlds are not fully inter-changeable concepts: 'Fictional worlds are not non-actual in the same sense that possible worlds are, that is, they are not alternative ways the world might have been' (Ronen 1996: 22). Possible worlds are non-actualised versions of our actual real world (they are actualisable in the sense that their events could have happened in the actual world); fictional worlds, on the other hand, depart from our actual reality and actualise a world themselves within their diegetic boundaries. Impossible puzzle films with their subtle and ambiguous deviation from actual world's reality seem to occupy a kind of twilight zone between fictional and possible worlds to create an enigmatic and perplexing experience: although clearly fictional and impossible, they also disguise themselves as somewhat 'possible'. Eco compares such experiences to the one that a glance at the famous Penrose figure elicits (Figure 3.2). Calling such diegetic universes impossible possible worlds, he describes these as a fictional realm that 'gives at the same time both the illusion of a coherent world and the feeling of some inexplicable impossibility' (Eco 1990: 77). Impossible

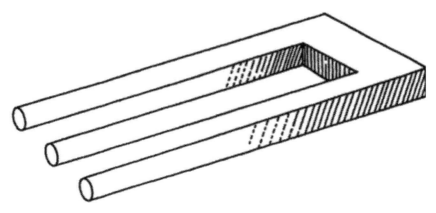

Figure 3.2

puzzle films are like impossible possible worlds: they present storyworlds that are seemingly coherent and in compliance with the logic of generic and real-world laws, but which, amidst this seeming coherence, also host narrative elements that will strike viewers as remarkably dissonant (with regard to both the internal laws of the storyworld and our sense of real-world logic). Their effect is comparable to the dissonant co-presence of a two- and/or a three-branched figure in Penrose's deceptive, but seemingly 'realistic' drawing.

Another explanation is that physical impossibilities often form an accepted and expected part of the *generic conventions* that culturally regulate narrative reception. The discursive generic context of science fiction, for example, readily naturalises the presence of spaceships, as our gathered knowledge about and expectations related to the sci-fi genre hand us the interpretive routines to make sense of those flying objects. Readers or viewers therefore only need to make specific local alterations to real-world models and real-world logic to accommodate a physically impossible event within the constructed storyworld – for instance by adopting a modified view of the scientific possibilities in astronautics to justify the existence of spaceships. The generic conventions and laws of genres like science fiction and fantasy allow a particularly high number of such modifications, maintaining a high degree of flexibility with regard to real-world possibilities. Of course, logical impossibilities too can be expected to be part of certain generic conventions (as, for example, happens in time-travel narratives within the science-fiction genre). The difference, however, is that whereas physically impossible events can easily be understood by expanding the specific laws of a particular story-world (for example, by assimilating laws of nature, biological categories or scientific possibilities), strong logical impossibilities constitute a violation of the fundamental laws of world building itself. They evade some of our most elementary strategies for constructing and making sense of a narrative, and are therefore prone to causing disturbances in comprehension.

Why is it that we seem to experience logically deviant storyworlds to be relatively 'impossible' to construct? An explanation for this relative inflexibility regarding basic real-world logic does not need to be sought in modal logic only (after all, most moviegoers do not behave like logicians), but could also be attributed to the elementary workings and limitations of human cognition (as will be discussed shortly in section 3.4), as well as to the ingrained dependence of hermeneutic procedures on the embodied nature of cognition (3.5).

3.4 Cognitive access to impossible storyworlds: immersed and reflected operations

Strong impossibilities tend to obstruct elementary mental processes of narrative comprehension. In cognitive narratology, it is assumed that all narratives – including even the most extraordinary fantasy stories – are understood by recourse to everyday knowledge acquired through real-life experience. This knowledge is clustered in what have been called frames or schemas (sometimes also scripts), which are memorised and habitualised structures of information related to prototypical events and situations.[9] Viewers, often unconsciously, bring in a broad variety of such predetermined knowledge structures when mentally (re-)constructing the different elements of a story. In the words of David Herman (who uses the term 'script'),

> comprehension of a text or a discourse – a story – requires access to a plurality of scripts. In the absence of stereotypes stored as scripts, readers could not draw textual inferences of the most basic sort . . . It is not that stories are recognizable only if and insofar as they tell me what I already know; rather, stories stand in a certain relation to what I know, focusing attention on the unusual and the remarkable against a backdrop made up of highly structured patterns of belief and expectation. (Herman 2002: 90)

Cognitive frames play an elementary role in comprehending storyworlds, as viewers use information and memorised patterns to structure incoming information, to regulate their own expectations, to determine what is salient and to fill in gaps of missing information. Readers and viewers tend to initially construct a fictional world on the basis of the assumption that the fictional world

---

[9] For explanations about these underlying structures of meaning-making see, among others, Marvin Minsky's (1975) *frame theory*, Roger Schank and Robert Abelson's (1977) *script theory*, Frederic Charles Bartlett's (1932) *schema theory* and its embodied explication by George Lakoff (1987) and Mark Johnson (1990 [1987]).

corresponds to their everyday experiential reality of the actual world, unless cued otherwise. Drawing on John Searle's work on speech acts, Marie-Laure Ryan called this the *principle of minimal departure* (Ryan 1991), also described by Kendall Walton as the *reality principle* or the *principle of mutual belief* (Walton 1990). Viewers will construct a fictional world as being a mimetic extension of the actual world – unless the film gives indications that a particular story-world has alternative rules. Viewers respond to such cues by making the necessary inferences, altering or adapting relevant frames to mentally recalibrate and construct the storyworld and accommodate the alteration (for example, 'this world is like ours, but with spaceships').

Impossible puzzle films tend to make heavy demands on viewers in terms of such storyworld revisions. One reason for this is that whereas physical impossibilities appear instantly in a storyworld and through that directly cue viewers to make frame adaptations, the dissonant effect of logical impossibilities manifests more pervasively, gradually undermining the basic structures on which worlds are built. Impossible puzzle films tend to unfold their logical impossibilities progressively throughout their narration, often in the form of subtle but cumulative violations of the minimal departure principle. Their impossible possible worlds aim to host a string of events for which no explanation can be instantly devised by the viewer. One could say that their narrative progression is like a linear and temporally organised version of the Penrose drawing (Figure 3.2) – a kind of narrative 'long-term illusion' (Eco 1990: 78): although viewers can witness a smooth, step-by-step developing story, the unfolding experience does not consolidate into a fully coherent and lucid narrative on the whole.

In cognitive terms, the comprehension of a temporally developing global impossibility is rather difficult, demanding an intense interplay between short- and long-term memory use, while usually also requiring more active and inventive rationalisation efforts. In *Triangle*, for instance, halfway through the course of watching the film, viewers have probably already needed to radically revise their strategies of narrative construction multiple times. As the narrative's loop structure is not yet fully and clearly revealed in this phase, viewers cannot know – but they gradually learn – that four versions of the same protagonist are active within a time loop. The unexplicated (and seemingly inexplicable) character doublings, strange multiplications of objects and the repeated events aboard the ship thus do not only violate real-world frames of minimal departure, but they also challenge viewers' rational reasoning, burdening them with the task of devising an alternative story logic. The multi-layered and continuous stream of cognitively dissonant events exerts a pressure on immersed viewers, prompting them to find a reasonable, if not rational, explanatory hypothesis regarding the coherence of the narrative events. Only gradually does the film's narration reveal new bits of information that provide clues as to how its particular temporal anomaly might be understood.

The meaning-making operations that impossible puzzle films activate arguably demand a high amount of invested mental effort from viewers – not only because they call for more extensive and active sense-making, but also because they involve procedures that are of a different, more cognitively taxing kind than the ones that classical narratives request. In canonical, classical film narratives, the overall story logic and storytelling procedures are usually directly accessible to viewers through the readily available cognitive and narrative frames. Real-world exploration, acculturation and familiarisation with convention have made viewers acquainted with recurring narrative patterns and equipped them with appropriate responses in sense-making. In classical narrative films, most viewers know (in a very practical, often unreflecting manner) that there will be one or more protagonists who most likely pursue some clearly identifiable goals, who correspond to a more or less rational character psychology and who are situated in a spatio-temporally and causally cohering storyworld comparable to ours. Viewers are also generally familiar with the narrative devices through which a classical narrative film allows them to construct a narrative sequence, recognising different markers of spatial, temporal and subjective continuity as well as transitions. This synergy forms the 'fictional contract' on which viewers can rely when confronted with even the most complicated of classical structures and the most fantastic of storyworlds. This solidified knowledge and acquired sense for story logic forms a background against which viewers can focus on understanding the particulars of a given story. Understanding the story thus becomes mainly a deductive and top-down procedure: available knowledge on prototypical narrativity is used (and where needed modified) to understand particular narrative instances at hand. In impossible puzzle films, on the other hand, it is exactly these available narrative schemas and scripts that are often violated for complicating effects. When watching *Triangle*, it will become apparent to most viewers that certain key elements of conventional story logic do not make sense. As explanatory frames are not (yet) available, the initial confusion pressurises viewers to come up with new hypotheses to explain or resolve the emerging dissonances. The viewing thus turns into a more inductive, bottom-up operation: viewers must re-sample the available information, and find a way to integrate the conflicting particulars into a globally cohering narrative structure (which in *Triangle* ultimately turns out to be a paradoxical loop). Cognitive dissonances in story logic therefore pervade the viewing experience as a complicating effect, but at the same time function as a consistent drive to keep viewers enduringly engaged in the cognitively demanding formations and continuous revisions of narrative hypotheses.

This problematisation of regular, immersive sense-making routines prompts viewers to engage with impossible storyworlds' cognitive dissonances in a more reflective manner too. By inspiring audiences to form increasingly informed and precise hypotheses, films like *Triangle*, *Primer* or *Reality* challenge (and entertain) viewers through both story-immersive and self-conscious channels simultaneously. Following Eco, we claimed that these films offer *impossible possible worlds*: they provide both the illusion of a coherent and logical world and the feeling of some indecipherable and inexplicable impossibility at the same time. But how can a narrative experience be simultaneously story-immersive and self-conscious? We argue that impossible puzzle films pull off a kind of *narrative double perspectivation*,[10] playing upon motivational pressures of represented dissonant cognitions on the levels of both immersive and reflective engagement. Put otherwise, these films invite viewers to be immersed in the fictional world, while at the same time also being confronted with the impossibilities in the fiction's design, and with the problems that these impossibilities pose to their own sense-making (while Chapter 4 will elucidate viewers' reflective acknowledgement of storytelling manipulation, Chapter 5 will detail the balance between dissonant cognitions and viewer immersion in impossible puzzle films).

One could claim that no rational mind would engage in immersive problem-solving when it is about fictional narrative paradoxes and other clearly dissonant scenarios. Indeed, in theory as well as by intuition, it seems unlikely that intelligent adults would invest serious energies in resolving fictional dissonance, for instance by figuring out how it could be possible that an apparently chronological fictional timeline bites its own tail. Nevertheless, as the abundance of forensic fan activity on the internet demonstrates, and as the university seminars that we conducted also showed us in practice, viewers often *do* embark on an immersive quest for finding (quasi-)rational answers to clearly irrational events of impossible puzzle stories. Throughout this book, we will try to address the different reasons for this fascination. First of all, we begin by following Marie-Laure Ryan, who, in her paper entitled 'Impossible Worlds and Aesthetic Illusion', argues that even impossible fictional worlds elicit some immersive illusion.[11] Fictional engagement, according to Ryan, allows the possibility of 'making oneself at home on a Moebius strip' (Ryan

[10] Our expression of 'narrative double perspectivation' is a metaphor describing the parallel process of viewers' absorbed-immersive and distanced-reflective engagement, and does not refer to Sabine Schlickers' (2009: 245–6) more literally taken notion of double perspectivation, by which she distinguishes focalised and non-focalised versions of point of view in cinema.

[11] Ryan argues that 'the only readers who can be satisfied with a purely metatextualist interpretation are literary critics; most readers will do whatever they can to construct a world in which they can achieve at least some degree of aesthetic illusion because make-believe

Figure 3.3

2013: 142). Important in this respect is Ryan's observation that even in the most radically impossible storyworlds, parts of the world will remain 'possible' – that is, these narratives always balance their impossibilities with possible aspects (or at least with more plausible ones). After all, it is through the viewer's immersion in a seemingly possible world that the confrontation with the impossible becomes all the more striking. As a concrete example, Ryan refers to Maurits Cornelis Escher's 1956 lithograph *Print Gallery* (Figure 3.3) as

> an image that represents an impossible space. Through its use of perspective, it allows the spectator to imagine herself within its world. As the eye follows

corresponds to a basic need of the human mind, and it is simply more enjoyable than self-reflexivity' (Ryan 2013: 144).

> the path of the gaze of a character looking at a picture in an art gallery, we
> see the world of the picture unfold in a perfectly normal way, until, suddenly,
> we realise that we have been thrown into another world, without noticing
> the transition – a world incompatible with the one we started from . . . It is
> our immersion in the three-dimensionality of Escher's picture that eventually
> leads to the recognition of the impossibility of its space. (Ryan 2013: 142)

A textually unfolding version of Escher's perceptual experience similarly
requires the reader to have the ability to oscillate between incompatible
spaces and plot trajectories. For such texts, Ryan suggests, readers may use a
strategy that she calls the creation of a 'Swiss cheese ontology':

> In this ontology, the irrational world is contained in delimited areas that
> pierce the texture of the fictional world like the holes of a Swiss cheese, but
> the laws of logic remain applicable in the solid areas and the reader can make
> regular inferences. (Ryan 2013: 143)

What is true for indirect textual simulation is doubly true for visual cinematic
representation. Given audiovisual representation's more direct address, displaying logically impossible worlds, like in impossible puzzle films, can make
the logically impossible perceptually available, thereby providing viewers
with an actual diegetically 'inhabitable' Möbius strip. Films like *Lost Highway*,
Triangle, Timecrimes, Primer or *Reality* provide a narrative and audiovisual versions of baffling but immersive experience similar to Escher's lithograph.
When vividly presenting realistic and life-like storyworlds, impossible puzzle
films assist viewers in their willing suspension of – narrative – disbelief
(Coleridge 1975 [1817]: 169), or, as Torben Grodal puts it, these films do
not impair viewers' disposition of suspension of belief (Grodal 2009: 154).
Through their narrative double perspectivation, impossible puzzle films
might violate Werner Wolf's second principle of world-making – '[t]he
principle of consistency of the represented world' (Wolf 2009: 151) – but
seem to not fully disturb viewers' immersion; instead, they often successfully lure viewers into various puzzle games of make-believe (Walton 1990),
encouraging them to try to resolve the cognitive dissonances.

3.5 'IMPOSSIBILITIES' AND EMBODIED COGNITION

Beyond the complex cognitive demands of a strategically built narrative
double perspectivation, other reasons behind the difficulty of comprehending
impossible puzzle films can be identified. We argue that logically impossible
scenarios do not only deliberately upset viewers' (1) *conscious and reflected knowledge* based on their everyday experientiality; these stories' strong perceptual
impossibilities and unconventional abstract narrative structures often also

challenge (2) *cognitively impenetrable deep-seated embodied underpinnings* of our sense-making operations (as introduced in Chapter 2). Further elucidating the second option (in subsections 3.5.1 and 3.5.2), we will demonstrate that in creating cognitive dissonance, impossible puzzle films often play on the universal operations and limitations of our *embodied minds*, challenging ingrained sense-making routines that are based on some of the most fundamental aspects of our lived experience.

Regarding option (1) above, we have already discussed how logically impossible stories can mess with viewers' acquired knowledge patterns to create dissonant viewing experiences. Yet what is important to emphasise is that the 'impossibilities' in impossible puzzle films often do not concern arbitrary or conventional aspects of narrative, but rather disrupt parameters that are also constitutive of everyday, real-life experientiality and consciousness. Think here of elementary dimensions such as space, time, action, causality, linearity, continuity and character identity. Disruptions of these dimensions seem to pose serious challenges that are pervasive and not easily resolvable for viewers. This can be related to the fact that we have minds fundamentally embedded in and adjusted to real-world actions and possibilities. As Jan Alber notes,

> [r]eaders have certain assumptions about the temporal and spatial organization of the actual world as well as its inhabitants, and this knowledge plays a crucial role when we try to make sense of narrative texts. Among other things, we *know* that human beings are either alive or they are dead; we *know* that time moves forward; we *know* that (unless there is an earthquake or a tornado) the spaces we inhabit do not suddenly change their shape; and so forth. (Alber 2013a: 71 – our emphasis)

Consequentially, when 'confronted with physically, logically, or humanly impossible scenarios or events . . . we have to conduct seemingly impossible mapping operations to orient ourselves within storyworlds that refuse to be organised with the help of our real-world knowledge' (ibid.: 71–2). Monika Fludernik has conceptualised the importance of the dimension of *embodiment* to such elementary knowledge in narrative sense-making. As she argues,

> [e]mbodiedness evokes all the parameters of a real-life schema of existence which always has to be situated in a specific time and space frame, and the motivational and experiential aspects of human actionality likewise relate to the knowledge about one's physical presence in the world. Embodiment and existence in human terms are indeed the same thing. (Fludernik 1996: 22)

Many of the governing principles of narrative (and of understanding narrative) are based on fundamental features of our consciousness, and hosted by the physiology of our human bodies situated in a world with specific physical characteristics. Embodiment, following Fludernik's view, thus informs the most elementary of narrative parameters – the so-called *narratemes*. Narratemes form the basic building blocks of any narrative.[12] The core of these narratemes, as devised by Gerald Prince (1999) and listed in detail by Werner Wolf (2003), include experientiality, representationality, temporality, setting, character, action, specificity, concreteness, meaningfulness, chronology, repetition, causality and teleology. Radically complex and unnatural narratives such as impossible puzzle films seem to deliberately undermine some of these basic ingredients of story logic (usually one or a few – but not all, as this would block any sense of narrativity altogether). For example, characters may duplicate, transform or transgress the limits of human possibilities; time may be looped, reversed, contradictory, fragmented or travelled; spaces may be expanding, contracting, endless, looping or more than three-dimensional, and so on. In the example of *Triangle*, the looping story clearly undermines our intuitive understanding of chronological time, of causal action and of the unicity of human beings. To a mind trained in a world with unidirectional time, causal relations and stable self-perceptions, such violations are relatively difficult to comprehend, as viewers have no phenomenological experience or concrete, real-world understanding of such a temporal loop. As Torben Grodal has noted,

> [t]he more concrete the phenomena we deal with – the more easily they can be comprehended through schemas derived from our basic interaction with external reality – the easier the thought processes involved, because they are both conceptually and emotionally backed up by our basic embodiedness. (Grodal 2009: 210)

Action patterns, for which no such basic schemas exist because they have no basis in concrete phenomena or lived experience (like an endless time loop), or for which these schemas do not work, will as a result be much more difficult to grasp cognitively. Such patterns can also require more extensive mapping operations, as in *Triangle*, for instance, where one has to blend one's understanding of the film's temporality with the more familiar and concrete spatial experience of being in a loop.

As for option (2), impossibilities do not only concern consciously available real-world knowledge and action patterns. That is, they do not simply negotiate viewers' cognitively aware access to their experiences regarding space, time, action, causality, linearity, continuity and character identity. Impossible

---

[12] 'As factors of narrativity . . . "narratives" designate the basic traits, the "building blocks and syntax rules" of the frame narrative and hence also of concrete narratives. The number and importance of these narratemes . . . determines the degree of narrativity that an artwork/text or parts of it can be seen to have' (Wolf 2003: 183).

puzzle films also induce perplexity by disturbing deep-seated, cognitively impenetrable embodied operations of sense-making.[13] Let us first briefly recap the main arguments of the embodied cognition thesis (as introduced in section 2.1), and then see how exceedingly complex films play upon these bodily determined and cognitively isolated processes.

As our interactions with the environment are of a bodily nature, our mental world, through which we (re-)construct and understand this environment, is bodily determined also. Various branches of research have confirmed this view, focusing on the feeling of one's body as it exists in close connection to one's mind. According to the basic tenet of the embodied-cognitive approach, the human body's continuously utilised motor programmes and repeated environmental interactions give rise to deeply rooted embodied knowledge structures in the mind. These embodied knowledge structures have been called *embodied image schemas*, referring to the results that come as the habitualised feelings of one's own body solidifies in 'structures for organizing our experience and comprehension' (Johnson 1990 [1987]: 29). When we actively assign and project fitting image schemas to actual experiences, embodied-cognitive structures function as top-down governed frames providing cognitive shortcuts for our understanding (see also Kiss 2015: 47).

Bodily being-in-the-world thus gives rise to basic cognitive patterns that also inform higher-order cognitive frames. Impossible puzzle films, however, simulate experiences that do not allow the projection of any fitting image schemas to them, thereby bringing formal-structurally intricate riddles to the fore. In the following we discuss two different modes – a local-perceptual (3.5.1) and a global narrative one (3.5.2) – through which confusingly complex films disrupt the customary link between the underlying schematic structures of our embodied cognition and the meaning-making mechanisms that such schematic structures normally allow.

3.5.1 Disrupting viewers' reliance on image schemas by perceptual impossibility[14]

The pervasively convoluted global story structures of impossible puzzle films often manifest themselves in specific local impossibilities. That is, these films frequently present concrete situations or events that exert a strong feeling

---

[13] By 'cognitively impenetrable', we refer to those primary (therefore mandatory) operations that underlie cognition and precede conscious awareness.

[14] This section is a recapitulation of our paper about the effect of impossible perceptual events on experienced narrative complexity in film (Coëgnarts et al. 2016).

of 'impossibility' in viewers. We argue that such explicit, often perceptually available moments of dissonance form 'local anchors' of complexity, meaning they serve to vividly exemplify and foreground the unfolding complexity of an impossible story.

In an article co-authored with Maarten Coëgnarts and Peter Kravanja, we focused on local moments of dissonance in complex film narratives, examining cases of what we called 'perceptual impossibilities' in character perception (Coëgnarts et al. 2016). Drawing upon earlier insights from conceptual metaphor theory (Coëgnarts and Kravanja 2014, 2015b) and from situation-model theory (for example, Johnson-Laird 1983; Magliano et al. 2001), the article examined the cognitive principles underlying such complex cases of character perception.

First, we showed how patterns of style and narration that represent character perception (such as point-of-view shots) normally follow a logic that is fundamentally based on conceptual blending and extensions of embodied image schemas.[15] These extensions may work metonymically (for example, showing a shot of a character's eye before showing the object of his or her perception), but also metaphorically, eliciting perception through conceptual mappings across different experiential domains (a point-of-view shot, for example, utilises the logic of the CONTAINER schema (inside/outside) to convey that a perceived object is being 'contained' inside the visual field or mind of a subject). In short, we argued that image schemas 'are vital in facilitating the viewer's comprehension of character perception, as they structure the concept of perception metaphorically by mapping the inferential logic of sensory-motor patterns (for example, CONTAINMENT, SOURCE-PATH-GOAL) onto the inferential logic of (character) perception' (that is, in terms of the relationship between perceiver and object perceived) (see Coëgnarts et al. 2016: 132). Furthermore, these patterns of character perception are also frequently metaphorically mapped onto other concepts, like time, for instance, when creating flashback point-of-view shots. Here, the same conceptual mapping logic is followed to metaphorically represent time, for instance by showing characters 'seeing the past' (Coëgnarts and Kravanja 2015c). Drawing on situation-model theory, we further assumed that viewers construct coherent representations of character perception by monitoring or indexing continuities on five dimensions: time, space, causation, entities (characters and objects) and motivation or intentionality.

Following the claims that the cinematic representation of character perception is grounded in metonymical and metaphorical extensions of human sensory-motor knowledge, and reliant on viewers' creation of continuity in

---

[15] For a detailed elaboration on this claim, see Coëgnarts and Kravanja 2014; 2015b; 2015c.

situation models, we can note that films might also seek to undermine this common logic for perplexing effects. We have observed that in complex films, disruptive character perception is often used to break with the elementary laws of viewers' visual perception. Unusual representations of character perception often particularly include discontinuities along the entity and/or temporal dimensions of a situation model to create complex viewing effects. This typically involves three types of disruptions: (1) scenes in which characters directly see events that took place in the past or will take place in the future (creating a temporal discontinuity); (2) scenes in which characters directly see themselves (creating an entity discontinuity); and (3) scenes in which characters directly see themselves in the past or future (eliciting both temporal and entity discontinuity). Some notable examples of scenes that involve such disruptive discontinuities in character perception occur in *2001: A Space Odyssey* (Stanley Kubrick 1968), *Le locataire* (*The Tenant*, Roman Polanski 1976), *Timecrimes* (Nacho Vigalondo 2007), *Coherence* (James Ward Byrkit 2013), *Interstellar* (Christopher Nolan 2014), as well as in *Triangle* (Christopher Smith 2009).

Scenes of disruptive character perception problematise viewers' embodied image schema-driven routines of sense-making, offering specific discontinuities along temporal and/or entity dimensions that violate elementary perceptual essences like the simultaneity and ontological separateness of the perceiver and the perceived. As an example, in the article we analysed a key scene from *Triangle* wherein narrative experimentation (the loop) leads to a violation of the rule of essential ontological separation of characters (their doublings), and thereby to a collapse between perceiver and perceived (an impossible percept). In this specific scene three versions of the same protagonist see each other, while all occupy a different moment on the looped narrative timeline. In this particular scene (at around 1:07:18 in the film), Jess (no. 3), from the upper deck of a ship, directly sees another version of herself (Jess no. 2), who is supposed to be in the past, standing on the lower deck of the same ship, while, in turn, this past self also directly sees yet another, even earlier version of herself (Jess no. 1), who approaches the ship standing on a capsized yacht (all three versions of Jess are played by Melissa George). The first confrontation, between Jess 3 and Jess 2, is elicited through editing, while the confrontation between Jess 2 and 1 is shown within a single frame (Figure 3.4). As we analysed,

> [t]he underlying image schema at work is that of the CONTAINER in which Jess 3's visual field can be conceived as a bounded physical space (i.e., the frame) containing the perceptual relationship between Jess 2 and Jess 3. By contrast, the second perceptual relationship between Jess 2 and Jess 1 is elicited homospatially by the strategy of framing. The contact between PR [the perceiving character] and OP [the object perceived by the character]

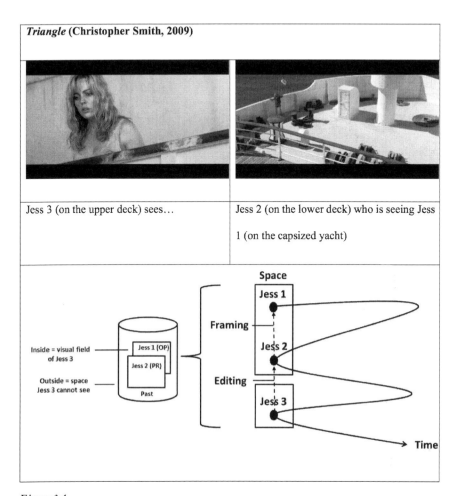

Figure 3.4

is construed cinematically by showing both elements together in one shot. More specifically, the FRONT-BACK image schema is extended metaphorically to express the idea of Jess 2 (FRONT-PR) seeing Jess 1 (BACK-OP). Moreover, the scene describes a static Ego-Reference-Point model of time in which the space in front of Jess's eyes is twice mapped onto the past (i.e., the space in front of Jess 3 and the space in front of Jess 2). The audience is able to infer both mappings from perception onto time because the inside content of Jess's visual field overlaps with events that were previously shown in the film. (Coëgnarts et al. 2016: 132)[16]

[16] The metaphorical model, in which the spatial location of the observer specifies (mapped onto) the moment of *now*, is called the system of Ego-Reference-Point model of time (see, among others, Lakoff and Johnson 2003 [1980]; Gentner et al. 2002).

Moments like these thus use the seemingly transparent, familiar logic of classical film style to represent content that will be felt to be 'impossible'. That is, the complexity of these scenes lies not only in their conceptual strangeness or formal deviance (in their treatment of narrative temporality, for example); the reason of their confusing effect is that they actually problematise the interrelation between conceptual knowledge, formal filmic representation and basic embodied image schemas (blocking the relations by which these usually rely on each other). By disrupting the underlying logic and embodied-cognitive structures of filmic representation, narration and comprehension, such concrete and confined dissonances in character perception often form 'local anchors' to global complexity: they serve to contribute to, reveal or even foreground the complexity of the larger narrative structure in which they are embedded (as is the case with *Triangle*'s global time loop and pervasive character-duplicating logic).

3.5.2 Disrupting viewers' reliance on image schemas by formal impossibility[17]

Besides perceptual challenges' local disruptions, the complexity of impossible puzzle films often also stems from global manifestations of confusing scenarios, labyrinthine plots and intricate formal narrative logic. Convoluted formal structures may be difficult to comprehend because they problematise – that is, they intensify or fully hamstring – viewers' reliance on schemas of embodied knowledge.

George Lakoff's (1987) and Mark Johnson's (1990 [1987]) seminal works were the first to discuss how human beings are capable of mapping schematic structures (image schemas), emerging from their experienced sensory-motor interactions to a non-imagistic abstract concept. 'Abstract conceptual structures' – Lakoff recapitulates – 'are indirectly meaningful; they are understood because of their systematic relationship to directly meaningful structures' (Lakoff 1987: 268 – about the emergence of image schemas see our section 2.1 above). Building on this theoretical heritage, the embodied-cognitive approach to narrative turned the traditional explanatory model of narratology inside out, claiming that it is not stories that structure experiences, but, on the contrary, that our bodily experiences shape narrative structures in the first place. For example, the SOURCE-PATH-GOAL image schema – grounded in our real-world experience of bodily movement from one point to another

---

[17] This section builds on our work about the general relation between film narrative and embodied cognition (Kiss 2015); here we only deal with the specifics that complexification brings to this relation.

along a path in a certain direction – can lead to our readily understanding a linear narrative structure. How exactly? In Richard Menary's succinct words, 'embodied experiences have a pre-narrative structure that lends itself to narration' (Menary 2008: 64). This means that the sensation of bodily determined perceptual patterns, such as a felt order through relation, repetition, closure or balance, can lead to a mental creation and solidification of elementary formal schemas, which can be seen as the most fundamental formal gestalts of a narrative (Kiss 2015). Elementary formal schemas facilitate narrative comprehension in several ways. In our case of the linear narrative structure, the real-world experience of bodily movement can be converted to apprehend stories as 'experiential paths' with a chronology that involves a beginning, a development and an end. By metaphorical extension, this schema also allows comprehension of fictional agents as they move along narrative paths, engaging in '"purposive activity", including questing and story-telling' (Forceville and Jeulink 2011: 37). Accordingly, stories are understood as offering a source that triggers the action, a path that is paved with obstacles, struggles and side tracks, and a movement towards certain goals that characters are determined to achieve. Classical films will often closely correspond to this basic schema. Our model example is John McTiernan's 1988 *Die Hard*, in which we follow a highly goal-oriented central agent, John McClane (Bruce Willis), who has a clear aim: he wants to make up with his wife, Holly (Bonnie Bedelia). However, following a terrorist attack, he must revise his plans, and instead embarks on an action-filled journey with several concrete objectives (rescuing the hostages, including his wife) in order to ultimately achieve his initial goal. This basic plot structure recurs in countless classical narratives, with variations, resulting in consolidated cognitive schemas of classical plot structure, linearity, causality and chronology.

What follows from this is that certain intricate plot trajectories evoke experiences that – temporarily or more permanently – can either problematise or question the customary link between viewers' underlying embodied cognition and narrative comprehensive routines. These plots can be varyingly intricate in a sense that they can either hinder or fully prevent viewers' habitualised reliance on their elementary formal schemas. While most complex films only challenge or in fact intensify this reliance, impossible puzzle films go beyond mere complication: they seriously upset the congruous relations between their overly intricate narrative forms and the embodied gestalts that are at hand, which normally allow for sensing and creating something organised and meaningful. In more radical cases, films can delay or fully revoke the 'feeling of meaningful order', resulting in a confusing experience that can be understood and theorised as a disturbance of the natural congruity between incoming stimuli and schema-based embodied resonance.

On the one hand, most moderately complex narratives only stretch (but do not disrupt) viewers' reliance on image-schematic thinking. For example, their reliance on the CONTAINER schema (characterised by the perception of a boundary between the inside and outside of our bodies that facilitates comprehension of an in and out logic and a clear distinction between nested layers) warrants them an understanding of embedded, stories-within-stories narrative scenarios. Among others, the CONTAINER schema ensures viewers' understanding of the specific type of embedding of a flashback story. Such a moderately complex embedded flashback story is famously exemplified by Orson Welles' non-chronological analeptic structure in *Citizen Kane* (1941), or by Danny Boyle and Loveleen Tandan's alternating flashback plot of *Slumdog Millionaire* (2008). More demanding but cognitively still manageable (that is, clearly signposted and moderately embedded) flashbacks can further stretch one's reliance on the CONTAINER schema. Examples of more bold experimentations with embedded flashbacks span over film history, such as John Brahm's four-layers-thick flashback-within-flashback-within-flashback classic *The Locket* (1946),[18] eventually finding their way too into contemporary television programmes – see, for instance, the double flashbacks in series like *Person of Interest* (season 1, episode 21: *Many Happy Returns*, Fred Toye 2012) or *The Following* (season 1, episode 6: *The Fall*, Marcos Siega 2013). The same CONTAINER schema also affords the comprehension of cases of simple, 'ordinary and innocent' (Genette 1980: 235) transgressions between embedded story layers (for example, omniscient narrators' rhetorical metalepses in Herman Melville's *Moby-Dick* or in Cervantes' *Don Quixote*), allowing viewers to grasp what happens inside one story and outside another through somewhat intensified mapping efforts.[19]

Impossible puzzle films, on the other hand, do not simply problematise or question conventionalised story patterns and viewing routines; they often fully revoke the overall explanatory potential of both image and formal schemas, and thereby induce viewer confusion on the most fundamental, embodied level of cognition. For instance, by revelling in a playful ontological metalepsis, Spike Jonze's *Adaptation* freely criss-crosses among extradiegetic,

[18] Brahm's formula: [A meets B] [A gives fire to B] [B talks about a woman, gets close up, blurs into his flashback] [B meets C] [B gives fire to C] [C talks about the same woman, gets close up, blurs into his flashback] [C meets the woman] [The woman gets close up, blurs into her flashback].

[19] Marie-Laure Ryan (2006a: 247) outlines the difference between unintended and thereby 'innocent' level-contaminations (*rhetorical metalepses*) and deliberate, overtly playful transgressions (*ontological metalepses*). As for analyses of rhetorical metalepses, see Henrik Skov Nielsen (2004) about Melville's *Moby-Dick*, and Brian D. Patrick (2008) on Cervantes' *Don Quixote*. For more about metalepses' relation to complexity, see section 2.2.

diegetic and hypodiegetic narrative layers, resulting in an Escherian short-circuit between character(s) being the writer and also the protagonist of one and the same story.[20] Looking at it from the embodied-cognitive analytical perspective, the film's bewildering trompe-l'œil narrative is at dissonance with both the basic explanatory courses of our SOURCE-PATH-GOAL schemas (allowing for chronology and causality) and CONTAINER schemas (regulating hierarchical relations among embedded parts). Even if it would be possible to untangle the hierarchy between the film's manifold embedded and looped layers, it would be impossible to establish a logical and coherent relation among them, let alone put their related events on a chronological timeline. Scrutinising *Adaptation*, Chris Dzialo (2009: 111) quotes Paul Cilliers on complex systems and summarises the effect brought about by these narrative intricacies as an overview on 'a whole [that] cannot be fully understood simply by analysing its components' (Cilliers 1998: viii). Cilliers' observation interestingly dovetails with Branigan's original classification of the impossible puzzle film, by which Branigan meant to discern films that 'appear perfectly correct but whose largest perspectival representation proves impossible' (Branigan 2014: 234).

An escalated version of the same effect is achieved in Quentin Dupieux's *Reality*, which not only transgresses the boundaries of different storylines and story levels, but, paradoxically, also embeds its multiple stories within each other. In one of its most remarkable and baffling scenes, we see a test screening of a movie, attended by the film's director and producer. The movie shows a little girl watching a video on a TV screen, which shows protagonist Jason Tantra (Alain Chabat) making a phone call to the producer, who takes this call *at the test screening*. By merging the distinct narrative temporalities of the recorded past and the actual present, and by violating the boundaries between embedded, even mediated hypodiegetic and actual intradiegetic realities, the scene simultaneously and cumulatively mounts an offensive on its viewer's reliance on both SOURCE-PATH-GOAL (which normally controls the unidirectionality of time experience) and CONTAINER (which generally maintains the hierarchy among embedded levels) schemas.

Duncan Jones's *Source Code* provides a subtle and cunning diegetically motivated version of *Reality*'s more overt playfulness. Unlike *Reality*, *Source Code* does not revel in confronting its characters and viewers with the absurdity of its impossible narratives; instead it obscures the distinction between the

---

[20] *Adaptation* is a film about the struggles of a fictional character, Charlie Kaufman (Nicolas Cage), a clear alter-ego of the film's real writer Charlie Kaufman, writing about himself writing about a writer Susan Orlean (Meryl Streep) writing about the roughneck florist John Laroche (Chris Cooper).

notions of possible and impossible. In order to achieve this, Jones actually pulls off not one, but two twists. The first twist reveals the film's concealed embedded structure, including the uppermost reality of a governmental experiment laboratory, and an embedded virtual reality, rendered by this lab's source code program. Here we learn that even though in virtual reality our protagonist Captain Colter Stevens (Jake Gyllenhaal) is a hale and hearty hero, in the story's upper reality, he is a severely mutilated war veteran, existing merely as a torso in an airtight chamber and an envatted brain stimulated by the lab's software. As a second twist, the film entertains the idea of an impossible parallel universe, opened up by an earlier unknown glitch of the software, where Stevens can continue to live his virtual life beyond the software's original eight-minute limit. As an effect, by deliberately ambiguating the relation between its narrative levels, that is problematising the permeability between the (supposed) intradiegetic reality of the laboratory and the (assumed) hypodiegetic reality of the simulated world, Jones's film dismantles its own constructed embedded structure, and thereby disrupts viewers' reliance on the inside-outside logic of their CONTAINER schema that could have provided them with a science-fictional, but at least coherent explanation for this puzzle.

Of course, it is highly unlikely that a narrative film would be able to fully secede from any governing power and positive match of underlying elementary image schemas. First, such a film would risk losing the sense of meaningful order that is implied in 'narrativity' and 'narrativisation' as an organising activity. Second, one might also wonder if it is at all possible to cut ourselves loose from our underlying embodied-cognitive comprehensive routines. We would argue that even the most experimental movies still invoke some correspondence with our basic embodied schemas, and still lend themselves to our bodily implied disposition of meaning-making and structuring (see also Kiss 2015: 59). Moreover, even when all the available embodied schemas are blocked (which, in the case of narrative experiences, sounds more like a mere theoretical option), alternative modes of information structuring can emerge. Viewers may substitute embodied image schemas for other metaphorical mappings that can help them to structure 'non-embodied' and 'non-experiential' narrative patterns. Thinking of George Lakoff's remark that all abstract structures are only understood metaphorically – that is, through their direct relation to meaningful structures – narration may encourage the invocation of other alternative meaningful schemas to make sense of its information. The plot of *Triangle*, for instance, internally employs a basic spatial dimension, that of a circle or loop, to host its highly abstract temporal dimension. Visualising the plot using this spatial metaphor – in the form of either a mental sketch or a physical drawing – may in this case help viewers to

structure the complex web of narrative cues and to understand the contradictions created by the different timelines.[21] Such structures thus do not secede
from but, on the contrary, actually demand an intensified form of schematic
reasoning, by which viewers organise the information, constructing a potentially infinite and self-spiralling version of the SOURCE-PATH-GOAL schema.
The increased effort that viewers must invest into mapping a loop plot can
play a significant role in making a story feel complex.

Nevertheless, there are many cases where primary rationalising and analytic approaches fall short in rendering impossible puzzle films intelligible.
As we hope to have shown throughout this chapter, impossible puzzle films
are exactly characterised by the presentation of paradoxical and confusing
scenarios for which no clear resolutions are offered (contrary to most contemporary complex movies). More precisely, impossible puzzle films achieve
their confusing effect by evoking strong and persistent feelings of dissonance
in viewers, using both internal incongruities (that is, contradictions between
narrative elements) and projected impossibilities (that is, resistance to sense-
making that follows from the disruption of elementary fictional and real-life
logic, laws and schemas). Such sensations of dissonance exert on viewers a
drive to be reduced or made consonant, but impossible puzzle films obstruct
the satisfaction of this need by withholding the required explanations and
solutions. Viewers may respond to this challenge in various ways. Some will
simply abandon the cognitively demanding activities of patterning, structuring and analysing information (especially when these efforts seem to be
futile), others will keep devising rational hypotheses (even though they realise
the impossibility), whereas others again may choose to apprehend dissonant
elements on more hermeneutic grounds instead (for instance, by focusing
on the thematic, symbolic, reflective or artistic merits of the dissonance).
Discerning this range of different meaning-making operations will be the
focus of the coming chapter, where we theorise the possible interpretive
responses to complexity and dissonance, offering an overview of coping
strategies that viewers can resort to.

---

[21] Complex films particularly invite such mapping activity. Seeing the abundance of concrete visual examples available online by which forensic fans have tried to untangle – 'iron
out' – these films' intricate plot trajectories, it is safe to assume that viewers are willing to invest
cognitive resources into creating mental models or even draw sketches of narrative maps if
their investment, presumably, contributes to their understanding of the complex narrative at
hand. For examples, search images for 'plot map *Memento*' or 'timeline *Lost*' or see our own
heuristic map of *Timecrimes* (Figure 3.1).

CHAPTER 4

Taming Dissonance: Cognitive Operations and Interpretive Strategies

> There is no problem being momentarily confused if you feel you're in good
> hands.
>
> Quentin Tarantino on *The Charlie Rose Show* (1994)

*A smooth aerial shot over the skyline of Toronto is interrupted by the beeping sound of a
voicemail. A worried mother leaves a message for her son. At the end of the call we see a
young pregnant woman sitting on a bed, turning around and then looking straight into the
camera. We cannot identify her – it is too dark in the room. The image fades to black and
reveals the opening line of the film: 'Chaos is order yet undeciphered.' Switching scene, we
now see two men enter a sinister erotic seance where a female stripper, wearing nothing but
a high-heeled shoe, is about to step on a tarantula spider . . . The story begins, introducing
Adam Bell (Jake Gyllenhaal), an introverted, if not depressed, college history teacher, who
is living with his girlfriend Mary (Mélanie Laurent). Following his colleague's recom-
mendation, Adam rents a movie, in which, to his astonishment, he spots a supporting
actor who seems to be an exact lookalike of himself. After some research, he learns that the
actor is one Anthony Claire (also Jake Gyllenhaal), who also happens to live in Toronto
with his pregnant wife, Helen (Sarah Gadon). Adam starts to stalk and finally confronts
Anthony – physically indeed his perfect doppelgänger, right down to a scar on his chest.
In character, however, Anthony is quite the opposite of Adam: successful, extroverted
and assertive. Seeking an explanation for this bewildering situation, Adam visits his
worried mother (Isabella Rossellini), but is assured that he does not have a twin brother.
In a cutaway scene a gigantic spider towers over the city. Meanwhile, having done his own
stalking investigation, Anthony has set his eye on Mary. Accusing his double of cheating
on him with Helen, Anthony forces a deal on Adam: he will take Adam's identity (and
Mary) for a single night, and then will disappear from his life forever. Adam complies, but,
while Anthony is with Mary in a hotel, he decides to visit Helen. While making love with
Anthony, Mary suddenly freezes, seeing a mark of a wedding ring on Anthony's finger; as
Adam, her boyfriend, doesn't wear a ring, she demands to know who this man really is.
Driving home, Mary and Anthony get in a fierce quarrel and have a serious accident that
leaves them both dead. The camera zooms on the wrecked car's broken window, which has
a pattern like a spider's web. The next morning Adam, taking Anthony's now-vacant
identity, pockets a key – clearly that to the hidden seance – and, before saying goodbye,*

he checks in on Helen. Instead of 'his' pregnant wife, he finds a giant tarantula filling the entire room, to which he responds looking more desperate than shocked.

Based on José Saramago's 2002 novel *O Homem Duplicado (The Double)*, Denis Villeneuve's *Enemy* composes a puzzling mystery from its suggested and cleverly nurtured dissonance. Circling around its central character, or characters, being simultaneously similar and different, the film seems to exchange Saramago's bizarre biological anomaly of a 'real double' for a confusing narrative riddle. *Enemy* opens and maintains a thoughtful balance among several analytical and interpretive possibilities regarding the relationship between or within Adam and Anthony. In Villeneuve's likewise carefully chosen words: 'You don't know if they are two in reality, or maybe from a subconscious point of view, there's just one . . . It's maybe two sides of the same persona . . . or a fantastic event' (Lewis 2014). Indeed, the film seems to juggle at least three possible readings, all present in Villeneuve's subtle spoiler,[1] but that does not mean that one could not come up with other credible analyses or evenly plausible symbolic interpretations. The point for us is not to determine an appropriate interpretation or to establish any hierarchy among the different hermeneutic options; rather, we are interested in the processes and strategies of meaning-making itself. How do viewers usually cope with and tend to make meaning out of such ambiguous narrative dissonances? Where do the balanced possibilities in *Enemy* come from? And wherein lies the engaging potential of the strategically sustained interpretive puzzlement? While so far our aim has been to describe and explain the confusing effect of impossible puzzle films, now it is time to find out what viewers actually can do to make sense of dissonant stories.

---

[1] Perhaps the least likely among these options adheres to Saramago's original supernatural idea, and sees *Enemy*'s story as a kind of (magical) realist tale of a real character duplication; however, this strange but realistic scenario is problematic due to a photo that Adam and Anthony both own, which appears as an impossible lapse between them. Another option is that Adam is Anthony, or that Anthony is Adam, in which case the film's primary question is who is whose hallucination? In this option the film ambiguates between two possible subjective realist scenarios. It could be that there is no history teacher, and Adam exists only in the imagination of Anthony, who simply cannot commit to his married adult life and impending fatherhood. The girl's panic concerning the wedding ring and his true identity might be seen as a projection of Anthony's own doubt. Or what if the entire film is a frustrated vision of Adam, the wannabe actor à la Betty Elms/Diane Selwyn of *Mulholland Drive*, who became no more than a miserable history teacher? From this prospect the advice of his mother sounds like a key to the story: 'I think you should quit that fantasy of being a third-rate movie actor!' Perhaps once Adam had a pregnant wife whom he cheated on and then lost in a car accident (hence his scar), and now his traumatic guilt fuels the dissonant dream-scenario of his successful self, having a career and an expectant wife.

In the previous chapter, we argued that complex film narratives can evoke cognitive dissonance by confronting viewers with conflicting cognitions (incongruities, impossibilities) in narrative comprehension. We argued that this may nonetheless result in an engaging viewing experience, as such dissonances send viewers on a quest to make sense of them. After all, as Festinger theorised, cognitive dissonance often exerts on individuals a pressure to reduce the tension elicited by the conflict. To conform our domain of interest to the logic of Festinger's original idea, this chapter seeks to address how viewers approach and cope with conflicting cognitions in narrative fiction. We will argue that in narrative comprehension, dissonance-reduction strategies almost invariably involve changes in interpretation. This chapter will therefore outline the different cognitive operations and interpretive strategies that viewers can employ when facing the challenge of dissonantly complex story situations. We highlight three general – interpretive – paths by which most viewers deal with cognitive dissonance in narratives. These are (4.2) dissonance reduction through naturalising interpretations; (4.3) engaging in a frame-switch as a more general change in viewing stance (such as a shift from narrative to poetic modes of meaning-making); and (4.4) frame-switching as a cognitive hesitation between different interpretive options, which allow for certain kinds of hermeneutic play (4.4.1), and which may give rise to viewing effects and 'theoretical genres' like Tzvetan Todorov's notion of the fantastic (4.4.2).

Of course, the problem with theorising interpretation is that any interpretive action is fundamentally subjected to myriad differences in terms of individual, cultural and contextual conditions. Determining definitive interpretations is a futile and consequently not very desirable endeavour, especially not in relation to borderline cases of complex narratives, since different viewers might opt for different ways of meaning-making. It is, however, possible to examine and specify the possible strategies that viewers commonly have at their disposal to make sense of complex stories – the 'interpretive toolkit' from which viewers can choose, so to speak. Following Liesbeth Korthals Altes, we could speak, in a 'meta-hermeneutic' manner, of certain 'interpretive pathways' that viewers use to negotiate the meaning of texts (Korthals Altes 2014). These are general strategies of interpretation that are deemed appropriate and acceptable in response to certain narrative patterns. Such pathways of interpretation are habitualised and distributed (socio-)culturally, for instance through film criticism, artistic socialisation and institutional contexts (such as journals or film festivals). Or, in David Bordwell's words, in making sense of texts and films, 'the inductive process is guided by particular, socially implanted hypotheses about how texts mean' (Bordwell 1989: 133).

Complex films often invite, rely on or play with such interpretive routines. Discerning the most commonly utilised and accepted strategies for making meaning of complex stories will therefore be the focus of this chapter. We will primarily draw on concepts from literary theory and literary narratology. This is mainly because these fields have already conceptualised the role of interpretation in relation to narrative more extensively. Some of the theories and taxonomies discussed may thus be familiar material for narratologists; we will nevertheless discuss them in some detail, as they may be less evident to scholars from other fields. Furthermore, these existing theories will be elaborated further to relate them to film and narrative complexity specifically. Applying this chapter's findings, we will in Chapter 5 turn back to the niche of impossible puzzle films, and address how their narration may strategically cue viewers to use certain strategies and abandon others. Chapter 6, the final chapter, will conclude with an attempt to explore some of the possible underlying reasons that make such fictional experiences engaging or attractive. In short, the ultimate goal of these last three chapters is to disclose how viewers engage with the cognitive struggles of impossible puzzle films, as well as what the possible appeal such an engagement with complexity could have.

4.1 COGNITIVE DISSONANCE VERSUS NARRATIVE COHERENCE

Up to this point, our theorising of dissonant cognitions in fiction has contained a potential discrepancy. This tension lies in the apparent incongruity between the presumed engaging quality (or even attractiveness) of cognitive dissonance in story comprehension, and a viewer's inherent drive to reduce the dissonance. The potential paradox – or 'dissonance' in the effect of dissonance, if you like – would be in claiming that viewers would enjoy or appreciate a mental state that they simultaneously strive to eliminate or reduce. After all, if we truly 'enjoyed' cognitive dissonance in narratives for its own sake, there would be no urge to reduce it – on the contrary, we would probably seek to create and maintain it. Conversely, if we readily reduced all dissonance in favour of soothing consonance, cognitive dissonance would be nothing more than an undesired obstacle in our path to narrative enjoyment.[2] Clearly, these two mental drives would be incompatible. So how could we say that the two notions co-exist within our hypothesis? To examine this, the current chapter will look into the coping strategies by which viewers deal with the effect of cognitive dissonance in fiction. After all, one may wonder, do the same real-life rules of dissonance reduction also apply when we are watching

---

[2] This contradiction shows some similarities to the 'paradox of negative emotions' in art, which we will also touch upon in Chapter 6.

a narrative film? Do viewers generally avoid dissonance and readily seek to get rid of all incongruities encountered in a story? And if this is the case, then how do they do so?

Looking into narrative and cognitive theories, and considering our own experiences with fiction, it seems justifiable to assume that viewers indeed strive for *consonance* in their understanding of stories. It is a widely shared assumption in literary and hermeneutic theory that readers and viewers – by disposition – always expect and, as a result, try to render works of art to be narratively meaningful and congruent as a whole. As Noël Carroll puts it in the conclusion of his functional approach to film, 'it is not strange to treat objects of human design teleologically' (Carroll 1998: 400).[3] Viewers actively strive towards making a text or film intelligible, even if the narrative at hand seems to resist their efforts at ascribing meaningful coherence. David Bordwell has called this basic viewer presumption the 'hypothesis of *minimal coherence*' (Bordwell 1989: 134). By the principle of minimal coherence, viewers and critics assume that all elements of a text are significantly related. What is more, even contradictory parts are conceived as cohering units, since 'in practice most contradictory text readings do not posit a thoroughgoing fragmentation', and therefore usually do not constitute a 'radically disunifying device' (ibid.: 134).

Both this passive disposition and active bias can be seen as stemming from our cognitive make-up as well as being culturally governed. It is cognitive in the sense that cognition can be characterised as a problem-solving activity that is geared towards establishing relatively unambiguous meaning from an information-rich environment. Within this, narrative fulfils a key role as an instrument of the human mind to organise information on actors, events, space and time, to assert coherence and continuity, to track changes, to establish causality, to recognise goals and obstacles, to memorise and navigate one's own experiences or to understand the actions and mental processes of others – and so on.[4] In short, making elements cohere and establishing meaningfulness can be claimed to be the core task of narrative as a cognitive instrument (and, consequently, one of its key functions as a social tool).

On the other hand, the tendency to assume that the elements of a text are significantly related is also a central cultural convention of art. As a socially

---

[3] Indeed, artworks are after all 'created by "narratively wired" humans to other "narratively wired" humans. If narrative artworks are products of a ("narratively wired") human mind, then it is logical that they resonate naturally with a ("narratively wired") human perceiver. Because of this loop between creativity and comprehension, "narrative functions" are just as much of the internal features of an artwork, as of the embodied mind's [sic] that creates, appropriates, then recognises, and ultimately labels the experience as "narrative"' (Kiss 2015: 54).

[4] For illustrations of this view of narrative as a fundamental human cognitive instrument, see, for instance, Jerome Bruner (1991), Mark Turner (1996) or David Herman (2003).

established expectation, it is distributed and reinforced through various channels including narrative habitualisation, literary and cinematic socialisation,
and art criticism. This convention surrounds not only the reception but also
the production of (narrative) artworks, exerting the predominant expectation
that the work forms a more or less unified, composed whole that should
communicate to its beholders a point. On the reception end, this cognitively
inherent and culturally strengthened narrative propensity causes viewers to
take a co-operative stance in making sense of a complex story, which we
could characterise as an aesthetic 'charity'. In the words of Liesbeth Korthals
Altes:

> Such a general intention attribution includes what has been nicely called 'the
> principle of charity'. Readers will do their best to make sense of narratives
> with strange gaps in information transmissions (whole murders eluded),
> implausible narrators (horses, unborn babies, needles), ontological incon-
> sistencies (houses that can expand or shrink, in narratives that strongly cue a
> realist reading), apparently pointless stories (about individuals without quali-
> ties, engaged in nonactivities), and ethos incongruities (sincere ironies, ironic
> sincerities). (Korthals Altes 2014: 108)

The expectation of a singularly meaningful point is a fundamental aspect of
our culture's view of art, and its origins are difficult to pinpoint. It may for
instance be seen partially inherited from romantic notions of art and criticism, but it can in different forms also be traced back to a variety of earlier
prominent theories of art and narrative (cf. Aristotle's *Poetics* and its notion
of the unified plot).

Narratives that evoke and maintain dissonant cognitions can be particularly threatening to this viewer anticipation of congruence and cohesion,
and thereby seriously challenge the limits of viewers' charitable viewing
disposition. When a viewer encounters elements in a story that are incongruent, or which do not resonate with his or her cognitive frames of narrative
comprehension, and hence provide a sensation of cognitive dissonance –
be it through some inconsistency in the story, or logical impossibilities in
the diegetic world – one may expect that the viewer's initial response will be
to readily seek ways to reason out the discordance. As in real life, dissonant
elements in a story often trigger the viewer's active engagement to reduce
the conflict. However, as we argued in section 3.2, to reduce dissonance in
a pre-structured and non-interactive medium like cinema, viewers only have
choices in terms of interpretations formed and attitudes taken with regard to
the experience at hand (rather than, for instance, having the option of taking
real actions or making changes in the film itself). This means that viewers will
strive for a consonant interpretation by changing their attitude to particular

elements of the film text, or to the film as a whole. A viewer will, for example, try to attribute an appropriate meaningfulness to the anomaly, infer that the story will cohere thematically or conclude that the story's experienced incoherence might perhaps be the work's intended function.

In the following sections (4.2 to 4.4), we aim to discern several types of interpretive operations by which viewers can reduce dissonance in narrative fiction. We believe that the below options constitute some of the most common and widely used pathways to make meaning out of complex narrative experiences. They make up a large part of the 'interpretive toolkit' that viewers have at their disposal. Naturally, different viewers will choose or prefer different strategies. Moreover, while some films explicitly and unambiguously cue their viewers to use specific interpretations (by providing intratextual motivations that support a certain meaning), other works will leave more freedom to the viewer to make meaning and to try out different strategies. As we will see in the last sections of this chapter, impossible puzzle films tend more towards the latter option, often retaining ambiguities in their potential readings and interpretations. We will argue that applying or testing different interpretive strategies may become a gratifying viewing activity itself, forming one of the possible reasons behind the engaging quality of dissonant viewing experiences (see more about the engaging potential of impossible puzzles in Chapter 6).

4.2 REDUCING DISSONANCE: INTERPRETATION AND NATURALISATION

First of all, there are various strategies by which a viewer may understand the cognitive dissonance evoked by a film to have a function, thus rendering the dissonance consonant within the work as a whole. Such strategies are old news to narratologists. Already in 1975, Jonathan Culler wrote on readers' efforts of *naturalisation*. Naturalising a text means that readers and viewers form new paths along which they can make textual incongruities 'intelligible by relating [them] to various models for coherence' (Culler 1975: 152). The term covers the interpretive strategies through which viewers or readers reconcile local textual inconsistencies by fitting them into overarching sense-making patterns. These patterns are often derived from cultural frameworks and discursive contexts. Applying a new interpretive stance or inventing another discursive context to an encountered inconsistency can render the experience meaningful again. For example, one can choose to interpret a textual incongruity as a sign of irony or parody, or as an expression of a thematic concern, or one may attribute it to the conventions of the work's genre. In any case, by changing the interpretive frame surrounding the inconsistency, we effectively change our attitude towards the experienced dissonance (for example, 'this must be ironic', 'this is meta-fictional', 'the author is playfully making us reflect on the medium of film' and so on). Viewers exercise such naturalising negotiations up to a point when there is no longer a dissonance (or at least less of a disturbing dissonance) between the film's represented inconsistency and our interpretation attributed to it – or, as we will see in some cases, up to the point where viewers run out of such naturalising possibilities.

Other theories on complex and counterintuitive narratives offer similar insights. In his work on impossible storyworlds (see also Chapter 3), Jan Alber (2009, 2013a, 2013b) builds on Culler's theoretical heritage when scrutinising reader responses to *unnatural narratives* – that is, stories that feature physically, logically or humanly impossible scenarios or events. Alber outlines a cognitive model that describes nine strategies by which readers and viewers can make sense of impossible events in fiction (Alber 2013a: 76–9). These strategies are also relevant for narrative complexity in cinema, since most complex films (from moderately challenging to impossible puzzle films) form distinctly 'unnatural' narratives of which viewers need to make sense in some way. In the following we will outline the strategies discerned by Alber, adding in what ways we believe film viewers may use these in response to variously complex and cognitively dissonant film narration.

(1) *The creation of unnatural frames*: to mentally adapt to a fictional impossibility, viewers can blend or enrich existing frames (see also section 3.4), and by that might create new, 'unnatural' frames. In this process, viewers recombine, alter, update or extend available previous knowledge in such a way that a world model is constructed that allows them to make some sense of the encountered impossibility. For instance, the cognitive concept of a cat and the concept of a narrating person can be combined to understand the unnatural scenario of a narrating cat (as it appears in Miranda July's 2011 *The Future*). This is due to a cognitive principle known as conceptual blending, which has over the last two decades received notable attention in the context of literary studies (for example, Turner 1996; Fauconnier and Turner 2002). Additionally, the notion of frame enrichment has been used by narratologists to refer to the idea that accepting fictional departures from real-world parameters can in itself create new fictional frames that allow the unnatural to persist, for instance in a conventionalised form (Alber et al. 2010: 118). By these principles, viewers can form new 'unnatural' frames or stretch pre-existing frames to make sense of a complex narrative structure.

Complex story structures and impossible storyworlds often cue their viewers to update, revise or reform their knowledge on the narrative they are watching (or on narratives in general). To make sense of a film like *Triangle*, for instance, viewers have to blend the idea of a linear narrative path with that of a circle; they need to constantly adapt and update their mental model of the story structure to include multiplying versions of the protagonist; they must keep track of these different protagonists as they are required to map and integrate their different paths in the story; and so on. As Jason Mittell has noted, puzzle films often 'require the audience to learn the particular rules of a film to comprehend its narrative . . . inviting audiences to play along with the creators to crack the interpretive codes to make sense of their complex narrative strategies' (Mittell 2015: 51). This process of puzzling one's way through a complex story by unravelling its internal laws can be understood as a constant blending and updating of frames. Successfully adapting one's knowledge and hypotheses to a challenging narrative logic may resolve (or at least tone down) cognitive dissonances and may make the story (more) coherent and meaningful; this can ultimately afford viewers a distinct sense of narrative gratification.

(2) *Generification*: readers and viewers may also 'account for certain impossible scenarios or events by identifying them as belonging to particular literary genres and generic conventions' (Alber 2013a: 77). Indeed, many fictional impossibilities, like speaking animals in fairy tales or time machines in science fiction, do not pose problems because viewers are able to assign their 'unnaturalness' to a generic context (and perhaps do not even perceive them as 'impossible' in the first place). Therefore, it makes sense to distinguish between two types of unnaturalness: on the one hand, there are the 'physical, logical or human impossibilities that have already been conventionalized and are now familiar forms of narrative representation' (Alber 2013a: 70) like time travel in science fiction; on the other hand, there are the impossibilities that have not yet been conventionalised, 'and, therefore, still strike us as odd, strange, disconcerting, or defamiliarizing' (ibid.: 70).

Impossible puzzle films by definition include one or several elements that belong to the latter category, as they are dependent on such strange, striking and challenging impossibilities for their effects. Viewers will, after all, be much quicker in grasping and making sense of narrative patterns with which they are familiar, as they already possess cognitive frames (in the form of a known genre or other internalised generic conventions) to make sense of them. Moreover, formal strategies that were once found complex and strange may over time and through recurrent use also become conventional generic cognitive frames, which reduces their capacity to create challenging or complexifying effects (see, for instance, the popularisation of the unreliable twist film around the turn of the millennium). However, logically impossible scenarios are arguably more resistant to such conventionalisation, since they challenge more deep-seated and inflexible embodied-cognitive schemas and sense-making processes (as we discussed in section 3.5).

(3) *Subjectification*: viewers can ascribe impossibilities to the subjective experience and interiority of a narrator or character. By this strategy,

impossibilities are explained as internal states, that is, as dreams, fantasies, hallucinations, distorted perceptions and so on. This strategy is an effective dissonance-reduction tool, because it helps viewers to bring seemingly impossible events back to the realm of the physically and psychologically possible. Moreover, it may allow viewers to invest these subjective events with meaningfulness, through, for example, 'psychoanalytic' readings that relate the impossibilities to the actual psychological state of a character in a diegetic world (for example, as expressive of a character's jealousy, frustration or desires). Seeing *Enemy*'s Adam and Anthony as two sides of the same person is a good example of such a psychological reading of dissonant narrative events.

Subjectification is a prominent strategy in making sense of complex narrative structures because, historically speaking, many puzzle and art films have explicitly cued viewers to take this stance (whether through narrative patterns, stylistic markers or explication in narration). Matthew Campora has identified the historical tradition of films that combine subjective narration with complex or embedded multiple-storyline structures. He has labelled this line of movies as *subjective realist multiform* narratives (Campora 2014) – a category that includes films ranging from Robert Wiene's *Das Cabinet des Dr. Caligari* (*The Cabinet of Dr. Caligari*) (1920) to David Lynch's *Mulholland Drive* (2001), and from Federico Fellini's *Otto e Mezzo* (*8½*) (1963) to Christopher Nolan's *Inception* (2010).

(4) *Foregrounding the thematic*: sometimes viewers do not treat impossibilities as being mimetically motivated (that is, not as a diegetic element of the storyworld), but rather as 'exemplifications of particular themes that the narrative addresses' (Alber 2013a: 77). In these cases, the thematic function of the unnaturalness overrides its mimetic (or, actually, diegetic) impossibility. The impossibility then is held to serve a more thematic or rhetorical function that relates to the point that a given work is found to convey. This, of course, is also ultimately in some ways mimetic (in the broader sense of being expressive of something), but this mimetic function is a somewhat meta-fictional one, relating to the work as a constructed, composed whole.

For instance, the impossible metaleptic structure in Spike Jonze's *Adaptation* (in which Nicolas Cage plays actual screenwriter Charlie Kaufman who writes himself into his film script, which becomes the film that the viewer is watching) can be seen as a narrative reflection of the film's central theme about a writer's block. By foregrounding the thematic function in interpretation, viewers can understand the experienced complexity as an expression of the work's concern beyond its actual story, attributing a meaningfulness that makes dissonant elements consonant within the work as a thematically composed whole. This strategy is usually more appropriate in art-cinema narration, which (as we will argue in the next chapter) is more encouraging of thematically expressive readings; the classical mode of narration (to which we claim that most contemporary mainstream complex films belong) tends to remain somewhat more focused on *mimetic, intradiegetic motivations* to account for formal story experimentations (for instance, by including storyworld elements like time machines, mental illness, hallucinations and so on). Yet classical narration does not exclude thematic motivation, and as the example of *Adaptation* confirms, contemporary complex narratives represent a particular niche that has frequently utilised such thematically motivated narration within the post-classical domain.

(5) *Reading allegorically*: readers and viewers 'may also see unnatural elements as representing abstract ideas in allegories that say something about the human condition or the world in general' (Alber 2013a: 77). The difference between thematic and allegorical readings – as we see it – is that whereas the strategy of foregrounding the thematic function relates the unnatural to the intratextual composition of themes and patterns within the work, allegorical reading assigns it to *extratextual* frames and knowledge. Allegorical readings are thus *naturalising explanations* that invoke extratextual frames of knowledge (experiential, cultural, philosophical and so on) against which textual oddities can be understood or given a function.

Perhaps even more than thematic foregrounding, such allegorical readings tend to be more commonly used in art cinema as a means to motivate formal narrative experimentation. For instance, a confusing narrative structure in Resnais' and Robbe-Grillet's *Last Year at Marienbad* can be naturalised by treating the film's intricate plot as an allegory of the human condition, in which the contradictory and troubling elements serve as a reflection on (the limitations of) human memory, perception and emotion. Mainstream narrative complexity, however, is sometimes read allegorically too. For example, stories involving the unnatural scenario of a character duplication, like *Being John Malkovich, Enemy, The Double* or *+1* have been read as allegories of the effects of new technologies, the internet and social media on the fundamental experience of the unity of our selves (Wilkinson 2014). Such allegories, materialised in doppelgänger and other schizophrenic stories, are argued to be fuelled by our everyday experiences with new technological affordances, including our habitualisation with the practice of lossless digital copying, the virtualisation of our selves through online second lives and videogame avatars, our creation and maintenance of different user profiles on different digital platforms represented by different thumbnail pictures of our multiple selves and so on (we will further explore the cognitive backdrop and engaging potential of character multiplications in section 6.5). Likewise, forking-path and multiple-draft narratives have been understood to allegorically expose the effects of digital technologies on modern subjects, such as the non-linearity of network or database logic, the non-destructive digital text processing and video-editing technology or the immortal agency (in terms of having many lives and endless attempts) that the modern subject can assume in videogames. However, probably '[t]he most popular reason given for unusual narration', as Elliot Panek notes, 'is that such narration is part of the film's critique of Enlightenment values, specifically the values of order and reason' (Panek 2006: 67).

(6) *Satirisation or parody*: Alber further notes how 'narratives may also use impossible scenarios or events to mock certain entities. The most important feature of satire is critique through exaggeration, and grotesque images of humiliation or ridicule may occasionally merge with the unnatural' (Alber 2013a: 77). This option shares some overlap with the generification principle (since the generic context of comedy may allow impossibilities in such a way that they are not experienced as disturbing in the first place; after all, parody films may constantly transgress real-world possibilities for comic effects), and with allegorical readings (as the exaggeration can be understood to stand for something extratextual, that is, something in the real world to be ridiculed).

Although not particularly common, complex and impossible narrative structures too may be understood primarily in terms of their comic effects, allowing them to be naturalised as exaggerations or caricatures. For instance, the otherwise little motivated time loop in Harold Ramis' 1993 *Groundhog Day* can be seen as a comic exaggeration of protagonist Phil's (Bill Murray) cynical attitude, and particularly as a hyperbolic punishment for his arrogant dislike of celebrating Groundhog Day in the small town of Punxsutawney, a day he has to relive over and over again. Also, moments of impossible metaleptic transgressions in film, such as breaking the fourth wall, can function as an often rhetorical tool for sophisticated mockery, as happens for instance in Woody Allen's 1977 *Annie Hall* (think of the sudden, more or less impossible appearance of Marshall McLuhan, who helps Allen's character prove a point to a snobbish intellectual, followed by Allen directly addressing the audience). Moreover, complex narrative story formats can themselves also be the target of parody. Examples of this can be found in television shows like *Community*, which in the episode *Messianic Myths and Ancient Peoples* (Tristram Shapeero 2010, season 2, episode 5) has parodied several complex story formats, including Charlie Kaufman-esque metaleptic and self-reflexive filmmaking, or *South Park*, whose episode *Grounded Vindaloop* (Trey Parker 2014, season 18, episode 7) provided not only a tongue-in-cheek comment about narrative complexity, but also a clever illustration of the experiential confusion that multiply embedded narrative modes can cause. Some viewers may attribute a similar satirical intention to Quentin Dupieux's *Reality* – probably the most overtly playful and self-conscious of all impossible puzzle films. Given the film's overall absurdity, its excessively complex dissonant structure can be seen as a caricature, reflecting on the trend of narrative complexity rather than asking viewers to actually untangle its impossibly intertwined narrative levels.

(7) *Positing a transcendental realm*: in some situations, 'we can make sense of impossibilities by assuming that they are part of a transcendental realm such as heaven, purgatory or hell' (Alber 2013a: 78). This principle can help viewers to resolve strong narrative incongruities and impossibilities by imagining a type of storyworld in which real-world parameters do not apply, and in which anything impossible might be considered possible. Positing a transcendental realm can become a particularly tempting strategy when there seems to be no other diegetic and mimetic motivation to account for a complicated narrative structure or an impossibility-ridden storyworld. For instance, Alber notes how a seemingly inexplicable time loop could be motivated as 'a continuous cycle as a form of punishment' (ibid.: 78) in an afterlife.

Indeed, viewers have used this interpretive strategy in response to the loop of *Triangle* for instance, understanding the film's unexplicated impossible loop structure as a form of atonement that the protagonist must perpetually undergo; this reading is also reinforced by some clues in the film, such as the name of the ship, *Aeolus*, on which the loop takes place (in Greek mythology, Aeolus is the father of Sisyphus, who has been fated to roll a massive boulder up a hill and is forced to fruitlessly repeat his action forever). We might also add that the strategy of positing a transcendental realm can conflate with Alber's principle of subjectification. By this, we mean that viewers may treat an entire storyworld as a kind of 'mental landscape', thereby understanding the entire narrative as taking place in a transcendental mental realm that represents sub- or pre-conscious or symbolical psychological struggles – a strategy we will discuss later (in subsection 4.4.1) with regard to impossible puzzle films such as *Enemy* and *Mulholland Drive*.

(8) *Do it yourself*: this is a principle that Alber borrows from Marie-Laure Ryan, who has noted that in some texts contradictory and mutually exclusive versions of events are offered to the reader or viewer 'for creating their own stories' (Alber 2013a: 78 quotes Ryan 2006b: 671). Contradictory storylines can sometimes ask viewers to adopt a 'quasi-interactive' stance, leaving them with the task of arranging the story or choosing which version of events they consider the 'true' outcome. 'Do it yourself' works exchange authorial control for a wider interpretive freedom. Alber's literary example is Robert Coover's 1969 short story *The Babysitter*, for which '[o]ne might argue that this narrative uses mutually incompatible storylines to make us aware of suppressed possibilities and allows us to choose the ones that we prefer for whatever reasons' (Alber 2013a: 78).

This option opposes Bordwell's seventh storytelling convention, according to which, in cognitively manageable complex film narratives, 'parts [of the multiple-draft storyline] are not equal; the last one taken, or completed, is the least hypothetical one' (Bordwell 2002a: 100). A 'do it yourself' narrative, as Alber defines it, would thus have to go beyond Bordwell's examples of relatively 'simple' complexities like Tom Tykwer's 1998 *Run Lola Run* or Krzysztof Kieślowski's 1987 *Przypadek* (*Blind Chance*), as in these films the final draft seems to have a privileged reality status (that is, the one last presented is the 'true' outcome). The radical type of contradictory 'do it yourself' option that Coover's story exhibits, however, seems to be rare in contemporary complex cinema. An overt optionality that fully entrusts the viewer to make his or her choice from the presented unresolved contradictions is probably beyond the (post-)classical domain, and remains restricted to art-cinema narratives. In movies like *Last Year at Marienbad*, 'the transparently purposive avoidance of closure' (Carroll 2009: 214) works less as a narrative question to be answered, let alone a puzzle to be solved, but more like an explicit call for meta-narrative reflection and interpretive creativity. One could, however, argue that strategically ambiguous open endings in mainstream complex cinema can have a somewhat similar effect: an ending like that of *Inception*, for instance, creates a multi-stability of interpretations that outsources the decision to settle on any single, unambiguous outcome to the viewer. Yet, it does so while keeping its viewers within their immersion; moreover, Nolan presents the options (Cobb accepts to live in a dream to be reunited with his children versus he has finally found a way to meet his children in reality) as if they could be deciphered by a sharp-eyed viewer from within the narrative storyworld.

(9) *The Zen way of reading*: the final strategy discerned by Alber interestingly represents somewhat of a departure from all of the above strategies. Whereas the previous strategies are all focused on resolving cognitive dissonances through various interpretive moves, the Zen way of reading is about accepting the dissonance. In Alber's words, this way of reading (or viewing, for that matter) 'presupposes an attentive and stoic reader who repudiates the above mentioned explanations and simultaneously accepts both the strangeness of unnatural scenarios and the feelings of discomfort, fear, worry and panic that they might evoke in her or him' (Alber 2013a: 78). Narratologists (among others, Tsur 1975; Abbott 2008; Richardson 2011; Nielsen 2013) have called for the emancipation of this open-ended strategy, stressing that rather than coming up with interpretive closure, viewers, critics and academics should be more open to celebrate the polysemy of such challenging instances, that is to accept and revel in the unnatural as such (Alber 2013a: 78–9). Of course, the willingness of readers or viewers to engage in something like the Zen

way of reading depends strongly on individual preferences, and is arguably also related to individual variables in one's personality traits – such as what is known in psychology as the need for cognitive closure, a scale of people's individual tendency to accept or need to resolve ambiguous situations (Webster and Kruglanski 1994). Yet, we would argue that the more a given film problematises traditional narrative comprehension and naturalisation, the more appealing this viewing stance can become. We would further assume that strategies like the Zen way of viewing form 'last resort' strategies, meaning that viewers are particularly prone to take this stance if all other strategies to deal with the impossibilities and dissonances fail. It must however also be noted that this viewing stance is usually no longer a strictly 'narrative' engagement, in the sense that viewers who find themselves in this situation tend to 'give up' on the formation of an actual concrete narrative and go for more affective, lyrical or associative formations of meaning (although little 'threads of narrativity' may still be teased out). We will further explore how this viewing stance reduces dissonance in the next section (4.3), where we discuss what we call aesthetic and 'poetic' stances and other similar 'recuperative' frame-switches that serve to deal with irresolvable dissonance.

Prior to Alber's work, narratologist Tamar Yacobi (1981) described five *integrating mechanisms* with which viewers can naturalise textual inconsistencies. For Yacobi, dealing with textual tensions is essentially related to various degrees of 'reliability' that readers attribute to a text or narrator (as in any other communicative situation). When readers run into incongruities or other difficulties, they reconsider their assessment regarding the level of 'fictive reality' on which they hold the text to take place, and evaluate the inconsistency as having a specific function or traceable origin. In terms of 'dissonance reduction', we could thus say that Yacobi's principles cover different attitude changes that viewers can utilise in response to texts' evoking dissonant cognitions. According to Yacobi, readers utilise the integrate inconsistencies by (1) genetic, (2) generic, (3) existential, (4) functional and (5) perspectival strategies (Yacobi 1981). The *genetic* principle (1) covers the strategy by which readers resolve oddities by relating them to the origin of the text's actual production (as coming from a different cultural background, or as the result of a mistake in production for instance); the *generic* mechanism (2) relates to naturalisation through genre conventions (that is, inferring appropriateness within a work's generic context, like with Alber's strategy of generification); the *existential* principle (3) solves inconsistencies in terms of the structure of reality that a viewer attributes to the work in question (as part of the work's particular storyworld; for example, within the world of Kafka's *The Metamorphosis*, readers have to come to terms with a storyworld logic in which, apparently, people may suddenly turn into large insects); through the *functional* principle (4), viewers take the work's thematic, aesthetic or persuasive goals as the reason behind the text's peculiarities (for example, interpreting the inconsistency as an intended aesthetic effect, comparable to what Alber calls thematic reading); and, lastly, by the *perspectival* principle (5) (analogous to Alber's subjectification) viewers connect inconsistencies to the internal focalisation of the narration, treating diegetic anomalies as part of a character's subjective perception, dream, hallucination or fantasy (Yacobi 1981: 115–17). These strategies are all aimed at integrating the dissonance by attributing a function to it; furthermore, Yacobi also holds open the option that viewers may seek an unintended reason behind the dissonance, for instance by attributing it to a production error, or to cultural differences in terms of the work's context of production.

4.2.1 Foregrounding

Sense-making in response to textual oddities has also been subjected to empirical literary work. In a psychological study, Katalin Bálint and Frank Hakemulder have related the perception of textual deviancies – among them narrative dissonances – to the notion of *foregrounding*.[5] The concept of foregrounding has been used frequently in literary and aesthetic theory, and holds some similarity to ideas such as Russian formalism's notion of estrangement (*ostranenie* or *ostrannenie*). Foregrounding occurs when viewers perceive a strong deviancy (such as narration that is clearly dissonant) which draws their attention to the text's narrative strategy itself. In their study, Bálint and Hakemulder argue for the (somewhat unexpected) hypothesis that such foregrounding may enhance (rather than just disrupt) narrative absorption, as it can trigger more active meaning-making in viewers (absorption here may be defined as immersion, but also as a sensed 'presence', or as character identification).

Blending a phenomenological perspective with approaches from empirical psychology, Bálint and Hakemulder developed an empirical study to test their hypothesis and to categorise viewers and readers' responses to moments of foregrounding. Working only with narrative artworks that the participants had selected as personally meaningful, the researchers used qualitative methods to collect participants' meaning attributions in moments that the subjects identified as striking. The results have led to a (preliminary) taxonomy of how viewers engage with and make sense of troubling (narrative and/

---

[5] Bálint and Hakemulder's 'Phenomenology of the foregrounding experience in film and literature' was presented as an invited lecture at the University of Groningen, the Netherlands (2013), and at the conference of the International Society for the Empirical Study of Literature and Media, in Torino, Italy (2014). A published version of this work is currently under review (Bálint et al.).

or stylistic) textual strategies. Distinguishing seven general options, Bálint and Hakemulder find that readers and viewers interpret strong deviations as being (1) *symbols* carrying added meanings (these meanings can be subjective, relating to the diegetic world and characters, or may have a symbolic relationship to the real, external world); (2) *obstacles* to be overcome (an example would be a text that is written backwards, which offers momentary challenge or frustration in the reading experience, somewhat in the sense of a 'puzzle'); (3) *blanks* to be filled in (a film scene that suddenly lacks sound, for instance, asks viewers to actively construct or imagine the missing elements); (4) *ambiguities* to be disambiguated (as perceived ambiguities spawn different possible interpretations in the viewer, they may set in motion interpretive activities that can create a stronger mental connection between the viewer and the text); (5) *novelties* to be considered as striking and appreciated for their uniqueness; (6) *strangenesses* in the form of bizarre 'attractions' (such as those eccentric and grotesque oddities that are abundant in the films of David Lynch); and lastly, (7) as *immersive forces*, occurring, for instance, in 'stream of consciousness' fiction, where the deviancies are – somewhat counterintuitively – meant to construct a smooth, life-like reading that is closer to real-life experience.[6]

The above findings by Bálint and Hakemulder thus collectively emphasise how moments of strangeness, dissonance and deviance need not be entirely disruptive; rather, by inviting viewers to actively engage and come to terms with them, such moments may lead to a higher appreciation of and a stronger or more prolonged mental connection to the text. We may conclude from their findings that dissonant textual strategies can be appreciated by viewers for the sake of the dissonance, provided that the viewer can recognise an aesthetic effect or find a textual function in it.

4.2.2 Narrating agency and authorship

In addition to the range of strategies outlined above, we would like to emphasise the prominence of the option of attributing certain intentions to a film's narrating agency, or, by extension, to a film's 'author' (as in Yacobi's 'genetic

---

[6] Such a naturalising reading of the modernist aesthetic in film was examined in our paper 'The perception of reality as deformed realism' (Kiss 2010). By scrutinising the viewing experience of Jean-Luc Godard's 1965 *Pierrot le fou*, the text highlighted the similarity between the experience of the film's violation of representational realism on the one hand, and the real processes of viewers' perception and comprehension on the other. If our claim that in moments of emotional stress 'physical reality might be linear and chronological, but the experience of this reality is non-linear, achronological' (ibid: 171) is correct, then Godard's neo-cubist montage works not as a deviance to but exactly as a 'technical – and therefore poetic – restitution of reality' (Pasolini 1966: 42).

principle'). Attributing intentions to an (inferred) film author or to the narration itself may form a key strategy in coming to terms with dissonances. This may however need some explanation, as film narratology has had a somewhat polemic history in defining the role of narrators and authors.

Unlike novels, most films do not make use of an actual narrator who presents the story to us viewers. However, some theorists have posited the notion that film must have a *narrating instance* – some agent responsible for selecting and arranging the presented material. Seymour Chatman argued for the notion of the cinematic narrator (comparable to Wayne Booth's 1983 [1961] literary concept of the implied author) to theorise the sending, organising and controlling agency in the communicative process of film viewing; after all, Chatman claims, the act of watching and receiving a film needs to include the postulation of a sender or creator (Chatman 1978: 146–51; 1990: 109–23). Several other theorists have followed Chatman, working with comparable concepts like the implied filmmaker (see Alber 2010: 163–4 for an overview), or, in a somewhat less anthropomorphic fashion, the filmic composition device, defined by Manfred Jahn as 'a theoretical device that need not be associated with any concrete person or character, particularly neither the director nor a filmic narrator' (Jahn 2003: F4.1.2–F4.1.3). These theoretical models all assume that there must be a sender (actual or inferred) for the communicative process of film viewing and interpretation to work. At the other end stands David Bordwell, who has questioned the need to construct such a theoretical communicating agency. According to Bordwell's *inferential model*, a film narrative can also be understood as emerging in the reception process. A film narrative can be simply seen as 'the organization of a set of cues for the construction of a story. This presupposes a perceiver, but not any sender, of a message' (Bordwell 1985: 62). According to Bordwell, it is better 'to give the narrational process the power to signal under certain circumstances that the spectator should construct a narrator . . . No purpose is served by assigning every film to a deus absconditis [sic]' (ibid.: 62). To wind up his debate with Chatman, Bordwell concludes:

> Of course, we don't think that narratives fall from the skies. They are created by humans. But the relevant agents in this context are real people, not the postulated agents that Chatman argues for. To undergo the experience of a roller-coaster ride, I don't have to imagine a ghostly intelligence standing between the engineer and me, shaping the thrills and nausea I feel . . . The very concept of a storyteller doesn't entail a virtual storyteller of the sort that Chatman proposes. (Bordwell 2008: 128)

Leaving aside the question of whether film narratology is fundamentally in need of defining a filmic narrator or not, the interesting question for this book is whether actual viewers use such a concept to make sense of complex and dissonant narration. Can the invocation of narrating or authorial agency help viewers to interpret complex and contradictory narratives? We will argue that narrating agencies and authors can function as *interpretive constructs* (no matter whether they correspond to actual authors or not) that may help viewers to understand certain qualities of a film by inferring intended meanings on behalf of the film or its creators. Viewers often attribute intentions to the film's narration itself (for instance when saying that '*Memento* mimics antero-grade amnesia'), however, implicitly, they naturally see all such experiences as results of a human design, manifested as a result of what they perceive to be the intentions of the film's author (for example, 'Christopher Nolan is posing us a puzzle'). As Jason Mittell summarises, despite the highly collaborative nature of film production, notions on film's authorship remain closely connected to a reconstruction of the intentions of a single (or a few) author(s). As Mittell notes,

> [u]sing approaches such as biographical criticism or close textual and inter-textual analysis, critics strive to understand what a text means by discovering what the author's intended meaning was. Although such traditional notions of explicit intentionality are less common within criticism today, a looser form of intentionality follows from the auteur model of film criticism, where a director's body of work is analyzed for consistencies of theme and style – while these authorial markers need not be identified as explicit 'intent,' such criticism assumes that directors bring particular concerns and approaches to their work, and that the critic's job is to uncover those commonalities to reveal an authorial presence. (Mittell 2015: 96)

This interpretive practice is not limited to critical discourse; many non-professional viewers also interpret in terms of authorial intentions, building on their film literacy, previous knowledge and expectations (such as the director's background, a specific body of work, a visible 'authorial signature', intra- and intertextual references), and the viewing context (for example, in an arthouse cinema, as part of a DVD boxset and so on). Finding a compromise between Chatman and Bordwell's conflicting theories, Jason Mittell calls this interpretive construct the *inferred author function*. To differentiate this from notions like the implied author, the choice of the term 'inferred' highlights 'that authorship is not (solely) being construed through textual implication, but is constituted through the act of consumption itself' (ibid.: 107). As a definition,

> *the inferred author function is a viewer's production of authorial agency responsible for a text's storytelling, drawing on textual cues and contextual discourses.* In more practical terms, when we watch a program and wonder 'why did they do that?' the inferred author function is our notion of 'they' as the agent(s) responsible for the storytelling. (ibid.: 107)

Mittell follows Bordwell's account, at least in theory, by agreeing that 'viewers do not *need* to construct an authorial figure to comprehend a narrative' but, he emphasises, in practice, 'per pervasive fan discourses and accounts of personal viewing practices, many often do' (ibid.: 115). Mittell's inferred author function seems to be particularly suitable to more complex forms of narration, as these tend to require more interpretive activity and invite more viewer inferences, often reaching out to the extratextual domain and asking an authorial agency to lend a hand.[7]

As we have seen in this chapter so far, many interpretive strategies in fact involve explanations of narrative complexity as being intentional (for example, deeming it an authorial expression of the work's themes; as carrying a covert symbolic meaning that must be denoted; as a consciously placed puzzle for the viewer to solve; and so on). The guiding hypothesis of authorship entails that viewers anticipate that complexity will be in some way meaningful, since, presumably, it has been intentionally built into the narrative's design (by 'narratively wired' and purposefully communicating human agents). This anticipation guides the process of interpretation: it helps viewers suspend or tolerate momentary feelings of dissonance for a later payoff, and encourages them to actively speculate on the possible point or on possible outcomes. No matter how strong the perceived dissonances in a narrative are, this stance can cause some viewers to believe that there must be a 'masterplan', some purposeful construct that ultimately integrates every-thing consonantly and provides it with meaning. After all, as Mittell notes in his discussion of contemporary complex serial television,

> many viewers want to imagine a creator with full knowledge and mastery guiding the outcomes, and in moments of doubt or confusion, they put their trust and faith in this higher power . . . The inferred author function offers a model for the pragmatic use of an imagined, all-powerful creator to guide our faithful narrative comprehension. (ibid.: 116–17)

The overarching hypothesis of inferred authorship – what Jan Alber has called *hypothetical intentionalism*[8] – may thus support viewers' hope in resolving

---

[7] Mittell's original research domain concerns television series and serials, whose formats entail long-term narratives. Viewers of long-term narratives will be more inclined to create a kind of authorial construct that allows them to hypothesise where the show is heading or what its creators intended with certain choices. This heightened attunedness to authorship also enables actual viewer-author correspondence while a show is in production.

[8] Alber's notion of hypothetical intentionalism provides another interesting alternative to theories of the filmic narrator (Alber 2010). Drawing from cognitive theories on folk psychol-ogy and everyday mind-reading, Alber assumes that 'we all attribute intentions and motiva-tions to films in order to find out what they might mean' (ibid.: 167), and suggests that in film

complex narratives, as the assumption of a controlling author-figure with a coherent vision may help to retain their faith in a rewarding outcome. It also goes without saying that film authors' public personas can also include certain expectations with regard to narrative complexity. This may help more experienced and 'auteur literate' viewers to cope with recurring complexity within a director's or screenplay writer's oeuvre.[9] Compare, for instance, the possible variety of expectations that an informed moviegoer might bring to a complex film directed by Christopher Nolan, David Lynch or Terrence Malick. Knowledge of these directors' bodies of work and idiosyncratic auteur approaches will presumably influence what intentions viewers initially assume to underlie moments of narrative dissonance, since they may be expecting, for example, a mind-bending puzzle, a disorienting subjective realist experience or a (pseudo-)profound philosophical exploration, respectively. In such situations, authorship functions as a cognitive frame connected to certain expectations, as well as interpretive and evaluative routines.

4.2.3 Artefact emotions and meta-reflexive appreciation

Notwithstanding the above, it must also be stressed that viewers need not be familiar with a film's director or writer to appreciate its narration. Moments of strong narrative deviance can also be scrutinised and valued for their own sake: a challenging enigma, a strikingly unconventional structure or an unexpected resolution can all be understood by viewers as moments of 'narrative spectacle'. Mittell calls such instances the narrative artwork's *operational aesthetic* – a notion he borrows from Neil Harris (1973). The term means the discernment of a mode of viewing that invites viewers to engage in a pleasure that is 'less about "what will happen?" and more about "how did he do that?"' (Mittell 2015: 42). Some complex films indeed seem to aim to 'outsmart' or 'trick' the viewer. Their operational aesthetic extends the fictional engagement with 'artefact emotions', triggering 'fascination with the construction of a film narrative or production design' (Plantinga 2009: 89). Complex films often invite us to marvel at their cleverness, unexpectedness, uniqueness or other striking qualities demonstrating their ingenious narrative construction. As Mittell notes in his seminal article 'Narrative Complexity in Contemporary American Television',

---

viewing spectators create cohesion and make meaning by inferring a kind of 'hypothetical filmmaker' to whom such intentions may be ascribed.

[9] For the latter, see, for example, Chris Dzialo's (2009) analysis of Charlie Kaufman's complex screenplays.

> [t]hrough the operational aesthetic these complex narratives invite viewers
> to engage at the level of formal analyst [sic], dissecting the techniques used
> to convey spectacular displays of storytelling craft; this mode of formally
> aware viewing is highly encouraged by these [complex contemporary serial]
> programs, as their pleasures are embedded in a level of awareness that
> transcends the traditional focus on diegetic action typical of most viewers.
> (Mittell 2006: 36)

The operational aesthetic of narrative artworks thus invokes a partially 'meta-
reflexive' appreciation; with complex films, viewers, through their confusion,
become aware of the intricate storytelling techniques being applied, and begin
actively trying to resolve the narrative puzzles. And yet this meta-narrative
exploration does not necessarily hamper them in their immersion in the fictional storyworld. Back to Mittell's words:

> what seems to be a key goal across videogames, puzzle films, and narratively
> complex television series is the desire to be both actively engaged in the story
> and successfully surprised through storytelling manipulations. This is the
> operational aesthetic at work – we want to enjoy the machine's results while
> also marveling at how it works. (ibid.: 38)

With the rise of mainstream narrative complexity, such partially meta-reflexive
modes of viewing have arguably become more commonplace in popular film
consumption (see also our discussion in Chapter 1).

4.2.4 Interpretation as dissonance reduction

In conclusion to all of the above, it must first be noted that the discussed
rationalising and sense-making activities are not restricted to complex or
dissonant films and texts. Viewers and readers, in their strenuous search for
meaning, always and constantly naturalise even the most basic of stories, relating texts to available cognitive schemas and knowledge of genres, as well as
to the real world and to actual contexts or authors. It is by reference to these
cognitive and cultural frames of knowledge that it becomes possible to understand and interpret any text in the first place. Such elementary hermeneutic
processes are arguably a key part of the mental activity that makes reading
a narrative or watching a film an engaging and even pleasurable activity.
However, complex stories, we would argue, often deliberately emphasise our
reliance on these strategies by resisting habitual sense-making (either locally,
through perceptual paradoxes and other instant modes of foregrounding, or
globally, by more pervasively affecting contradictory events) in such a way
that interpretation becomes a conscious, central and ultimately engaging or
rewarding activity. This can function 'online', while watching the film (as the

formation of interpretive hypotheses is often implicated in the act of complex film viewing), but also 'post-hoc', in the form of reflective engagement after the viewing – for instance when we look back on a film, discuss it with a friend or spend extra time on online message boards and review platforms to read or share different interpretations.

This insight constitutes the first possible explanation that can account for the seeming paradox of the attractiveness of cognitive dissonance: it is not the felt dissonance itself that appeals to readers and viewers, but the creative act of finding and applying strategies or ascribing meanings to reduce the dissonance that may constitute the fascination with (and assumed pleasurability of) complex narrative experiences. Several reasons could underlie this explanation.

First of all, successfully reducing dissonance may be rewarding, if not pleasing, because it allows viewers to feel competent and insightful – in having solved the puzzle, in comprehending the narrative machinery, in mastering the appropriate interpretive moves and so on. This explanation can account for a significant part of the gratification of complexity in art, something we will further explore in Chapter 6.

Second, naturalising interpretations can have a rewarding and satisfying effect because they bring formal narrative complexities back to the realm of the mimetic. The interpretive work serves to (re-)connect abstract, formal complexity to the realm of the humanly meaningful, as naturalisations make the dissonance expressive of, or relevant to, some aspect of everyday lived experience.

Lastly, viewers' naturalising interpretations can also have another, intellectually 'reflective' dimension. By foregrounding potential ambiguities and ambivalences, dissonances in narrative artworks invite viewers to consciously apply different cognitive and cultural frames to resolve them. This means that viewers are asked to try out different knowledge frames, to consciously process them, to examine them and to reflect on them. Engaging in such intensified (and manifold) acts of interpretation may have a philosophically reflective side-effect, as they can make us aware of our own interpretive activity, and may, in the process, reveal as much about the interpreter as they do about the work interpreted. These reflective opportunities to be hermeneutically and interpretively critical and creative can form an important part of the gratification of art experiences.

All in all, however, claiming a central role for these naturalising or reduction strategies does not yet solve our paradox entirely – at least not with regard to impossible puzzle films. As we have noted, these films often exploit the effect of cognitive dissonance more enduringly. Films like *Donnie Darko*, *Enemy* or *Mulholland Drive* do not offer the type of local impossibilities and incongruities that one can easily naturalise – sometimes not even after pro-longed efforts. The paradoxes and counterintuitive events they present are stubborn, and the evoked effect of their cognitive dissonance tends to be more global and lastingly disconcerting. Impossible puzzle films often do not hand their viewers the above pathways to naturalise their strangeness in an unambiguous manner, nor do they give viewers the ultimate gratification of having 'solved the puzzle'. Instead, they seem to rely on the bewildering and perplexing effects of enduring and pervasive dissonances, like the ones created by paradoxes and other impossible incongruities. The question thus remains: when a narrative resists straightforward modes of naturalisation and ration-alisation, then how do viewers engage with highly unnatural, paradoxical or counterintuitive story elements? In the below, first we will outline how dis-sonant film narratives may inspire viewers to take different aesthetic stances towards the work as a whole – laying less stress on narrativisation efforts and rather focusing on a film's aesthetic, poetic or lyrical qualities (see section 4.3). This will be followed by the unpacking of the hypothesis, according to which some complex films – including impossible puzzle films in particular – may encourage repeated switching between different interpretations (rather than settling on a single interpretive strategy) in response to their persistent dissonance (in section 4.4).

4.3 COPING WITH DISSONANCE: FRAME-SWITCHES AND POETIC AND AESTHETIC READINGS

A high degree of dissonance or unnaturalness can cause a more fundamental shift in the apprehension of a text, triggering an altogether different kind of interpretive response. We will call this kind of viewer activity a *frame-switch*: when local textual conflicts become too severe or numerous, and naturalis-ing strategies fail, viewers often alter their stance towards a text as a whole. That is, they change the 'macro-frame' through which they apprehend the work. Sometimes, such frame-switches direct viewers' assessments to differ-ent (but in some ways 'neighbouring') types of narrative engagement, such as 'poetic' or 'aesthetic' modes of viewing and reading, but also modes of viewing that abandon narrativity altogether, or what Jan Alber called the Zen way of reading, all of which allow different aesthetic effects than traditional narrativisation.

One such theory comes from Torben Grodal, who has described the viewer mechanisms that are active in the confrontation with dissonant narrative experiences from an embodied-cognitive angle. According to Grodal, movies 'presenting paradoxes and counterintuitive events . . . arrest the PECMA flow and overactivate the association areas' and, by doing so, provide 'experiences of deep significance' (Grodal 2009: 149–50).[10] For Grodal, dissonant experiences trigger a frame-switch in viewers' evaluations of a given narrative: he suggests that rather than focusing on concrete action, viewers will take a different stance and look for more symbolic and higher-order meanings in such narratives. This means that they detach their interpretation from immersion in the 'online', embodied and concrete actions of a story, and rather focus on the more abstract, 'disembodied' realm of 'higher-order' meaning-making systems. This frame-switch partially suspends the mimetic make-believe in the storyworld, and exchanges it for a more interpretive apprehension, a shift that ultimately justifies the categorisation of these experiences under a reception-defined label of art film, which, according to Grodal, is 'a subcategory within film art in general' (Grodal 2009: 207). In this sense, according to Grodal, art cinema is not just a set of conventional principles and representational modes (that is, not only a genre), but also forms a label for describing actual viewers' embodied-cognitive film experiences (that is, a particular stimulation of viewers' cognitive faculties that results in their specific labelling of a film as an art film).

In her cognitive-narratological volume *Towards a Natural Narratology*, Monika Fludernik argues for a similar strategy of frame-switching, albeit without the 'hard' neuroscientific and embodied-cognitive claims that characterise Grodal's work. According to Fludernik, when dealing with a (potentially) narrative artefact, readers and viewers engage in an act of *narrativisation*. Narrativisation comprises the reading and viewing routine of assigning a cognitive macro-frame that imposes narrativity onto a text; it naturalises the artefact as a story by recourse to narrative schemas (Fludernik 1996: 34). This process involves both culturally acquired schemas (for instance, familiar storytelling situations and generic patterns) and natural embodied-cognitive parameters (such as embodied knowledge about human action, communication, perception, emotions and so on) to render certain artefacts or events 'narrative' (ibid.: 22–5). For Fludernik, narrativity is thus primarily a natural cognitive act, a frame that viewers apply (actively, but typically subconsciously) to artefacts or real-life events. Some texts, however, resist this process of narrativisation. Fludernik uses the term 'non-natural' texts for works of art that challenge mimetic models, routines of comprehension and

---

[10] Grodal's PECMA (Perception, Emotion, Cognition and Motor Action) model 'describes how the film experience relies on a processing flow that follows the brain's general architecture, namely a flow from perception (ear and eye), via visual and acoustic brain structures, association areas, and frontal brain structures to action (motor activation) . . . In films . . . it is the perception of activities on the screen that cues the viewer's simulation of the flow' (Grodal 2009: 146, 151). For a detailed analysis of narrative complexity's disruptive – blocking – effect on a seamless PECMA flow, see Ros and Kiss (under review).

real-life cognitive parameters: 'Recuperation of narrativity from non-naturally coded texts . . . becomes possible through recourse to a variety of natural cognitive parameters . . . [However, w]here narrativity can no longer be recuperated by any means at all, the narrative genre merges with poetry' (ibid.: 36).

Like Grodal, Fludernik's notion also allows for a kind of interpretive 'last resort' strategy by switching to a different frame altogether. When the dissonance is too insolubly large, or the incongruities are too numerous, viewers will often abandon the mental formation of a prototypical narrative, and construct meaning and assign significance on a level that is not strictly narrative. Such a shift towards a (more) poetic reading can provide a satisfying recourse when the story(-logic) of a text is no longer recuperable through conventional story patterns or mimetic parameters. This frame-switch arguably entails a fundamentally different viewing stance – one that is no longer aimed at forming prototypical narrativity (that is, constructing a causal and chronological chain of events around agents in a spatio-temporal setting), but also allows more connotative and reflective modes of interpretation. When defining the third pillar of his four-tier model of cinematic meanings, David Bordwell has called this viewer-inclination the *symbolic impulse* (see our discussion in section 2.2). 'The spectator,' Bordwell notes, 'may seek to construct implicit [that is, symbolic] meanings when she cannot find a way to reconcile an anomalous element with a referential or explicit aspect of the work' (Bordwell 1989: 9).

These strategies can work to reduce dissonance because a poetic frame of assessment will lay less stress on the importance of narrative coherence and logic. It thus downplays the magnitude of the dissonance that is caused by incongruent, incoherent or impossible narrative elements. At the same time, it allows for a wider interpretive range to make meaning, to produce consonant readings and to assign significance to the work. Moreover, modes of viewing that allow such attitudes (like the aforementioned Zen way of reading discerned by Jan Alber) can also serve to give way to the more affective dimensions of a cognitively problematic narrative. Arguably, one possibly enjoyable (side-)effect of a cognitively baffling story is that it can make room for viewers to simply undergo the perceptual or affective sensations of wonder, strangeness, beauty or anxiety that the work evokes. In the next chapter (subsection 5.1.3) we will come back to these frame-switches with regard to art-cinema viewing, where such strategies seem to be more prominent and sometimes even the desired effect.

Interestingly, the implicit consensus among the above models of naturalisation and narrativisation seems to be that whereas physically impossible features can usually be explained or naturalised as part of a storyworld or genre, strong logically unreasonable scenarios (like those in impossible puzzle films) are supposedly usually tamed through more 'distancing' frame-switches – that is, by transforming their unbearable paradoxes into associational, allegoric, symbolic, symptomatic and other extradiegetic domains of meaning-making. Such frame-switches are generally characterised by a certain decrease of immersion in the mimetic qualities of a text, and, in turn, by an expanded emphasis on more meta-fictional or extratextual modes of meaning-making. Yet, again, when regarding impossible puzzle films, it seems that viewers' *narrative* inclination usually remains stronger than the reflective aesthetic pleasure that a symbolical interpretation or other frame-switch can provide. These films do present logically unreasonable and mutually incompatible events, but do not seem to trigger art-cinematic feelings of 'deep significance', as Grodal assumes, nor do they encourage viewers to direct fully their meaning-making activities towards the poetic, associative, aesthetic or lyrical dimensions. Instead (as we will argue more extensively in the next chapter) it seems that impossible puzzle films often rather tempt viewers into a more intensive narrative investigation, encouraging them to closely map the plot and carefully scrutinise the storyworld in an insistent endeavour to reveal possible, logically reasonable solutions.

4.4 FRAME-SWITCHING AS HERMENEUTIC PLAY IN IMPOSSIBLE PUZZLE FILMS

Lastly, a third strategy, in some ways complementary to the previous two but arguably more suitable to the particular challenges of impossible puzzle films, has been proposed by literary theorist Liesbeth Korthals Altes. She relates puzzling narrative experiences to the idea of repeatedly switching between different explanatory and assessment frames as an aesthetic effect in itself. According to Korthals Altes, 'some kinds of texts, and some kinds of reading strategies, require that we hold in mind alternative conflicting framings and oscillate between them, as this may result in pleasurable ("aesthetic") mental activity' (Korthals Altes 2014: 33 – our emphasis). This view acknowledges that switching between interpretations – rather than settling on one exclusively assigned meaning – can be a rewarding mode of reception too.

Indeed, complex stories may appeal to readers and viewers by requiring them to apply and test different frames of knowledge, thereby inviting them to check the flexibility of their interpretive and critical competences. This oscillating frame-switching activity can function as a kind of *hermeneutic play* in the process of making meaning of complex narratives. Dissonant cognitions, in the form of unresolvable ambiguities, impossibilities or contradictions, can present powerful triggers to engage viewers in this hermeneutic play, as such challenges can be particularly stimulating for viewers' need for resolution and their general urge to construct meaning. By allowing the application of different hermeneutic frames, this creates an opportunity for viewers to be imaginative, reflective, philosophical or meta-cognitive, or to simply try out and train any combination of these sensibilities.

Some impossible puzzle films enhance such effects by leaving strong ambiguities in terms of the possible meanings (that is, framing options) they warrant to their dissonances. For instance, they may create and maintain uncertainty between the objective or subjective nature of their narration, or between the appropriateness of concrete narrative readings and more asso-ciative, poetic or allegorical ways of making meaning of the events. When viewers experience such ambiguities, we can roughly discern two general types of narrative frame-switching activities that they may resort to. These concern (4.4.1) *switching between macro-frames* (that is, deciding on, for example, 'What text type or genre is at hand?'; 'How should it be watched?'; 'What meaning-making and evaluative procedures are appropriate?') and (4.4.2) *local frame-switching* between possible interpretations and naturalisations of local textual elements (addressing questions such as, for example, 'How should this particular contradiction be understood within the represented boundaries of the narrative world?' or 'Is it a subjective representation, an aspect of the storyworld, a symbol or a meta-fictional reflection?'). The divide is, of course, not so clear-cut, as these two levels of framing operate in close connection: a change in the chosen macro-frame (for example assessing the text as a detec-tive story, as lyrical poetry or as a political manifesto) also entails the applica-tion of different local naturalisations. Conversely, local problems and shifts in meaning-making can cause viewers to take a different stance towards the text as a whole. Nevertheless, in the sections below, we outline the two options independently, as they may relate to different (albeit closely related) possible viewing effects of impossible puzzle films.

4.4.1 Switching between narrative and symbolical readings: *Enemy* and *Mulholland Drive*

In some cases, viewers may remain in disagreement not just on specific interpretations, but also in terms of which macro-frame is most appropri-ate to understand the narrative at hand. Denis Villeneuve's *Enemy*, our case study at the start of this chapter, is an example of an impossible puzzle film that knowingly plays with the options of reading its story through different macro-frames. Upon first viewing, the initial apprehension and interpretation of most viewers of the film will be that of a mimetic, perhaps magical-realist narrative, comparable to the original story of José Saramago's novel *The Double*, on which the movie is based. This means most viewers are likely to first see the story as a (semi-)realistic tale of Adam Bell (Jake Gyllenhaal) who discovers that he has a perfect double, Anthony Claire (Jake Gyllenhaal), who looks indistinguishably similar to him.

The fundamental difference between Saramago's novel and Villeneuve's film is the way in which they approach the same idea of someone being confronted with his exact double. While the original novel takes the bizarre situation as a strange but real anomaly of the fictional storyworld, the film, by playing on its protagonist(s) and viewers' natural scepticism about the very possibility of such unnaturalness, focuses on the intrinsic ambiguation of the (im)possible character duplication. While Saramago's treatment evokes rational questions like 'How can you deal with or resolve such weird simultaneity?', Villeneuve raises more ontological concerns, asking 'How is this possible at all?', 'Who is who? and 'Is what we see real?'

As we get lost in *Enemy*'s schizophrenic spider web, it becomes clear that the film does not settle upon the novel's realistic treatment and rational contemplation of this strange phenomenon. Instead, by cumulating incongruities and ambiguities, the film version gradually challenges the realistic reading of the story's strange (or magical) elements. The two physically identical characters seem to conflate increasingly throughout Villeneuve's rather free adaptation. Moreover, the suggestion of strong psychological themes and recurring motives and symbols (such as the spider figures and cobwebs) underline the ambiguity as to how the story could be read as a whole: perhaps the two men form a duality of two aspects of the same person, manifesting an old interpretive trope that is often present or implied in the literary theme of the doppelgänger. Or, some would say, there is actually a single protagonist, and his apparent physical split – focalised through a subjective realist point of view that creates an alter ego – is an unreliable representation of his mental disintegration (fuelled by his insecurities of being unable to commit to his family and to his soon-to-be-born child, or, according to another possible interpretation, by his guilty conscience causing a fatal car accident in which he lost his pregnant wife).

By cumulating dissonances, the narration in *Enemy* thus suggests a second, psychological or symbolical framing of the events, creating the ambiguity that all events may possibly be subconscious, sublimated or imagined. This offers an alternative viewing stance to solve the film's internal narrative conflicts: one that abandons classical narrative routines and embraces more psychological readings that treat the offbeat elements as symbols of guilt, fear or desire. The possible appropriateness of the latter stances is further reinforced by the film's puzzling, if not shocking, final scene (in which the film's narrative spider's stratagem – literally – corporealises, turning the protagonist's pregnant wife into a giant spider). Whereas, on the surface, the film seems to be a 'narrative' film in the rather classical sense, its narrative dissonances and stylistic suggestions gradually pull the viewer towards alternative symbolical or allegorical readings that may possibly yield a more coherent interpretation. *Enemy*'s balanced ambiguity between equally possible global interpretations thus brings into effect an engaging hermeneutic play of switching between classical narrative and symbolic explanatory assessments.

In some of the most ambiguous of these cases, the viewing experiences evoked by impossible puzzle films may border on viewing routines that we associate with art cinema. An illustrative example of such framing ambiguity is offered by the case of David Lynch's *Mulholland Drive*. In a paper on the film's origins as a potential television series, Jason Mittell outlines the debate between academics, critics and fans on how the film's enigmatic complexity should be understood. Mittell notes that the readings of Lynch's highly complex narrative can be filed under two general positions:

> The first is a question of *comprehension*, trying to understand the literal coherence of the film's narrative events . . . The most common explanation for the film's narrative is that the first 80% of *Mulholland Drive* is Diane Selwyn's dream, and that the final act portrays the reality she is trying to escape, but many other explications argue for various versions of dreams, reality, deaths, and parallels. (Mittell 2013)

This position, we would argue, is the one that follows from maintaining a more or less 'classical' narrativising viewing stance. Relying on the subjectification or perspectival principles of sense-making outlined above, it favours structural narrative orientation on a mimetic level, and aims to provide traditional naturalisations and motivations (subjective realism, dreams, mental illness) for the narration's complex formal functions, while accepting the film's paradoxes as part of the game. From this analytical angle, the film's confusing effect emerges from the film's narrative complexity that operates on two interlocked levels. First, Lynch provides an exceedingly complex structure that combines a severely shattered non-linear chronology with a self-contained metaleptic structure, juggling with and jumping in and out from the levels of the reality frame of dreaming (Naomi Watts as Diane Selwyn) and the dream itself (Naomi Watts as Betty Elms). Second, adding another layer to the film's complexity, Lynch conceals the plot's non-linearity or looped metalepsis, refusing to signpost any transitions or transgression moments along its bumpy narrative ride. As a result, the viewer faces the rather impossible task of deciphering an excessively complex game without the help of any manual that would at least reveal the rules of such an intricate game.

Alternatively, Mittell notes, 'the other way to answer the question about *Mulholland Drive*'s meaning, is to engage in *interpretation*, looking for the meanings beneath the surface, at the level of symbolism, thematics, or sub-textual significance' (ibid.). The explanations offered by this second group of viewers employed poetic, allegorical or other more 'art-cinematic' apprehensions that favoured the invocation of extratextual, connotative or philosophical frames of knowledge to tame the film's narrative dissonances. As Mittell notes, in the abundant critical and scholarly writings on the film

> we can find readings of the film as illustrating Lacan's theories of fantasy, desire, and reality; evoking contemporary technologies of virtual reality; dissolving the boundaries between semiotic oppositions; offering a lesbian tragedy as an indictment of homophobia; and critiquing the dream-crushing logic of Hollywood cinema, among many others. (ibid.)

Such readings place the film's dissonance in a discursive, naturalising context, downplaying concrete narrative readings in favour of extratextual frames and other hermeneutic solutions to make its dissonant elements cohere.

The case of *Mulholland Drive* and these two viewing attitudes demonstrate how narrative and cognitive macro-frames do not only underlie different interpretations, but can also shape very different *viewing experiences* and modes of engagement. It is on these thin and sometimes fuzzy boundaries that the differences between impossible puzzle films and art cinema often become articulate (or where the differences may dissolve, for some viewers). Due to this difficulty in categorisation, we will pay more attention to the specification of the differences between art cinema and impossible puzzle films in the next chapter, where we will discuss their divergent narration strategies. Most impossible puzzle films, we will claim, do not primarily encourage poetic, lyrical or allegorical readings, but remain (at least partially) rooted in the general confines of 'classical narrative' engagement.

4.4.2 Cognitive hesitation and the fantastic

The potential ambiguity between naturalising options does not always only concern shifts in macro-frames, which alter viewing stances altogether. Within a more or less established classical narrative macro-frame of engagement, viewers may still experience local conflicts in naturalising or rationalising routines. These may concern uncertainty over determining how local incoherencies can be seen as a functional part of the narrative (see also the models of Jan Alber, Tamar Yacobi, and Katalin Bálint and Frank Hakemulder discussed earlier). Viewers can, for instance, remain unsure as to whether a certain element of the storyworld should be seen as an ontological fact of the diegetic world, or as the subjective perception of a character, or perhaps as a symbol that is to be interpreted in terms of a thematic, metadiegetic meaning constructed by the author – and so on.

Impossible puzzle films sometimes strategically retain such ambiguities with regard to different naturalising options. One common strategy is to not make explicit whether certain events, moments or plotlines are subjective internal states of a character or objective external facts of the fictional storyworld. Such ambiguity is similar to the one related to *Enemy*, but with the difference that here it need not concern the status of the narrative as a whole. As Allan Cameron has noted, 'these [that is, David Lynch's LA trilogy] and other [then] recent films, including *Donnie Darko* (Richard Kelly 2001) and *Fight Club* (David Fincher 1999) create ontological uncertainty between "subjective" and "objective" narrative modes' (Cameron 2008: 11). Even within seemingly subjective scenes, Cameron notes, 'we are not always sure whether we are witnessing a memory, a hallucination or an alternative reality' (ibid.: 11).

Indeed, creating and strategically maintaining uncertainty between objective and subjective modes of naturalisation is a key strategy of many impossible puzzle films. In this sense, impossible puzzle films can facilitate a kind of cognitive hesitation – a cognitive dissonance that, as Matthew Campora describes it, 'results from the lack of sufficient information required to make a decision regarding the nature of the event' (Campora 2014: 60). This cognitive hesitation is a viewing effect that can be seen as closely related to what narratologist Tzvetan Todorov defined as the 'theoretical genre' of the fantastic. In fantastic fiction, troubling impossibilities occur in a seemingly normal storyworld. More precisely, within an immersive, realistic and natural storyworld, the fantastic presents viewers with

> an event which cannot be explained by the laws of this same familiar world. The person who experiences the event must opt for one of two possible solutions: either he is the victim of an illusion of the senses, of a product of the imagination – and the laws of the world then remain what they are; or else the event has indeed taken place, it is an integral part of reality – but then this reality is controlled by laws unknown to us. (Todorov 1975: 25)

The category of the fantastic, Todorov argues, is not defined by the choice for either one of these options (a subjective illusion or a supernatural storyworld) but rather by the uncertainty that follows from the 'equitenability' of both options. In other words,

> [t]he fantastic occupies *the duration of this uncertainty*. Once we choose one answer or the other, we leave the fantastic for a neighbouring genre, the uncanny or the marvelous. The fantastic is that hesitation experienced by a person who knows only the laws of nature, confronting an apparently supernatural event. (ibid.: 25 – our emphasis)

A text thus belongs to the category of the fantastic when it persistently maintains a puzzling ambiguous effect as to how its presented oddities should be understood: that is, 'until an explanation is provided, or until a decision is made by the viewer regardless of the provision of an explanation, the spectator remains in the mode of the fantastic' (Campora 2014: 61). Texts that ultimately do offer a reasonable option to rationalise the supernatural elements (restoring the laws of a realistic world) belong to the genre of the uncanny, whereas texts that ultimately accept the supernatural as part of the laws of the storyworld belong to the marvellous (Todorov 1975: 41).

Besides the presence of impossible or supernatural elements, Todorov notes that the effect of the fantastic requires immersion ('an integration of the reader into the world of the characters') and must be sustained by ambiguity ('that world is defined by the reader's own ambiguous perception of the events narrated') (ibid.: 31). The fantastic, it can thus be argued, is essentially a cognitive dissonance – it is a viewing effect characterised by a maintained cognitive hesitation that readers experience with regard to a troubling impossibility in a storyworld: '[t]he reader's hesitation is therefore the first condition of the fantastic' (ibid.: 31). Moreover, the fantastic – like impossible puzzle films – does not allow viewers to make a definitive frame-switch that would modulate the storyworld's mimetic and immersive qualities for a more thematic or poetic reading. In Todorov's words, the fantastic implies 'not only the existence of an uncanny event, which provokes a hesitation in the reader and the hero; but also a kind of reading, which we may for the moment define negatively: it must be neither "poetic" nor "allegorical"' (ibid.: 32). In sum, Todorov defines the fantastic as a genre as follows:

> The fantastic requires the fulfilment of three conditions. First, the text must oblige the reader to consider the world of the characters as a world of living persons and to hesitate between a natural and supernatural explanation of the events described. Second, the hesitation may also be experienced by a character; thus, the reader's role is so to speak entrusted to a character, and at the same time the hesitation is represented, it becomes one of the themes of the work – in the case of naive reading, the actual reader identifies himself with the character. Third, the reader must adopt a certain attitude with regard to the text: he will reject allegorical as well as 'poetic' interpretations. These three requirements do not have an equal value. The first and the third actually constitute the genre; the second may not be fulfilled. Nonetheless, most examples satisfy all three conditions. (ibid.: 33)

All three of Todorov's criteria for the reading effect of the fantastic hold for impossible puzzle films too. It seems that these films also achieve their viewing effects by evoking in viewers a cognitive hesitation, as they keep open certain interpretive options to deal with the presented dissonances. Also, in impossible puzzle films, both the protagonist and the viewers often experience comparable confusion and uncertainty with regard to the diegetic impossibilities (as happens in *Triangle* or in *Enemy*, for example). Lastly, a viewing stance that settles for a poetic (rather than narrative) engagement will downplay the hesitation in such a way that the hesitation effect is lost. Impossible puzzle films therefore walk a similar interpretive tightrope of specific conditions which need to be balanced to trigger and preserve a particular hesitation in their viewers with regard to the narrative's non-natural elements.

Matthew Campora believes that fantastic narratives, in both literature and film, will invariably resolve themselves into one of Todorov's categories of the *uncanny* or the *marvellous* (or into one of the other two subgenres of the *fantastic uncanny* or the *fantastic marvellous*). According to him, '[e]ven if *Mulholland Drive* offers no explanation, for instance, the spectator *must* decide how to explain the event' (Campora 2014: 61 – our emphasis). Campora reasons that *Mulholland Drive* lifts its fantastic mode by offering naturalisation through positing a narrative mode of subjective realism (for example, Betty's unexplainable disappearance can be understood in the context of a dream). We argue that impossible puzzle films like *Mulholland Drive* indeed may demand, but actually do not reassuringly allow the offloading of their dissonant elements into the (fantastic) uncanny or (fantastic) marvellous domains of naturalisation. Although impossible puzzle films may indeed evoke certain naturalising explanations to some viewers, they do not fully commit to a single one and retain ambiguities. Through this refusal, they maintain a degree of cognitive hesitation instead, and are therefore capable of providing a perpetually fantastic mode of viewing. For instance, as Dennis Lim, author of *David Lynch: The Man from Another Place*, has argued,

> [m]uch more than an enigma to be cracked, *Mulholland Dr.* takes as its subject the very act of solving: the pleasurable and perilous, essential and absurd process of making narrative sense, of needing and creating meaning. Whether or not they explicitly pose the question, Lynch's late films ponder the role of story at times when reality itself can seem out of joint. (Lim 2015)

Readings like this one – which take hesitation itself as their subject – are equally possible for many impossible puzzle films. They do however require an ability to suspend interpretive closure that, following Reuven Tsur, we call 'negative capability' (Tsur 1975) – a stance which we will discuss further in section 6.1. It is true that movies like *Mulholland Drive* or *Triangle* could be naturalised as a subjective dream or hallucination (for Campora *Mulholland Drive* belongs to the fantastic uncanny). This option may be tempting for some viewers, because it brings the troubling dissonances back to the realm of both the humanly possible and the symbolically meaningful. However, it is not necessarily the only possible, most attractive or 'maximally meaningful' of the options. As for *Triangle*, for instance, although the vicious loop in which the protagonist finds herself could be easily naturalised as a projection of a guilt-ridden and therefore schizophrenic mother's internally focalised subjective realist view (similar to that of *Enemy*'s protagonist), most viewers do not opt for this solution. Instead, keeping the fantastic mode in operation, they often maintain their close analytical engagement when permanently attempting to crack the puzzle, or enjoy the film's balanced play, regulating the oscillation between their pertinent explanatory frames.[11]

Lastly, the fundamental difference between Todorov's category and ours is that whereas the fantastic concerns questions on the ontology of the storyworld, such as the existence or non-existence of ghosts in the particular world of the fiction (that is, elements of the told), impossible puzzle films maintain the uncertainties on the level of narrative structure and narration (that is, in the telling). The fantastic can occur within relatively simple narrative structures too. Impossible puzzle films, on the other hand, do not have to play with the hesitation of the fantastic with regard to the unnatural elements of their storyworlds; for example, complex time-travel films like *Primer* and *Timecrimes* leave no ambiguity as to what causes their convoluted story structures, as they construct storyworlds that host the existence of time machines. Nevertheless, impossible puzzle films do almost invariably include some strange, supernatural or disturbing elements in their storyworlds, which often serve to heighten the evoked sense of puzzlement. Moreover, sustaining uncertainty over the ontological status of these impossible story elements can be an effective (additional) strategy to increase or maintain puzzlement and curiosity. In Roman Polanski's *The Tenant* (1976), for instance, the ambiguity of who is responsible for the impossibilities and supernatural occurrences in the story (either a haunted apartment, or the distorting paranoia and identity crisis of the focalising protagonist) is the same question as to what or who is responsible for the narrative's impossible loop structure. The effects of impossible puzzle films and the fantastic may thus function in tandem, with the hesitation and ambiguity of the fantastic serving to heighten the puzzling effect of an impossible narrative structure.

---

[11] Supervising more than ten seminar discussions about *Triangle* (between 2010 and 2014, at the University of Groningen, the Netherlands), our experience tells us that viewers do not easily settle on the simple subjective realist explanation. Rather, as their feeling of competence seems to be provoked by the brainy narrative, many viewers tend to continuously and persistently search for some reasonable solution.

All things considered, when examining the engagement with cognitive dissonance in impossible puzzle films, it does not suffice to conclude that the attractiveness of cognitively dissonant scenarios lies only in their successful resolution. After all, some of these films strategically obstruct and enduringly frustrate exactly these viewer attempts. Rather, one could go as far as to say that the engaging power (if not appeal) of impossible puzzle films partially stems from viewers' inability to reduce the dissonance. In the engaged situation of narrative immersion, and under the right narrative conditions, an enduring sense of cognitive dissonance can become a source of fascination rather than one of sheer frustration. Cognitive dissonances can trigger viewers to keep investing mental energy in the reduction of incongruities, whether in vain or not, urging these viewers to apply different frames and to test different interpretive solutions to the options and constraints afforded by the narrative. Whether it is through the successful naturalisation, integration or rationalisation of dissonance within the fiction (4.2), through a more poetic, lyrical, associative and affective apprehension (4.3) or through the constant hesitation and mental oscillation between different hermeneutic frames (4.4), coping with dissonance in narratives gives viewers the possibility to feel competent, to try out and reflect on different cultural, cognitive and mimetic frames, or to just be overwhelmed by the perplexing strangeness, complexity or beauty of impossible worlds and illogical stories. Maintaining ambiguities in naturalising and framing options, like impossible puzzle films do, can prolong these effects for longer periods of time, possibly even long after the actual viewing experience.

In conclusion, one can argue that impossible puzzle films are characterised by striking a balance between offering viewers challenging incongruities on the level of narrative on the one hand, while maintaining their immersion and willingness to engage in interpretive and analytic operations on the other. The focus of the next chapter will be on the narrative tactics that impossible puzzle films employ to achieve these specific conditions, addressing how such strategies maintain the viewer's analytical immersion in their exceedingly complex narrative scenarios. For now, we may conclude that evoking cognitive dissonance can be a key strategy to create a strong mental connection between the viewer and a narrative artwork – however incongruous, ambiguous or complex – as it enduringly occupies our minds with interpretive and analytic efforts.

Impossible Puzzle Films: Between Art Cinema and (Post-)Classical Narration

> The impossible is one thing when considered as a purely intellectual conceit . . . It is quite another thing when one faces a physical reality the mind and body cannot accept.
>
> Mark Z. Danielewski, *House of Leaves*

Dreaming about a breakthrough invention, four young, bright engineers struggle with small tech projects in a messy garage. While working on a box intended to reduce the weight of any object put in it, Aaron (Shane Carruth) and Abe (David Sullivan), the smartest of them, encounter a strange physical anomaly. As a side-effect of their experiment, the box has accumulated a protein-like fungus. It is not so much that the material is strange – what is weird is that under natural conditions, the amount of protein found in the box would need around five to six years to build up. Testing the machine by leaving a watch in it, they start to understand the enormous potential of their invention: according to their calculations, when in the activated box, time moves differently relative to the outside. Without saying it, they both realise that what they have built works, in effect, as a time machine. Shutting their partners out of the garage (using the pretext of spraying against bugs), the two excited engineers start to contemplate possible applications . . . One day, during their regular brainstorming sessions, the slightly distressed Abe hands a pair of binoculars to Aaron and warns his friend that what he is about to see is not a trick. While standing next to Abe, Aaron witnesses another version of Abe, around a hundred metres away, carrying an oxygen tank while approaching a suburban storage complex. They follow the 'other' Abe who enters one of the complex's storage rooms. Abe asks Aaron to wait exactly six minutes, after which they step into the storage room. It is hard to tell what is more disturbing: Aaron's realisation that the bigger box they just agreed to create has already been built and tested by Abe, or the fact that the 'other' Abe has disappeared from the room . . . Notwithstanding the first noticeable cracks appearing in their friendship, Abe and Aaron start to fantasise about the possible utilisations of their time machine box. They opt for the obvious: either winning the lottery or manipulating the stock market. But first Aaron wants to test the machine himself too. To stay in sync with each other, both Aaron and Abe take an oxygen tank and go into the machine for six hours. After they come out, instead of going for the lottery prize, they agree on cashing in on the stock market. They play it carefully (avoiding making any noticeable impact on the market, they go for stocks in the mid-cap funds), but things soon get out of hand: they earn more and more money, start dreaming about a new life, lie increasingly to their partners and colleagues, and even play heroes when saving the life of Abe's girlfriend. Their differing views on the use of the machine are ruining their friendship. On top of it all, it becomes clear that the machine has other repercussions too, causing more and more concerning health issues for its users. Their reading and handwriting skills deteriorate, Aaron starts to bleed from his ears and there are other symptoms that indicate a stroke and developing brain damage . . . Meanwhile, we also learn that the time traveller who is about to go back in time is already back from his trip and exists in overlap with his original self (who is about to go back in time). They co-exist, at least for the six hours during which the original self is studying the stock market. During this period this original is hiding in a hotel room in order to avoid any confrontation with his already returned self, who is then reaping the benefits of their 'clairvoyant' knowledge . . . We gradually learn that from the point when we saw Aaron and Abe watching their 'other' selves approaching the storage complex carrying oxygen tanks, it has been impossible to tell which version(s) of them we are following. Exploiting the full potential of its created logic, the film's plot spirals into a dizzying whirlpool of manipulations, deceptions, crossings and double-crossings of different versions of Abe and Aaron, including additionally rented storage rooms for secretly built 'failsafe' machines, and so on . . . And we are only halfway through the movie . . .

Confusing? Immensely. Not just explaining the film, but even providing a lucid plot synopsis for Shane Carruth's 2004 *Primer* is highly challenging, if not impossible.[1] No wonder that its immense complexity, constructed in a mere seventy-seven minutes of labyrinthine plot, makes this probably the most discussed (and debated) story among forensic film fans. The emerging cult status of *Primer* is due to the film's unique experience that resides somewhere between an intimidating test of its viewers' puzzle-solving skills and an astounding, basically experimental descent into the innermost depths of the time-travel paradox. Balancing these options, it seems as if the movie entirely entrusts its own assessment to its viewer's judgement – one can accept the challenge to search for logical explanations, or calmly enjoy the ride and let oneself be entertained by a kaleidoscopic mind trip. But how does Carruth create and maintain such balance in possible viewer responses? What does *Primer* owe to our routine in evaluating as well as interpreting film narratives, and how does it exploit these conventions?

So far we have discussed how impossible puzzle films offer puzzling experiences through paradoxes, ambiguities, character multiplications, and other narrative and cognitive incongruities and impossibilities. We have argued that

---

[1] Probably the best attempt at providing a nearly lucid explanation of the workings of the film (and its time machine), including a heuristic plot map, is on *Primer*'s Wikipedia site at https://en.wikipedia.org/wiki/Primer_(film)

both the telling modes and told stories of such complex narratives evoke a mental state that can be characterised as a 'cognitive dissonance', and that this mental state may inspire viewers to engage in various interpretive operations. Before we move on to further examination of the potential appeal of impossible puzzle films, we need to address two more aspects of particular traits that concern their formal make-up. The first aspect concerns impossible puzzle films' relation to art cinema, from which tradition of film narration these films seem to borrow extensively. If they widely overlap with 'complex' art films, as we will argue in more detail in this chapter, then the logical question is what makes impossible puzzle films different, or what makes them deserve a distinct narrative category? The second, closely related, aspect further distances the impossible puzzle film category from the art-cinematic mode, positioning its narrative functioning closer to (or even within) the (post-)classical paradigm. To do so, this chapter deals with the question of how these exceedingly complex narratives not only create dissonances, but also manage to maintain viewers' interest, immersion and willingness to engage with their extensive complexity.

One of the remarkable features of impossible puzzle films is that they seem to walk a tightrope in balancing their viewers' fascination and frustration. That is, these films aim to be challenging, perplexing or even overwhelming in terms of their complexity, while they must also simultaneously prevent viewers from losing interest in their stories or faith in the possibility that they might solve the puzzle presented to them. It seems that an enduring sense of cognitive dissonance can only become a source of sustained engagement and fascination under specific narrative conditions. In the following chapter, we will argue that impossible puzzle films are dependent not only on radically complex storytelling strategies for their effects, but also on traditional *classical narrative tactics* that maintain a notable degree of story-related interest and engagement. These classical storytelling tactics serve to maintain viewers' immersion in the mimetic dimensions of the story and their faith in the possibility of narrative recuperation.

One of the leading questions for this chapter can therefore be summarised as 'How do impossible puzzle films regulate viewer responses to their excessive complexity?' Crucial in this respect is that the effect of cognitive dissonance is not only dependent on the complex or confusing moment itself; it is also largely determined by the broader narrative context. The particular *narrative system* within which a given complexifying narrative device operates significantly influences how we experience, interpret and evaluate the film's complexity and our confusion. The mode and context of narration can exert a background of conventions and expectations against which the dissonance stands out, and therefore can influence what responses and hermeneutic routines (as discerned in the previous chapter) viewers determine as appropriate to explain and interpret the dissonance. Questions like 'Is it a classical genre movie or a modernist art film?', 'Is the film encouraging us to solve a puzzle?' or 'Does this film contain an allegorical message?' become crucial in the way one commits oneself to tame the cognitive dissonance at hand.

On this account, another goal for this chapter is to answer the question 'What kind of narrative and generic context do impossible puzzle films provide to embed their complex and cognitively dissonant narrative devices in order to create their distinct viewing effects?' This inquiry will lead us to discuss impossible puzzle films in comparison to the tradition of art cinema in more detail. The juxtaposition is crucial, as art cinema (the modernist art film in particular) also has a tradition in cognitively dissonant narration. This comparative perspective will take up the first half of this chapter (5.1), since we believe that distinguishing impossible puzzle films from the (neighbouring) class of art cinema presents one of the key aspects of defining impossible puzzle films' specificity within a more general set of complex narratives. In the second half of the chapter (5.2), we turn our full focus back to impossible puzzle films, analysing how their narrative make-up and techniques ensure distinct viewing effects through an appeal to and use of classical strategies of narration.

5.1 FROM ART CINEMA TO PUZZLE FILMS

Historically, there seem to be two general 'modes' of film narration (in the Bordwellian sense of the term, as we will soon see) in which cognitively dissonant storytelling strategies have frequently been used. First, the contemporary mainstream examples of complex storytelling that have been discussed in this book can be said to belong to the predominant classical narrative formal system – or, as some theorists would argue, to the 'post-classical' category, allowing a relatively higher degree of mediacy, complexity and self-reflexivity than that of the truly 'classical' storytelling paradigm (see, for instance, Thanouli 2009a, and our brief recap of the discussion about the classical, post-classical, even post-post-classical label in section 1.3). Second, dissonant effects have been prominently and frequently used in the tradition of art cinema – most notably in the modernist art films of the 1950s and 1960s: in films that Norman N. Holland originally labelled as 'puzzling movies' (Holland 1963). Impossible puzzle films draw elements from both these traditions, but, as we will argue in this chapter, tend to remain primarily rooted in the classical narrative system by relying on rather classical presentation modes and viewing routines.

Throughout film history, art cinema has traditionally been the prime site for experimentation with disruptive and complex storytelling. In fact, the complex narration strategies that we find in contemporary mainstream films can be understood as continuations, appropriations or modifications of techniques once pioneered in art-cinema narration. Even though many of the complex storytelling strategies and innovations in popular film were first used in art-cinema narratives, only relatively few theorists working on narrative complexity have pointed out this formal-historical dialectics (such as Cameron 2008; Klecker 2011; Campora 2014). In some cases, disruptive and complex techniques have entered the mainstream in watered-down form, while in others, they have re-emerged through sheer familiarisation and habituation. Interestingly, this process seems to have intensified over the last two decades, resulting in an increase of overlap between art cinema's experimental techniques and mainstream films' more exploratory (post-)classical narration. In the words of András Bálint Kovács:

> in the 1980s and 1990s some modernist narrative techniques became increasingly popular not only in European art films but also in America, and some of them were clearly appropriated by the Hollywood entertainment industry . . . David Lynch, Quentin Tarantino, the Coen brothers, or films like *Crash* or *Fight Club* are systematic manifestations of several sophisticated modernist narrative procedures 'infiltrating' probably the world of quality Hollywood production. (Kovács 2007: 60)

Striking overlaps in narrative strategies between (modernist) art-cinema and contemporary complex mainstream films include the use of elaborate flashback structures and other non-linear and fragmented temporalities; an emphasis on subjectivity in narration; unmarked point-of-view shots, dream sequences and fantasies; the presence of self-reflexive, metaleptic and metafictional narrative elements; as well as the use of ambiguous, dissonant and contradictory narrative structures. Acknowledging this richness of commonalities in used techniques, one may wonder whether contemporary complex films simply provide popular versions of 'art films'? Can these films be seen as art-cinema narratives that have crossed over into the mainstream, shifting their target audience? Or should one rather focus on the differences and scrutinise how the narrative (and institutional) context of art cinema facilitates different functions for complex storytelling than its mainstream counterpart?

In the following, we will proceed from the latter option and for that reason briefly develop a comparative perspective to examine the functions of narrative complexity within the imbricated domains of art-cinema and classical narration. To begin with, this will require some considerations on the slippery problem of defining 'art cinema' in the first place. We will suggest and discuss both narrative (5.1.1 and 5.1.2) and cognitive (5.1.3 and 5.1.4) approaches to this conceptualisation. Following this, in section 5.2 we will come back to impossible puzzle films, and see how these films achieve their specific viewing effects by balancing their complex dissonant elements, known from art cinema, with elements established and utilised within the classical narrative paradigm.

5.1.1 Art cinema as a narrative mode

Although the scope and particular interest of this book do not allow an exhaustive conceptualisation of the term 'art cinema', it is important to note that the notion, although often referred to, can become rather problematic under closer theoretical scrutiny. As Eleftheria Thanouli has pointed out, art cinema 'is one of the fuzziest and yet least controversial concepts in film studies' (Thanouli 2009c: 1). Indeed, viewers and critics can consider a wide range of films to be 'art films' for a variety of reasons.[2] The problem of defining 'art films' is in this respect closely related to the problem of defining 'art' itself, and different conceptions of art cinema often follow from different conceptions of 'art'. For these reasons, one should readily acknowledge that no singular encompassing definition of art cinema can be formulated satisfyingly. Rather, the phenomena that the term covers are best approached by applying Wittgenstein's concept of 'family resemblance' and acknowledging that even though there are certain overlaps and similarities in these films' characteristics, they lack a single essence in the form of a unifying trait or a set of features that is common to all cases.

Nevertheless, moviegoers customarily speak of art cinema and have some tacit notion of which films they are discussing. In film theory, however, some consensus has been established in identifying art cinema on the basis of its specific *narrative strategies*. In a narrower sense, the term 'art cinema' is often used to refer to the post-war – predominantly European – auteur films and national cinemas of the 1950s and 1960s. These prototypical art films include

---

[2] For instance, viewers and critics may consider a movie to be an 'art film' because of its narrative experimentation, but also because of its style or stylistic innovation (for example, films of Robert Bresson or Béla Tarr) as well as themes and subject matter (Jean Renoir or Yasujirō Ozu), a certain psychological depth (Michelangelo Antonioni or Ingmar Bergman), or social engagement (Vittorio de Sica or Jean-Luc Godard), specific historical or cultural importance (Roberto Rossellini or Satyajit Ray), symbolical allusions (Luis Buñuel or Lars von Trier), or phenomenological revealing power (Andrei Tarkovsky or Terrence Malick), through the status of its director as an auteur (*a* François Truffaut, *a* Luchino Visconti, or any of the above), its references or affinities to other art forms (like with Jean Cocteau or Sergei Parajanov), and so on.

the work of the renowned and strongly canonised auteur directors of the era, such as Federico Fellini, Ingmar Bergman, Michelangelo Antonioni, Luis Buñuel, Alain Resnais, Robert Bresson, Andrei Tarkovsky, Yasujirō Ozu, (self-)proclaimed 'movements' like the French Nouvelle Vague and other international new waves or auteur exponents from various other non-European national cinemas. Drawing on Clement Greenberg's notion of modernism as being art's 'aesthetic self-reflection' (Greenberg 1940), András Bálint Kovács has identified these post-war art films as a second wave of cinematic modernism (Kovács 2007: 12).[3] When defining its specificity, Kovács notes that '[b]y far the most spectacular formal characteristic of modern cinema is the way it handles narration and how that relates to storytelling' (ibid.: 56). More precisely, '[w]hen contrasted to Hollywood classicism, modernism may appear as an almost uniform set of *"disturbing" narrative practices*' (ibid.: 55 – our emphasis).

The most influential conceptualisation of art cinema as a set of narrative strategies has come from David Bordwell's work on film narratology. Outlined in his 1979 article 'The Art Cinema as a Mode of Film Practice', as well as in his seminal 1985 book *Narration in the Fiction Film* (205–33), Bordwell argued that 'the overall *functions* of style and theme remain remarkably constant in the art cinema as a whole. The narrative and stylistic principles of the films constitute a logically coherent mode of cinematic discourse' (Bordwell 1979: 57). As Kovács has summarised, Bordwell's taxonomy of the art film holds a middle ground between a historical inventory and a more ahistorical technical characterisation: 'Bordwell does not link any of his categories to historical contexts, and he leaves open the possibility for anyone to discover them in any period of film history' (Kovács 2007: 59). Over the past thirty years, Bordwell's conceptualisation of art cinema as a mode of narration has proven widely influential in film studies. The amount of criticism to its argument has been surprisingly small, with the most notable objections coming from scholars who have suggested that art cinema be understood as an institutional construct rather than as a formal category (see for instance Neale 1981; Thanouli 2009c; Andrews 2010).

The central aspect of art-cinema narration, according to Bordwell (1979), is that it defines itself explicitly against the classical narrative mode. Classical narration forms the historically and technically dominant mode of story representation in cinema. It presents a unified and construable chain of causes and effects, through which psychologically and rationally motivated characters strive towards clearly set and identified goals. In classical narratives, narrative time and space are subordinated to and governed by

---

[3] This second modernist movement followed avant-garde's first wave of the interbellum era.

the plot's causality, whereas stylistic devices serve to retain clear mimetic representation and immersion, relying on and reinforcing known narrative procedures and markers (Bordwell 1985: 156–204). The art-cinema mode of narration, on the other hand, uses a very different set of strategies. It often opposes or undermines the unobtrusive transparency of the classical style. Rather, art-cinema narratives use techniques that are motivated by a stronger sense of 'realism'. This can be *objective realism*, in the form of de-dramatised plots and episodic stories, which are justified as being 'truer to life'; or *subjective realism*, emphasising psychological or emotional states and trajectories of complex characters who often lack the clear-cut traits and undoubted motives of classical protagonists. The art-cinema mode also makes room for authorial expressivity, which manifests in an 'authorial signature' that favours overt auteurial display over immersive qualities of the classical mode. A wide range of narration techniques can be used to this end. As Kovács summarises:

> Here are the most important features that, according to Bordwell, character-ize narrative techniques as they diverge from the classical norm: non-redun-dant 'suzhet' (plot) structure; a story less motivated by genre rules, not so easily associated with a common genre; episodic structure; the elimination of deadlines as a temporal motivation of the plot; concentration on the character and the 'condition humaine' rather than on the plot; extensive representation of different mental states, like dreams, memories, fantasy; self-consciousness in stylistic and narrative techniques; permanent gaps in narrative motiva-tion and chronology; delayed and dispersed exposition; a subjective reality that relates to the story; a loosening of the chain of cause and effect in the plot; extensive use of chance as a motivation; a concern within the plot for psychic reactions rather than action; frequent use of symbolic rather than realist linkage of images; radical manipulation of temporal order; increased ambiguity regarding the interpretation of the story; open-ended narratives; 'retheoricizing' the *fabula*, that is, subordinating the plot to the development of rhetorical (mostly political) arguments; overt political didacticism; use of collage principle; the dominance of style over narration; and serial construc-tion. (Kovács 2007, 61–2)

Kovács divides the above strategies into two categories. The first category concerns those aspects of art films

> whose effect is to create a multilayered description of the characters, the envi-ronment or the story itself. The function of these traits is to create a *complex signifying structure* in which the viewer's attention is diverted from the direct cause-and-effect chain of the plot toward information that is only indirectly related or unrelated to causality. (ibid.: 62 – our emphasis)

These strategies encourage viewers to look beyond the concrete dimensions of the plot and to engage in more thematic, symbolical or psychological inquiries, establishing meanings beyond the concrete events in the diegetic cause-and-effect chain. Returning to Bordwell's typology of narrative meanings (discussed in Chapter 2), one could say that these art-cinematic strategies shift the emphasis from directly 'referential' and 'explicit' types of meaning towards inspiring viewers to search for more 'implicit' and even 'symptomatic' kinds. This is a classic trait of the art film (and, some might say, a precondition of any work with artistic pretence). Moreover, by de-emphasising and therefore discouraging the viewer's construction of a classical story, these techniques may also work to support more lyrical, contemplative or style-driven aesthetic modes of viewing.

The second category that Kovács discerns covers techniques more specific to the modernist tradition; to branches of literary modernism like the *nouveau roman*. It concerns those narrative techniques which relate to the

> three main principles of modern art: *abstraction, reflexivity,* and *subjectivity.* In other words, art-cinema narrative involves *ambiguity* of the interpretation, the spectator's conscious intellectual *involvement* in the plot construction, and the *subjective* character of the story. Those are the traits that are responsible for creating the modernist effect in narration. (ibid.: 62 – our emphasis)

Most art cinema's complexifying and cognitive dissonance-inducing narrative techniques can be filed under this second category. Art films have commonly included narrative incoherencies, incongruities and ambiguities to deliberately problematise and reflect on the straightforward construction of narrative meaning. These strategies serve to obfuscate meaning-making, sometimes already on the referential level, by undermining elementary narrative principles that go unquestioned in classical narration: linear time and unified space, rational agency, the clear epistemological divide between objective reality and subjective experience, the separation of memorised past and the present, or the general reliability of representation in the film medium. All of these aspects may be challenged by the self-reflexive strategies of modernist narration devices. Art films often openly use narrative dissonances and ambiguities to deconstruct classical mimesis and emphasise relative notions of truth, as well as to engage their viewers in an active, conscious co-construction of their denotative and connotative meanings. As Torben Grodal has noted, '[t]he term *idealist* could be applied . . . to many art film narratives. In art films, the problem of interpreting and understanding the world precedes concrete action and often renders it impossible' (Grodal 2009: 222).

5.1.2 Dissonance in modernist art cinema

In short, whereas classical narration's mimetic realism offers accessible, epistemologically clear, unambiguous but stimulating immersive stories, part of the enjoyment of many complex art-cinema narratives stems from a break with this mimetic clarity in favour of a (controlled) sense of confusion and ambiguity. In Kovács's conclusion, '[c]lassical art films make narration a multilayered, complex system, and the modernist art film makes this complex system essentially ambiguous or even self-contradictory' (Kovács 2007: 64). Materialising these ambiguous and self-contradictory tendencies, the modernist art cinema offers a variety of examples of cognitively dissonant narration. Many of the classic modernist art films are built on dissonant scenarios, such as Alain Resnais' *Hiroshima Mon Amour* (1959) and *Last Year at Marienbad*, Federico Fellini's *8½* (1963), Akira Kurosawa's *Rashômon* (1950), Michelangelo Antonioni's *Blow-Up* (1966) and Ingmar Bergman's *Persona* (1966). These 'puzzling films' (to return to Norman N. Holland's original use of the term – see Chapters 1 and 2) have arguably introduced and certainly established complex and dissonant stories and storytelling techniques in narrative cinema, along with the pre-war European art films from which these movies themselves took inspiration.[4] As for contemporary complex films, a traceable key influence too comes from the pre-war surrealist cinema in particular. Elliot Panek has noted (referring to Jonathan Eig) how 'many psychological puzzle films owe a great deal to the surrealist and avant-garde cinema of the 1920s and '30s, particularly the work of Luis Buñuel' (Panek 2006: 66). Buñuel, 'the grandfather of the modern mindfuck film' (Eig 2003), indeed seems to offer a fruitful case for illustrating the overlaps between early avant-garde, second-wave modernism, and contemporary complex narrative techniques, which all frequently represent 'ambiguous, occasionally contradictory relationships between diegetic events' (Panek 2006: 66).

Avant-garde and art films have indeed pioneered several ambiguous, subjective, self-reflexive and self-contradictory patterns of narration that later re-emerged in contemporary complex films, particularly in impossible puzzle films. For example, Fellini's modernist art film *8½* employed a style of 'subjective realist' narration, in which memories, dreams and fantasies are not demarcated from objective story representations (neither stylistically nor

---

[4] Particularly in terms of stylistic innovation, several aspects of the modernist art film can be traced back to avant-garde traditions of the 1920s and 30s (such as to the Soviet montage film, the French impressionism of Jean Epstein, Germaine Dulac and Abel Gance, the expressionist qualities found in the filmmaking in Weimar Germany or in the films of directors like Carl Theodor Dreyer, as well as to the work of film artists in *cinéma pur*, dadaist or surrealist film, including Marcel Duchamp, René Clair, Luis Buñuel, Salvador Dalí and Jean Cocteau).

narratively), but rather converge in the same narrative or sometimes even the same visual frame. Such narration evokes cognitive dissonances between conflicting versions of events or conflating timelines and spaces, and taxes viewers with the interpretive activity of having to determine which of the events are to be considered objectively 'true' and which should be understood as interior states or fantasies of the protagonist – or, perhaps, whether the difference can be made at all. This particular strategy, reminiscent of literary modernist techniques that emphasised subjectivity, has proven influential, and can be said to form the basis for the complexity in impossible puzzle films like *Mulholland Drive* or *Donnie Darko*. Impossible puzzle films similarly often create cognitively dissonant viewing experiences by blurring subjective and objective modes of narration.

The subjective dimensions of narration have been pushed further by other art films, such as Bergman's 1966 *Persona*. Bergman's most radically modernist film reaches a point where the ontological status of the film's entire narrative becomes enigmatically unstable (the film's mimetic properties are undermined already from its self-reflexive and meta-fictional opening scene onwards). In *Persona*, the option that the entire narrative could be seen as the projection of an individual's psychological conflict space is left open – much in the same way as the earlier discussed character conflation in Denis Villeneuve's recent *Enemy*. *Persona*'s experiment with a similar idea of melding its characters plays a subtle game on art cinema's recurring trope of the 'double' (Bibi Andersson and Liv Ullmann's psychological fusion can be seen as a suggested version of *Enemy*'s more direct confrontation of character doubling). As for further examples of more concrete and, through that, in their effect, more dissonant character duplications in art cinema, one can think for instance of Bernardo Bertolucci's 1968 *Partner* – doubling its protagonist (Giacobbe I and II, both played by Pierre Clémenti) in a Brechtian fashion – or a film like Krzysztof Kieślowski's 1991 *La double vie de Véronique* (*The Double Life of Véronique*), in which the Polish Weronika sees, for a brief moment, her French counterpart Véronique (Irène Jacob), or of Buñuel's doubled female variation of his 1977 *Cet obscur objet du désir* (*That Obscure Object of Desire*), which famously swapped actresses (Carole Bouquet and Ángela Molina) playing the same role of Conchita. Such character duplications are frequent occurrences in impossible puzzle films too, where the trope manifests in various ways that range from examples that viewers will most likely motivate psychologically (like in Villeneuve's *Enemy*, Lynch's *Lost Highway* or Richard Ayoade's *The Double*) to more supernatural and generically determined multiplications (as in science-fiction narratives like Carruth's *Primer*, James Ward Byrkit's *Coherence*, Christopher Smith's *Triangle* or Nacho Vigalondo's *Timecrimes*).

Art films have also experimented with evoking cognitive dissonances through contradicting storylines and narrative incongruities. A classic example is Kurosawa's *Rashômon*, which offers four incompatible versions of the very same event, recalled from the perspectives of four different witnesses. The different accounts of the event, a story of a murdered samurai, can never be integrated into a coherent and 'truthful' whole; they remain dissonant with each other, creating a central narrative mystery that emphasises a fundamental epistemological relativity. In art cinema, such 'mysteries' are often kept unresolved or unresolvable to preserve effects of ambiguity or dissonance – the pervasive effects and interpretive offshoots of which are the actual 'points' of these narratives: rather than exposing a particular truth, *Rashômon* is more about presenting the experience (the 'Rashomon effect') of relativity. The most radical instances of such techniques can be found in the post-war modernist tradition. In Antonioni's *Blow-Up*, for example, the central mystery propelling the film is a dissonance ('there was a dead body'/'there was never a dead body'), to which our epistemological access remains obstructed, retaining a fundamental ambiguity at the heart of the narrative. Another notable example is Resnais' and Robbe-Grillet's nouveau roman film *Last Year at Marienbad*. Here, too, the narrative revolves around a single dissonant ambiguity ('A and X met last year at Marienbad'/'A and X did not meet last year at Marienbad'): viewers are presented various contradictory versions of the past events, without an indication of any hierarchy of reliability among them. The boundaries distinguishing subjective and objective modes of narration seem to have been entirely blurred in Resnais' film. On top of that, the film also presents a highly fragmented spatio-temporal structure, mingling past and present in a single spatial setting. As Kovács notes, comparable to Robbe-Grillet's earlier literary work with the nouveau roman,

> [t]hese films work like a mental labyrinth with no way out. The different solutions for the plot are systematically destroyed as one plot is succeeded by another one until the viewer finds himself with a story that has *multiple solutions*, which are *incompatible with each other*. The contradictory nature of past, present, and future is homogenised by the continuous flow of narration, which simply makes passages between them without dissolving the contradictions. (Kovács 2007: 129 – our emphasis).

These storytelling experiments, Kovács further notes, have paved the way for narrative complexity in contemporary mainstream films:

> The fact that *Mulholland Drive* was not only made but that director David Lynch was awarded an Oscar nomination for it proves that narrative ambiguity, which was introduced into modern cinema by Alain Resnais and Alain Robbe-Grillet as a highly avant-garde artistic element, forty years later has finally become a mainstream norm. (ibid.: 60)

More generally, one could argue that the highly 'self-conscious' and 'meta-reflexive' approach to narration found in contemporary complex cinema is a repurposed inheritance of art cinema. Art cinema has traditionally had a tendency to work against classical narration, that is, art films have frequently sought to 'bare the devices' of classical narration and film style, to challenge the established norms and rules, to reflect on them or to work self-reflexively (cf. Bordwell's and Kovács's characterisations). One may, for instance, think of the modernist examples outlined above, or of the playful Brechtian self-reflexivity of a director like Jean-Luc Godard, whose films popularised a renegade approach to classical notions of narration, plot, editing, style and sound. Although contemporary complex films do not carry a similar 'hostility' or deliberate opposition against classical narrative norms and rules, the post-(post-)classical paradigm also allows (or even celebrates) modes of self-reflexivity to serve its interest in evoking cognitively challenging experiences. Films like *Adaptation* or *Mulholland Drive* invite incongruities and impossibilities to thematically reflect on and play with the style, form and conventions of Hollywood storytelling. Moreover, in their overt display of what Jason Mittell calls an *operational aesthetic* (discussed in subsection 4.2.3), many contemporary complex films frequently invite viewers to be aware of the techniques that are being applied, permeating meta-fictional modes of apprehension into the traditionally non-reflective engagement of classical narrative film viewing.

5.1.3 Art cinema as a cognitive reception frame

In conclusion to the above, it is clear that there are formal similarities and functional overlaps in the complexifying strategies of art-cinema narration and (impossible) puzzle films. But how should this commonality be interpreted? Does the overlap indicate that over time, the once radical art-cinematic experiments have 'trickled down' into mainstream complexity? Has the appreciation for complex storytelling techniques shifted from arthouse to mainstream audiences? Or are there still fundamental differences between the modes of (post-)classical and art-cinema narration, and between the ways in which they have embraced narrative complexity? Having discussed the similarities and overlaps, in the following sections we will point out some of the remaining differences and argue for their significance, thereby defining the idiosyncrasy of impossible puzzle films. To articulate these boundaries, we will first identify the particular viewing experience that is specific to the effects evoked by experimentation in art-cinema narratives, before moving on to itemise the distinctive complexification strategies that regulate viewer responses in impossible puzzle films.

According to Torben Grodal, two key aspects separate art cinema from classical narrative cinema: first, art films tend to be very different in terms of *stylistic innovation*, and second, they seem to trigger entirely different kinds of claims in terms of *higher meaning*. As Grodal has analysed,

> [a]n art film is supposed to express not only formal (stylistic) skills, but also skills relating to content: deeper 'visions,' for example, into certain central and permanent aspects of the world, society, or the human psyche . . . On the one hand, therefore, the concept of high art highlights the concrete perceptual level of style, but on the other it focuses on an abstract level of permanent (transcendental) meaning . . . the prototypical art film combines stylistic innovation with a claim to higher meaning. (Grodal 2009: 207–8)

Central in Grodal's argument is that art films are not just different in their formal make-up, but, through their combination of the above aspects, they also evoke very distinctive viewer responses. For Grodal, a key difference lies in the orientation of classical narrative films towards clear, concrete, transient, goal-oriented action with certain concrete embodied affordances (involving basic emotional patterns like love, survival or social status). Art cinema, by opposition, allows for 'higher-order' types of meaning that Grodal characterises as being more permanent and 'disembodied' (as already briefly discussed in section 4.3). He notes that, generally,

> [classical] narrative films are based on concrete embodiment; they concern actions carried out by human agents for whom mental processes are intimately linked with physical actions aimed at concrete goals. Style in such films thus serves to flesh out these concrete actions and the emotions that go with them. In art films, by contrast, style is often associated with the portrayal of a deviant reality, one that is not accessible through standard online interaction . . . The abstract, disembodied nature of this type of representation has emotional consequences, for here the viewer cannot have the tense emotional involvement that he or she experiences with concrete phenomena that allow for embodied action. Such disembodied categories may nevertheless exert a powerful fascination. (Grodal 2009: 208–9)

Grodal contrasts the two types of narrative cinema by calling attention to the fundamental difference between their emotional and narrative stimulation. Art cinema's lessened emphasis on the enactment of concrete action, as well as its distinct emotional stimulation, lead to different viewing experiences and prompted meanings compared to the ones that classical cinema provides and incites. 'Melancholia, nostalgia, and empathetic distance are among the emotions that art films tend to cue, because by blocking enactment, such emotions promote in the viewer a mental experience instead' (ibid.: 226–7). As Grodal further notes, '[w]atching films with extended scenes that cue saturated (mental, disembodied) emotions is a minority taste; most people prefer films that cue tense (embodied) emotions based on action tendencies' (ibid.: 210).

Although Grodal's characterisation of classical narration as 'embodied' and art films as 'disembodied' may sound somewhat overgeneralising, we will follow part of the argument.[5] Without fully subscribing to the more 'hard', neuroscientific claims of his work – as we are not in a position to either confirm or disconfirm these – we would agree that art cinema offers specific kinds of narrative stimulation, and that this often prompts viewers to take a different viewing stance compared to classical narratives. More precisely, we would argue that art-cinema narration encourages the application of some very specific cognitive routines that lead to distinctive strategies of meaning-making (regardless of whether such routines are prompted through embodied-cognitive effects or through convention and habituation).

In section 4.3, we called the oscillating shifts like the one between art-cinema and classical narrative apprehension *frame-switches*. As discussed, frame-switches can include shifts to viewing strategies, for example to aesthetic, allegorical, associative or symbolical readings that do not belong to classical narratives' referential and explicit meaning-making procedures. Indeed, in narrative film, art cinema seems to be the privileged site for alternative modes of narrative apprehension. Yet, one should be careful not to relate this narrative framing solely as a response to narration (to its complexity, recurring patterns, 'disembodied' representation or other formal aspects); the interpretive process of reception and cognitive framing is always more complex, and involves textual and contextual as well as paratextual features. We would therefore suggest reconceptualising 'art-cinematic' viewing stances themselves as 'framing judgements' – meaning that the act of framing should be seen as a dynamic interpretive response. This conceptualisation entails some minor but consequential amendments on structural and formalist, as well as strictly cognitivist approaches to the reception issues of concern. By suggesting that 'art-cinema viewing' is itself a mode of 'framing', we claim that when viewers mentally label a film as an art film, their judgement entails an assignment of a specific 'macro-frame' of knowledge. As noted, cognitive frames refer to sets of top-down schemas, scripts and information held in

---

[5] As clarified elsewhere, '[n]aturally, Grodal does not mean that the experience of art cinema is fully detached from embodied cognition. Although he talks about "disembodiedness" ([Grodal 2009] 208–11), what he describes is the detachment of our comprehension from an actual and concrete bodily immersion (see how mainstream narrative films offer "concrete embodiment" [208]), where the experience finds outlets in more abstract, somewhat "disembodied" meaning-making strategies (see how art cinema gives rise to feelings of "deep significance" [149–50])' (Kiss 2015: 310).

one's memory. They involve expectations, steer attention, determine salience and serve to govern appropriate interpretive and evaluative routines. Art cinema can be seen as such a frame in the sense that (re-)cognising (on whatever textual or contextual grounds) that a given film would be an 'art film' relates to the activation of a considerable set of knowledge involving expectations, conventions and norms – both culturally distributed and, with more or less experienced film viewers, cognitively operational. What is important to acknowledge is that an 'art-cinema frame' is assigned not only in response to textual cues, but also through contextual ones, as well as through different individual dispositions (these latter aspects all too often remain overlooked in strictly cognitive models).

As for contextual cues, the institutional setting of arthouse cinema may play a key role in assigning the frame of art-cinema narrative to the experience. In this sense 'framing' can take on the meaning that it acquired in the work of sociologist Erving Goffman, namely to denote socially shaped and transmitted constructs that guide the individual's cognition and experience (see Goffman 1974). After all, when we watch a film in an arthouse cinema or at an art film festival, such collectively presumed social contexts (reinforced by established institutional discourses) influence our individual meaning-making strategies. Involving cognitive, contextual, pragmatic and hermeneutic aspects, framing appraisals lead to judgements in the forms of interpretive choices.

Besides their cognitive basis and social transformability, frame attributions also involve more individual dispositions. The information content of frames will vary significantly according to an individual's acquired knowledge, personal competences, subjective conceptions and experience: the films that an individual has seen before, reviews that he or she has read, his or her degree of 'artistic' socialisation and personal life experiences – all such factors of interpretation can become relevant in framing operations. Yet the recognition that narrative understanding in art cinema may be partially dependent on an individual's preconceptions does not exclude the possibility of making valid generalising claims on how such strategies are brought about. To some degree, one can assume that the subjective response is embedded in socially and conventionally shared paths of narrative meaning-making (as addressed by both David Bordwell and Steve Neale in their respective formal and institutional characterisations of the term art cinema). After all, storytelling and film viewing, as well as general conceptions of 'art' or 'culture', are socially constructed acts; they follow conventionally established rules which enable and guide their cultural exchange and meaning. In sum, the art-cinema frame – distributed to viewers through specific formal traits and contextual embedding, and acquired through film viewing and general acculturation – provides an essential grip on certain (art) films' experience, and hands viewers the elementary pathways for narrative interpretations beyond referential and explicit meaning-making.

5.1.4 Narrative complexity and meaning-making in art cinema

Although there are many ways in which 'art cinema' can be said to be operational as a cognitive reception frame (which are related to the diversity of art cinema itself, and its various traits in terms of style, cultural context, psychology, plot construction, realism, authorial expressivity and so on), we will restrict our discussion here only to matters of narrative complexity. The question is: what kind of strategies does art cinema usually allow and encourage viewers to use in response to narrative complexity? And how it is that such strategies can elicit different experiences of complexity compared to that of the (post-)classical narrative mode prompts?

The art-cinema frame offers viewers distinct strategies to make meaning from specifically presented (and contextualised) puzzling narrative experiences. We argue that when traditional narrative coherency is persistently being hampered – by gaps, incongruities or incoherencies, for instance – viewers will be encouraged to interchange their traditional story-focused viewing stance for alternative strategies. Building on the theories of meaning-making in response to complexity discussed in Chapter 4, we claim that treating a film as an 'art film' can entail specific *coping strategies* to deal with the particular challenges of narrative complexity that appear in the art-cinema mode of storytelling. As this section will show, a number of viewing strategies can converge in the art-cinema frame when encountering complexity on the level of narrative. These include particular strategies for naturalising strange or deviant textual elements, such as (1) the possibility of employing a broader conception of mimetic properties; (2) the application of aesthetic and meta-fictional viewing stances; (3) the option of having recourse to non-prototypical narrativising efforts; and, lastly, (4) taking a more charitable stance towards stylistic excess.

First (1), in Chapter 4 we introduced Jonathan Culler's notion of *naturalisation*, the meaning-making process of assigning cultural frames and conventional reading strategies along which viewers shape their interpretation. Naturalisation is related to the tendency to attribute interpretations to texts in which every single element can ultimately be considered to contribute to the meaning as a whole. As Culler argued,

> we can always make the meaningless meaningful by production of an appropriate context. And usually our contexts need not be so extreme. Much of Robbe-Grillet can be recuperated if we read it as the musings or speech of

a pathological narrator, and that framework gives critics a hold so that they can go on to discuss the implications of the particular pathology in question. Certain dislocations in poetic texts can be read as signs of a prophetic or ecstatic state or as indications of a Rimbaldian 'dérèglement de tous les sens'. To place the text in such frameworks is to make it legible and intelligible. When Eliot says that modern poetry must be difficult because of the discontinuities of modern culture, when William Carlos Williams argues that his variable foot is necessary in a post-Einsteinian world where all order is questioned, when Humpty-Dumpty tells Alice that 'slithy' means 'lithe' and 'slimy', all are engaged in recuperation or naturalization. (Culler 1975: 138)

Culler's choice of examples already indicates that the process of naturalisation becomes more prominent in complex and experimental texts. Such works tend to present a higher number (and level) of inconsistencies that, in turn, inspire their audiences' creative sense-making mechanisms. The same can be said for modernist art cinema, especially when compared to classical narrative. David Bordwell discerned certain 'motivations' – objective realism, subjective realism, authorial expressivity and ambiguity – that are characteristic of art-cinema narration. Rather than as formal elements of a film, we will understand these as naturalising strategies of viewer responses (possibly, but not necessarily associated with specific formal narrative and stylistic devices).[6]

Objective and *subjective realism*, first and second, may both be called upon as a naturalising response to narrative complexity. As Bordwell notes, in art films, '[v]iolations of classical conceptions of time and space are justified as the intrusion of an unpredictable and contingent daily reality or as the subjective reality of complex characters' (Bordwell 1979: 58–9). In this way, any registered dissonance can be perceived as an inherent part of the mimesis: the incoherence is given an expressive function within the story, decreasing the need to reduce the dissonance or untangle the complexity.

The third motivational criterion around which art-cinema narration revolves is *authorial expressivity*. Art films, according to Bordwell, foreground their authors as part of their overtly self-conscious narration, presenting them in the form of an 'authorial signature'. This signature is a kind of 'trademark' that can be found in recurrent violations of classical filmmaking norms, as well as by an 'extratextual emphasis on the filmmaker as source' (Bordwell 1985: 211). Yet here, one can wonder how the art film could be able to foreground, on a formal basis, its author as a structural aspect of the text? We

[6] Although Culler stressed that the Russian formalist notions of 'motivation' and naturalisation are not exactly the same – as naturalisation is done by a reader or viewer individually, in response, but not as a binding relation, to textual elements (see Culler 1975: 137–8) – these 'generic' motivations can be seen as conventional 'naturalisation pathways' for art films.

would argue that authorship too is best understood as a naturalising inference made by a viewer, based on his or her application of knowledge and cognitive frames. Following Jason Mittell's (2015) proposition, we called this the inferred author function (see subsection 4.2.2). Film-literate viewers often use a known director's authorial persona to rationalise narrative intrusions, especially when these cannot be readily naturalised in a mimetic, diegetic manner. Many of Jean-Luc Godard's films, for instance, use the *Verfremdungseffekt* to consistently block the classical mimetic representational norms and rules of narrative filmmaking, creating distancing effects that most viewers will justify as rhetoric interferences of Godard's omnipresent authorial figure. As in art film 'a body of work linked by an authorial signature encourages viewers to read each film as a chapter of an oeuvre' (Bordwell 1985: 211), the convention of authorial expressivity reinforces the inferring of authorial intentions. Many practised viewers of art films are particularly attuned to this dimension of authorship, and naturalise the effects of diegetic or narrative complexities as a gesture of a consistently present – auteur – authorship.

Bordwell's fourth and last characteristic of art-cinema narration lies in its affinities to *ambiguity*. There seems to be a tension in art cinema between its focus on 'realism' on the one hand and the intrusion of a pervading 'authorship' on the other. Bordwell argues that it is the device of *ambiguity* that solves this conflict. While 'classical narration tends to move toward absolute certainty' (ibid.: 212), art cinema often conveys relativistic notions of truth that invite ambiguity into their narratives. As Bordwell playfully proposes, in terms of viewing strategies, the art film's procedural slogan could be '[w]hen in doubt, read for maximum ambiguity' (Bordwell 1979: 60).[7] The acceptance of ambiguity is an important feature of the art-cinema frame with regard to narrative complexity too. Art films generally encourage viewers to retain the ambiguity and dissonances, rather than to readily disambiguate or solve the puzzle – as they would be inclined to do in (post-)classical films, which commonly direct them to restore certainty in narrative situations. This 'narrativising lenience' lessens the pressure to resolve dissonances, or to untangle complex mysteries, as in art cinema viewers may accept dissonance and ambiguity as the intended narrative state of affairs, rather than as a puzzle that is to be solved.

In sum, the above four principles – objective and subjective realism, authorial expressivity and ambiguity – can all help to render narrative dissonances meaningful. Yet, arguably, these viewing strategies can lead to many

---

[7] Some years later, from a cognitive-constructivist perspective, Bordwell gives practically the same advice: 'Interpret this film, and interpret it so as to maximize ambiguity' (Bordwell 1985: 212).

different paths by which viewers naturalise cognitively problematic elements in art-cinema narratives. As a more general principle, we could say that the art-cinema frame allows a broader recognition of narrative mimesis than classical narrative engagement. Traditional conceptions of mimesis and narrative are often restricted to concrete, conventional narrative 'realism' – that is, 'make-believe' stories that mimic or evoke aspects, qualities or events analogous to 'everyday' human experience. The art-cinema frame, however, allows recuperation of mimetic meaning far beyond this restriction. Through a large variety of naturalising frames – including a profusion of allegorical, authorial, subjective or thematic readings – art films allow for mimetic experiences beyond the classical narrative presentation of a cause-and-effect chain of lifelike events. Viewers can make sense of art films by deeming them as primarily expressive of cultural, existential or experiential issues, for instance.

Framing a narrative as art cinema means that viewers open up their viewing stance to an arguably wider range of naturalising frames than they would in response to a classical narrative. When a relatively dense, concrete and logical narrative chain of events cannot be formed, the art-cinema frame can help viewers to recover different levels of mimetic content. By this, narrative complexity may not only be interpreted as subjective realism or an authorial poetics, but also as representing an existential predicament, as a symbolisation of philosophical issues, as reference to the cultural context of the film's production (social, political, historical), as a reflection on perception, cognition and emotion or on art and culture itself – and so on. For instance, in their reviews of Antonioni's modernist 1966 movie *Blow-Up*, different critics attribute different mimetic functions to the film's dissonant story. For Roger Ebert, for instance, the film's unresolvable mystery primarily highlights the nature of the protagonist, and his modern consumerist-materialist values:

> Antonioni uses the materials of a suspense thriller without the payoff . . . Whether there was a murder isn't the point. The film is about a character mired in ennui and distaste, who is roused by his photographs into something approaching passion. As Thomas moves between his darkroom and the blowups, we recognize the bliss of an artist lost in what behaviorists call the Process; he is not thinking now about money, ambition or his own nasty personality defects, but is lost in his craft . . . 'Blow-Up' audaciously involves us in a plot that promises the solution to a mystery, and leaves us lacking even its players. (Ebert 1998)

Geoff Andrew of the British Film Institute rather deems *Blow-Up* a 'metaphysical mystery', concerned with 'questioning the maxim that the camera never lies, and settling into a virtually abstract examination of subjectivity and perception' (Andrew, n.d.), while, according to the editorial of *Variety*, '[t]here may be some meaning, some commentary about life being a game, beyond what remains locked in the mind of film's creator . . . As a commentary on a sordid, confused side of humanity in this modern age it's a bust' (*Variety* staff 1965). Such naturalisations locate the unity and expressiveness of a work on different, more abstract levels than that of concrete narrative events, but ultimately also provide them with a *mimetic function*: the dissonant plot is seen as a socio-cultural critique, a reflection on representation, or as an expression of the enigma of subjectivity, the fallibility of perception or of the *condition humaine*. Naturalisations like these entail that viewers or critics accept narrative confusion or incoherence as mimetically expressive, in a manner that is more unrestricted than in classical narrative meaning-making. Curiously, refusing to attribute any such meanings can become a way of rejecting the artwork altogether. For instance, in an unfavourable review of *Blow-Up*, Pauline Kael expressed her dislike of the film by refusing to attribute any meaningfulness to it. Rather, she mockingly wondered: 'Will *Blow-Up* be taken seriously in 1968 only by the same sort of cultural diehards who are still sending out five-page single-spaced letters on their interpretation of [*Last Year at*] *Marienbad*? (No two are alike, no one interesting)' (Kael 2010). For her, 'Antonioni's new mixture of suspense with vagueness and confusion seems to have a kind of numbing fascination for them that they [the film's proponents] associate with art and intellectuality' (ibid.).

Second (2), some of the art-cinematic naturalisations have no mimetic grounding, and should rather be characterised as aesthetic or meta-fictional. Meta-fictional viewing competences are not concerned with attributing a mimetic motivation to inconsistencies (that is, understanding the narrative as representative or referential to something in the diegesis or outside of the artwork), but rather provide these with some (self-)reflexive aesthetic function. Consequently, viewers may conclude that the confusion they encounter in a film like *Last Year at Marienbad* is not about representing intricate events in the first place, but rather about offering them an opportunity to reflect on human experience. This means that viewers may treat their own confusion as an aesthetic effect that is, in turn, intended to create a distanced contemplation, for instance on the human condition, artistic practices or on the medium of film itself. Some complex structures can also be seen as part of a reflection on the process of filmmaking: for instance, the deranged narration in Fellini's *8½* may be naturalised as a somewhat autobiographical reflection on the process of creating a film (analogous to the director's actual writer's block). Since meta-fictional viewing stances are 'self-conscious' strategies, as a result viewers are utilising their meta-reflexive alertness in the process of meaning-making. For example, they may infer that complicating narrative devices are 'intended' to make them reflect on their participation in the narrative meaning-making, or that violations of narrative coherence may invite them to form philosophical reflections or critiques on the mimetic mode of representation. Film viewers, especially when equipped with an in-depth knowledge of art films, may possess all sorts of these meta-fictional competences and strategies that can help them to deal with the variety of complex disruptions of art cinema and modernism.

Third (3), in the most extreme of these cases, when narrativity seems to be temporarily absent or lost altogether, viewers may engage in an entirely different apprehension strategy. In some art films, recurring dissonances, overall incoherency or problematic (or simply absent) narrative cues can send viewers on alternative tracks of meaning-making. Viewers may give up the construction of a prototypical narrative in favour of more poetic, lyrical, associative or aesthetic modes of apprehension. We describe this particular frame-switch as *non-prototypical narrativising efforts*, as they seem to depart from narrativisation (naturalisation by recourse to narrative schemas) as conceptualised by Monika Fludernik in her 1996 volume *Towards a 'Natural' Narratology* (see also in our section 4.3). Fludernik argues that narrativity is attributed to a text by the reading (or otherwise spectating) subject, using a certain frame of perceiving and understanding that renders artefacts or events 'narrative' (Fludernik 1996: 22–5). For Fludernik, imposing the macro-frame of narrativity onto the (film) text means that readers (and viewers) will always

> try to recuperate the inconsistencies in terms of actions and event structures at the most minimal level. This process of narrativization, of making something a narrative by the sheer act of imposing narrativity on it, needs to be located in the dynamic reading [or viewing] process where such interpretative recuperations hold sway. (ibid.: 25)

When this process of narrativisation fails, Fludernik notes, readers (and viewers) may shift to a more poetic apprehension to integrate the information in question (Fludernik 1996: 36). In such situations, we may 'give up' on the story, but this need not mean the end of our engagement with the work. Rather, we may watch it for its associative, aesthetic, poetic or affective affordances, deliberately suspending our narrativising efforts to allow other effects and affects. 'Poetic reading', or strategies such as what Jan Alber called 'the Zen way of reading' (see section 4.2), constitute alternative macro-frames to retain or recuperate some mimetic dimensions, however, strictly speaking, the attribution of such frames should be seen as departures from the realm of 'narrative', since a story-concerned narrative is abandoned here. Aesthetically challenging avant-garde feature films from Jean Cocteau's 1932 *Le sang d'un poète* (*The Blood of a Poet*) to Carlos Reygadas' 2012 *Post Tenebras Lux*, 'fraught with ambiguities, paradoxes and multivalent messages' (Verrone 2012: 14), offer exuberant audiovisual experiences for effectuating naturalisations of the poetic kind. Positioning viewers to engage with the cinematic medium in alternative, less 'narrative' modes has after all traditionally been one of the key aims of the avant-garde (cf. the theoretical writings of avant-garde filmmakers such as Germaine Dulac or Maya Deren).[8]

Finally (4), sometimes as a last resort for our narrativising urge, problematic elements of art-cinema narration can also be evaluated as 'excessive' features of a film's style. This means that viewers accept them as stylistic exercises that are seemingly unrelated or non-contributive to the narrative. We would argue that viewers who recognise a film as 'art cinema' tend to be more charitable towards such stylistic excess.

The notion of 'stylistic excess' was coined by Kristin Thompson, marking films, or parts of and moments in films, in which style is displayed 'for its own sake' (Thompson 1977: 55) and can hardly be contained by the narrative. Although Thompson finds that such noticeable moments of stylistic excess might be 'counternarrative' (ibid.: 57), as the viewer may not be encouraged to unify the seen into a story, on the other hand she also acknowledges the more indirect contribution of such excessive moments to the unfolding narrative. While stylistically excessive moments 'provide *relatively* little causal material' (Thompson 1977: 55), they can augment the film's characterisation and complement motivation for its characters' behaviour. Agreeing with this amendment, we would like to further argue for a reconciling approach between the recognition of stylistic excess and the emergence of narrative meaning. First of all, strong classically cohesive narration can absorb some degree of stylistic excess and can neutralise its counternarrative effects. As David Bordwell notes,

> artistic motivation – taking an element as being present for its own sake – is not unknown in the classical film. A moment of spectacle or technical virtuosity, a thrown-in musical number or comic interlude: the Hollywood cinema intermittently welcomes the possibility of sheer self-absorption. (Bordwell 1985: 164)

Second, stylistic excess occurs more frequently in art films, as its counternarrative effects seems to better support the aimed aesthetic and poetic effects

---

[8] For examples of the 'non-narrative' ambitions of avant-garde filmmakers, see Germaine Dulac's 1926 essay 'Aesthetics, obstacles, integral cinégraphie', republished in Richard Abel's (ed.) *French Film Theory and Criticism* (Princeton, NJ: Princeton University Press, 1993), pp. 389–97, or Maya Deren's 1960s treatise 'Cinematography: The Creative Use of Reality', which originally appeared in *Daedalus* 89 (1): 150–67, and was republished in *The Avant-Garde Film: A Reader of Theory and Criticism*, ed. P. Adams Sitney (New York: Anthology Film Archives, 1978), pp. 60–73.

of the art-cinema narration. After all, as Peter Verstraten has noted, stylistic excess tends to emerge more easily when a film's narration is less concerned with providing a cohesive story in the first place (Verstraten 2008: 30–1). An art film like Antonioni's 1960 *L'Avventura*, for example, seems to abandon plot-centredness almost entirely in favour of 'excessive' stylistic contemplation. Underlining Verstraten's position, we would add that stylistic excess can also contribute to the framing of a film as an art film: an excessive emphasis on style can indicate that the particular film in question has other aesthetic aims than the presentation of a straightforward story, and, while activating the viewing stances discerned above, may therefore suggest a more pertinent framing of the experience.

5.2 Impossible puzzle films and (post-)classical narration

If art cinema has used contradictory narration and other dissonances to – in Bordwell's earlier quoted words – 'throw us off balance' (Bordwell 2008: 168), and to send us on a quest for thematic, psychological, symbolical, allegorical or meta-fictional meanings, then the relevant question for this book is how does this functioning compare to that of dissonance in impossible puzzle films? Does the complexity of impossible puzzle films have a similar effect? Surely one could argue that impossible puzzle films' contradictory and impossible stories can throw some viewers 'off balance'. However, beyond the commonalities discussed above, there are also notable differences that can be detected in the reception and meaning-making routines of art-cinema and impossible puzzle films. From what we have observed on online message boards, by interviewing university students and from our own viewing experiences, it seems that impossible puzzle films generally do not evoke the type of art-cinematic responses outlined above. That is, despite these films' clearly dissonant story structures, viewers tend to persistently approach impossible puzzle films using classical narrativising and rational sense-making strategies. Holding on to their narrativisation drive, viewers keep trying to make sense of these films on the diegetic, intratextual and often immersed level. They investigate 'how the film works' rather than asking 'what it means'; they attempt to 'crack the codes' of complexity, rather than extracting symbolic, symptomatic or meta-fictional meanings of the type associated with art cinema. Of course, this attitude varies among viewers, as well as across the affordances of different films: some viewers might consider a film like *Mulholland Drive* to be an 'art film' and will look for corresponding types of thematic, psychological, symbolical, allegorical or meta-fictional meaning. As we noted previously, the ambiguity of some impossible puzzle films does indeed allow them to be read through multiple strategies (see our discussion of narrativising versus interpreting approaches to

Mulholland Drive and *Enemy* in subsection 4.4.1), making them interpretive borderline cases that can be framed in multiple ways. For most impossible puzzle films, however, the divide is clearer. Films like *Triangle*, *Timecrimes*, *Coherence* or *Primer* are generally not approached by viewers as art films. Rather, we argue, these films are usually seen as complex versions of classical narratives, inviting the corresponding viewing routines that are habitualised by viewers' recurrent exposure to (post-)classical narrative films.

Where does this difference reside? We believe that differences in interpretive stances follow mainly from formal strategies of narration that impossible puzzle films employ, and from the viewer expectations that go with these. More precisely, we hypothesise that impossible puzzle films achieve their effects by countering their disruptive narrative tactics with classical narration strategies. This way, they encourage their viewers to retain a high degree of classical narrative engagement – despite the excessive complexity of the story – thereby discouraging them from switching to other, art-cinematic frames of apprehension. In the following subsections, we will introduce some key strategies which we generally find in most impossible puzzle films, and which persuade viewers to take a classical narrative viewing stance. These strategies include the use of stories with a high degree of tellability (5.2.1), offering classical character identification (5.2.2), showing a strong reliance on traditional genre elements (5.2.3), retaining an adherence to narrative cohesion devices on both the micro- and macro-levels of the narrative (5.2.4) and, lastly, introducing explicit diegetic suggestions for maintaining quasi-rational frames of naturalisation (5.2.5).

5.2.1 High degree of tellability

In narrative theory, the notion of *tellability* generally refers to the somewhat mysterious quality that makes a story 'worth telling' – or, from the audience's point of view, engaging enough to listen to. Usually, this comprises some 'noteworthiness' or a 'point' to the story. Of course, the degree of tellability is often subjective, and contextually as well as culturally dependent: it is, for instance, very likely that one will deem a story about the misfortunes of a close friend to be more 'tellable' than the exact same story about a total stranger. Nevertheless, some general cognitive and affective factors play a key role in enhancing tellability. First of all, as Jerome Bruner has noted, for a narrative to be tellable, some canonical script must be breached, meaning that something unexpected or out of the ordinary should happen in it. As Bruner writes,

> not every sequence of events recounted constitutes a narrative, even when
> it is diachronic, particular, and organized around intentional states. Some

> happenings do not warrant telling about and accounts of them are said to be
> 'pointless' rather than story-like. A Schank-Abelson script is one such case: it
> is a prescription for canonical behavior in a culturally defined situation – how
> to behave in a restaurant, say (Schank & Abelson 1977). Narratives require
> such scripts as necessary background, but they do not constitute narrativity
> itself. For to be worth telling, a tale must be about how an implicit canonical
> script has been breached, violated or deviated from. (Bruner 1991: 11)

The degree of tellability is thus greatly enhanced by the evocation and disruption of particular cognitive scripts and frames: the occurrence of an unexpected event, a character's exceptional behaviour, the twist of fate that befalls him or her, the complications that keep him or her from achieving a certain goal – much of what we enjoy or find engaging in stories is constituted by the breach of some ordinary script(s). Looking at impossible puzzle films, one can see how these films largely adhere to such classical story patterns. Evoking basic narrative templates or canonical scripts, impossible puzzle films usually focus on particular protagonists inhabiting a seemingly normal or recognisable storyworld. The plot is driven by a disruption of this familiar initial state through the occurrence of something out of the ordinary. On the surface of their stories, *Triangle* is about a young single mother who goes on a boating trip with friends, is caught in a storm and seeks shelter on a mysteriously abandoned ocean liner; *Mulholland Drive* introduces a woman who survives a car accident, suffers from amnesia and must re-find her identity; *Enemy* presents a young college history professor who suddenly discovers that he has a perfect physical double. All these situations evoke canonical scripts and noteworthy breaches; they could, in fact, also have been the start of very classical narrative films, evoking a strong sense of narrativity and a high degree of tellability. What is more, impossible puzzle films (by 'breaching the breached') raise their 'narrative stakes' even further when disrupting these familiar scripts by inserting something challengingly extraordinary (the young mother is trapped in a loop of endlessly recurring events; the amnesic woman turns out to be a fantasy of a suicidal girl struggling with her own identity crisis; the oddity of a double is not a biological, but a psychological or perhaps a non-diegetic narrative anomaly). After all, as Raphaël Baroni summarises, 'it is assumed that there is a general human interest for stories reporting events that have a certain degree of unpredictability or mystery' (Baroni 2011). Additionally, it should be noted that (moderate) story complexity may sometimes also enhance tellability: noteworthy or unexpected events (like running into one's doppelgänger), narrative elements of surprise or the successful evocation of curiosity resulting from a complex story structure may all enhance viewers' general interest and immersion in a narrative – even if the presented mystery ultimately proves unsolvable.

In short, by (initially) appealing to familiar story patterns of classical narratives, impossible puzzle films hook their viewer onto their stories through engaging plots, compelling mysteries or challenging dissonances. This augmented adherence to known and popular elements of classical plots forms one of the grounds on which impossible puzzle films can generally be distinguished from the kind of complexifications that art films and high literature host. Ultimately, as Marie-Laure Ryan notes, '[w]hereas popular literature invests heavily in the tellability of plots, high literature often prefers to make art out of the not-tellable' (Ryan 2010b: 590).

5.2.2 Identification with goal-oriented characters

Closely connected to, or for some a key part of, tellability is the role of narrative agents or characters in eliciting story-immersive viewer stances. Characters arguably function as our anchors within narratives: they provide the basis for action, empathy, emotion, interpretation and narrative orientation. Some narratologists, such as Monika Fludernik, have identified the role of human(-like) agents as the key component of narrativity and tellability. According to Fludernik it is not events themselves that are central to stories, but rather the ways in which these events gather meaning for the agents in a story, and by that allow immersion for the reader or viewer. This idea was conceptualised by Fludernik as experientiality, by which a definition of narrativity emerges as a mediated human experientiality (Fludernik 1996: 26). Building on Fludernik's notion, in his enactivist approach to the experientiality of narratives, Marco Caracciolo describes stories as 'imaginative experiences because of the way they draw on and restructure readers' [and viewers'] familiarity with experience itself' (Caracciolo 2014: 4). By drawing on our real-life experiences, experiencing agents of stories can be said to form our 'access points' into narratives, facilitating all our comprehension, communication, involvement and emotion.

The central characters in impossible puzzle films often belong to the type of 'transparent' protagonists, known from stories of classical narration, who allow high degrees of experiential resonation. Unlike the prototypical art-cinema protagonist, the main figures of impossible puzzle films have accessible rational motivations and clear goals, exhibit transparent psychology and relatively unambiguous behaviour, and are emotionally and actively invested in the unfolding story's concrete actions and events. This clear backdrop can serve viewers' immersion in and engagement with the story by providing a point of effortless identification with characters that populate the otherwise abstract and confusing narrative. As Torben Grodal notes,

[a] key to understanding the viewer's reconstruction of a narrative is the procedure by which he cognitively 'identifies' himself with the agents of fiction, using mental models and schemata from everyday psychology. Part of the motivation for the reconstruction is provided by empathy, that is, the viewer's cued simulation of emotions in identification with an agent of fiction. Cognition is intimately linked to emotions. (Grodal 1997: 87)

In impossible puzzle films, we closely follow one (or a few) protagonist(s) experiencing a strange storyworld. Usually, these characters have strong emotional responses; they experience the impossible and incongruent events as puzzling, disconcerting or even threatening – providing a model response for the film viewer for easy identification. *Triangle*'s Jess is in a perpetual state of perplexity and fear as she tries to escape from the anomalous loop; Adam in *Enemy*, as well as Rita and Betty in *Mulholland Drive* are distressed, but also embark on investigations to try to understand their mysterious predicaments (which ultimately only lead to more puzzling experiences). These characters thus invest the abstract narrative structure with experientiality for viewers to relate to, allowing a tense emotional and empathic involvement in the story. They can 'mirror' and by that reinforce viewers' own sense of surprise, perplexity or strangeness, and emulate their urge to investigate and rationalise the perplexing storyworld. Characters like Rita and Betty in *Mulholland Drive* function as diegetic manifestations of our own rational quest for sense-making. Comparable to the way by which, in crime fiction, we typically try to solve a crime alongside a detective, viewers can create hypotheses and make attempts to beat the narrative maze by relying on the information that is accessible to these focal(ising) characters.

Both tellability and character identification may be enhanced by the goal-oriented action patterns of classical narrative agents. Stories are often propelled by the desires and aims of a protagonist, which entail action patterns around the accomplishment or obstruction of concrete objectives (such as reaching a destination, overcoming an antagonist, being united with a love interest, taking revenge and meting out justice, and the like). Such action patterns offer viewers something concrete and familiar to relate to, enhancing their identification, narrative engagement and immersion. Most impossible puzzle films present characters who act in pursuit of such clear goals. Moreover, in many cases, these goals are of a very concrete nature; they involve what Grodal has called embodied action patterns which relate to strong ecological factors like survival, love or social status (Grodal 1997, 2009). Films like *Triangle* or *Timecrimes* are related to movies of the classical action genre in the sense that they focus on characters with very concrete and vital goals (such as survival), affording tense simulations and embodied affects (such as hunting, hiding or fleeing from threatening adversaries). In most impossible puzzle films, the labyrinth-like story often forms a threat, problem or obstacle to the central characters' goals, desires or general well-being. Once they have overcome the hurdle of their initial puzzlement, the characters typically respond to the challenges with clear action: they try to resolve the troubling situation, make plans and, when accepting and accommodating to the unnatural storyworld, look for alternative strategies – for example by fleeing, investigating or by somehow attempting to take matters in their own hands (remember *Triangle*'s Jess and her desperate attempts to escape the loop and the fate that comes with such anomaly). With art-cinema protagonists, on the contrary, the narration is typically not oriented towards such action patterns, but rather focuses on the psychological ramifications of distressing situations. For example, Delphine Seyrig's passive character in *Last Year at Marienbad* is seemingly paralysed, but at least does not take any proactive steps to ease the confusion of her dissonant situation. Her 'actions' entail what Grodal characterises as abstract, disembodied action patterns; as a result of the absence of goal-oriented experientiality, the film exchanges the option of narrative rationalisation for the emergence of higher-order meanings (see our previous discussion in subsection 4.3). For viewers, the lack of the concrete action component thus shifts the focus away from concrete narrative involvement, and gives way to psychological, symbolical or allegorical meaning-making options that art-cinema narration usually facilitates. Of course, some of the more psychologically oriented cases of impossible puzzle films, like *Donnie Darko*, *Mulholland Drive* or *Enemy*, may also be concerned with such higher-order meaning stimulation. Nevertheless, here too, engagement and identification with the central characters and their particular goals and problems keep viewers focused on the diegetic reality and mimetic world, despite the abstract and impossible features of the presented storyworld.

5.2.3 Strong reliance on classical genre elements

Another recurrent formal strategy of impossible puzzle films lies in their evocation of known and shared conventions of classical genres. As Jerome Bruner notes in his discussion of narrative tellability, breaches of canonical scripts are themselves 'often highly conventional and are strongly influenced by narrative traditions' (Bruner 1991: 12). Impossible puzzle films often appeal to such familiar narrative patterns. They draw on generic conventions, not only in their plots, but also by including particular narrative elements (such as prototypical characters, settings and story tropes), characteristic film style (such as conventional lighting, colour filters) and contextual and paratextual cues outside or around the films (such as film posters and taglines).[9] Typical impossible puzzle films combine their diegetic riddles with an action-driven classical genre, resulting in crossovers like 'mystery-horror' (for example, *Triangle, Chasing Sleep*), 'mystery-science fiction' (*Timecrimes, Primer*) or 'mystery-thriller' (*Lost Highway, Mulholland Drive*). The conventions of 'strong' genres are known to most viewers through acculturation and habituation, and this knowledge routinely guides them in their apprehension, comprehension and interpretation of films that exhibit some of these shared and prominent genre codes. In his article 'An Introduction to Genre Theory' Daniel Chandler highlights that '[g]enre provides an important frame of reference which helps readers to identify, select and interpret texts' (Chandler 1997). Chandler notes how this top-down guidance of genres can be compared to the general functioning of cognitive frames or schemas. In his words,

> [k]ey psychological functions of genre are likely to include those shared by categorization generally – such as reducing complexity . . . Genre theorists might find much in common with *schema theorists* in psychology: much as a genre is a framework within which to make sense of related texts, a schema is a kind of mental template within which to make sense of related experiences in everyday life. From the point of view of schema theory, genres are textual schemata. (ibid.)

Indeed, genres, like other cognitive frames (acquired knowledge structures that provide shortcuts for understanding), entail particular knowledge and interpretive routines in viewers. Impossible puzzle films often draw generic markers from classical Hollywood narration, including elements from horror, sci-fi, thriller, mystery or detective films. For instance, in discussing David Lynch's films and the serial *Twin Peaks*, Elliot Panek notes that director Lynch draws upon conventional generic plot patterns, revolving mostly around mysterious murders, to cue viewers to engage with his films and TV series as detective stories. Whereas the cognitive function of genres usually comprises a reduction of complexity (through pattern recognition and corresponding inference-making), in impossible puzzle films, such patterns and expectations are also present, but are used to put viewers 'on the wrong track'. As Panek puts it, films like

> *Lost Highway* and *Mulholland Drive* use the detective trope to provoke the audience into looking for answers that the film doesn't provide. Both of these films feature duos of detectives who appear in the first act, never to appear

---

[9] See, for example, the poster design of Shane Carruth's *Primer*, which displays an entangled web of cables that gives a visual indication of the film's convoluted plot, or the paratextual tagline of James Ward Byrkit's *Coherence* – 'Nothing is random' – that clearly directs viewers' expectations towards something logical and decipherable.

> again. Though these brief appearances can be written off as red herrings, the
> protagonists play roles comparable to detectives throughout the narratives.
> (Panek 2006: 76)

The effect of such textual (and possibly contextual) markers is that they exert
the corresponding 'classical' expectations that usually go with these genres.
In Panek's words,

> [c]learly some conventions exist for the mystery detective *noir* genre. These
> conventions cue the audience to look for an answer by seeing gaps as tem-
> porary and looking for clues . . . It is crucial that Lynch uses detective story
> tropes. Detective stories set the audience the task of searching for something
> alongside their diegetic proxy, the detective. (ibid.: 77)

Indeed, for viewers, traditional generic framings call forth and maintain the
assumption that the narrative is coherent and lucid, and that the energy they
invest in trying to solve the puzzling mystery will pay off. At the same time,
the recognition of elements from popular genres also restrains the emergence
and applicability of other interpretive responses, like those associated with
art cinema. After all, as Panek aptly concludes, regarding Lynch's narrative
strategy,

> [w]hether or not the viewer sees a film as a cognitive puzzle or an affective
> experience may shape his or her interpretation of the film. *Lost Highway*'s use
> of detective story tropes encourages the 'puzzle' reading strategy, but it does
> not provide a clear cut answer to the questions prompted throughout the
> diegesis. Audiences might be more likely to accept unresolved gaps and ambi-
> guity as authorial in motivation if such generic cuing were absent. The desire
> for closure and concrete answers is a function of the classical Hollywood
> mode of narration, but it is also, more specifically, a function of the detective
> murder mystery. (ibid.: 78)

Genre can be decisive in viewers' choice of meaning-making strategies even
when they face excessive amounts of complexity or confusion in a narrative.
Monika Fludernik discusses the 'narrativising' drive of a recognised genre in
relation to literary works that stubbornly resist sense-making. She argues that
'[w]hen readers are confronted with potentially unreadable narratives, texts
that are radically inconsistent, they cast about for ways and means of recu-
perating these texts as narratives – motivated by the generic markers that go
with the book' (Fludernik 1996: 34). Similarly, the generic markers of confusingly complex impossible puzzle films seem to exert such a guiding function.
For instance, in his DVD commentary to *Triangle* (Icon Film Distribution
2010), director Christopher Smith explains that he is aware of how his film's
appeal to horror genre conventions steers its viewers in a particular direction.

According to him, viewers tend to engage with his film's convoluted structure in a rational and analytical manner 'because it's a horror' – that is, 'because it's a movie that is watched primarily by an audience that are very into logic, and they want it to make logical sense'. Doubtlessly, in horror, detective or science-fiction films, generic expectations encourage diegetic investigation and induce a search for rational story logic. After all, most genre films reward such efforts. On the other hand, if viewers encountered similar complexities in an art film that lacked reliable generic markers, they would arguably be more prone to shift to authorial, symbolical or meta-fictional readings, or would foreground the affective dimensions of the experience, without expecting any classical narrative explanation or resolution. In short, by evoking and fostering genre-specific expectations, impossible puzzle films maintain viewers' inclination to adhere to the viewing routines that normally work for classical narratives – even if such reassuring resolutions or other indications of classical story logic remain absent. Genre expectations do not only invite viewers to rationally engage with excessive yet immersive narrative puzzles, but they can also be effective in encouraging viewers to choose certain meaning-making strategies over others.

5.2.4 Adherence to classical narrative cohesion devices

To suggest narrative transparency and coherence in their storytelling, impossible puzzle films also commonly draw on conventional techniques known from classical narration and film style. As David Bordwell has argued,

> [s]tories bear the traces of not only local and historical conventions of sense-making, but also of the constraints and biases of human perception and cognition. A film, while moving inexorably forward (we can't stop and go back), must manage several channels of information (image, speech, noise, music). It must therefore work particularly hard to shape the spectator's attention, memory, and inference-making at each instant. No wonder that filmmakers balance potentially confusing innovations like the multiple-draft structure with heightened appeal to those forms and formulas that viewers know well. Artists should test the limits of story comprehension, but those very limits, and the predictable patterns they yield, remain essential to our dynamic experience of narrative. (Bordwell 2002a: 103)

Even though impossible puzzle films go beyond the early 'unconventionally conventional' experiments with forking-path and multiple-draft plots that Bordwell is discussing here, his concluding words remain applicable to their highly complex narratives too. For the most part, the storytelling and style of impossible puzzle films comply with classical narrative schemes to keep viewers engaged with the diegetic events. Following a term used by Bordwell, we call these strategies 'narrative cohesion devices', which denote 'formal tactics that link passages at the local level – from scene to scene or from one group of scenes to another' (ibid.: 95). Such devices, we argue, can exert their cohesive effect on both these films' (1) *micro-narrative* level (in the use of local conventional style and narration) and their (2) *macro-narrative* level (in story structure and overall storytelling patterns). By gratifying our classical analytical routines on both these levels, such strategies help to keep the experience of impossible puzzle films within the (post-)classical paradigm.

First, on the *micro-narrative* level (1), it is apparent that many impossible puzzle films follow the representational norms and rules of classical narration and style. That is, they adhere to familiar formal and stylistic norms such as continuity editing, point-of-view structures and conventional narrative markers for scene-to-scene transitions, and follow classical principles including match on action, eyeline matches or the 180- and 30-degree rules – to name just a few. Similar to genre conventions, the presence of these familiar devices may already cue viewers to approach these films as classical narratives, evoking the corresponding expectations and analytical routines. As Elliot Panek argues, this discrepancy – between recognisable techniques of classical narration on the one hand and obfuscating complexity on the other – is a key feature of the popular contemporary puzzle film:

> the films exhibit many of the characteristics emblematic of classical narration such as continuity editing, local causal logic, and a high degree of verisimilitude. However, these texts clearly do not promote narrative clarity in the way that is typical of Hollywood fare, and thus call upon different sense-making procedures on the part of the audience. (Panek 2006: 65–6)

This adherence to conventional style and classical patterns of formal representation is clearly one of the features that set contemporary complex films apart from art films. Art-cinema narration is often concerned with foregrounding idiosyncratic variations in style (cf. Grodal's definition of the prototypical art film as displaying 'stylistic innovation'), and these stylistic exercises do not necessarily serve the plot. In the most experimental cases, style may even deliberately work to obfuscate or problematise narrative clarity, as often happens in modernist art films. Impossible puzzle films, on the other hand, do include conventional and classical patterns, exactly because of the suggestion of narrative logic and transparency that these entail. Local, micro-level use of recognisable classical devices supports viewers' overall classical narrative expectations and maintains their attempts at rational, causal inference-making. Moreover, classical formal devices and conventional style patterns may also help to 'camouflage' moments of narrative impossibility, which can (somewhat paradoxically) make these moments more effective. Comparable to how a Penrose or Escher drawing is partially dependent on immersive, life-like realism to draw us into a world that ultimately proves paradoxical, impossible puzzle films can use the promise of verisimilitude and transparency of classical film style and narration to construct accessible and 'inhabitable', yet baffling and impossible worlds. For example, in the scene from *Triangle* that we analysed earlier (see subsection 3.5.1, or, in more detail, Coëgnarts et al. 2016), protagonist Jess, caught in an impossible loop of events, is confronted with two versions of herself (these are earlier appearances of herself, already seen by the viewer at earlier moments of the film – see Figure 3.4); this scene uses very traditional point-of-view editing, representing this impossible state of affairs clearly and unambiguously. The traditional representational forms of classical realism are thus utilised to forward (neatly diegetised) events that otherwise clearly transgress reality. In another scene, at around the halfway point in the film, we see Jess on board the ocean liner watching herself in a mirror; distracted by a scream from outside, she looks away and walks off to explore the source of the distressed cry. Through the attentional continuity of her gaze, the pull of the mysterious offscreen sound, the natural connection of an eyeline match and some additional filmmaking trickery,[10] the film smoothly camouflages how, at the moment when Jess walks away from the mirror, the camera actually traverses into the mirror and continues following the events on the other side, into the second, doubled world of the mirror image – establishing the starting point of the film's consecutive loop (Figures 5.1–5.5).

Classical continuity style thus initially 'conceals' the impossibility. For those observant viewers who do notice the perceptual anomaly, however, the contrast between style and content in fact foregrounds the impossible nature of the events. Yet, the dissonant effect of such moments may be compensated for by the narration's operational aesthetic, as viewers may appreciate the cunning narrative trickery over the logical problems such scenes entail for the story.

Besides the use of conventional style and narration on local micro-narrative level, one can also find cohesion devices on the *macro-narrative* (2) level of films' plots and story structures. Individual storylines that remain linear, traditional developments in the plot or recurring patterns in storytelling may all suggest cohesion and causal connections, even among the otherwise highly complexified web of events. Several strategies can be used to maintain cohesion – or the suggestion thereof – in complex story structures, even if,

---

[10] The 'mirror scene' does not have any mirrors but a hole in the wall and a body double of Melissa George mimicking Jess. Also, the visible smudge 'on the mirror' was put there by CG during post-production.

Figure 5.1

Figure 5.2

ultimately, parts of the created cohering elements do not necessarily aggregate in a fully coherent story. Some of the macro-narrative cohesion devices are discussed by David Bordwell in his 'Film Futures' article. Analysing contemporary mainstream examples of forking-path films (see subsection 2.2.2), Bordwell notes how these plots use several strategies by which their potential range of complexity is 'trimmed back to cognitively manageable dimensions, by means of strategies characteristic of certain traditions of cinematic storytelling' (Bordwell 2002a: 91). Even though impossible puzzle films allow a much higher degree of narrative complexity than the examples that Bordwell

Figure 5.3

Figure 5.4

is discussing, they do make use of similar macro-cohesion strategies to evoke a sense of order amidst their confusing scenarios (although, as we will see, they draw on these devices in a usually less prominent and sometimes more ambiguous form).

First, Bordwell notes how in forking-path films, individual plotlines are always kept linear, meaning that 'each path, after it diverges, adheres to a strict line of cause and effect' (ibid.: 92). As a trade-off between their displayed complexity and maintained sense of logical coherence, impossible puzzle films, like most narratives, usually keep large portions of their narrative or

Figure 5.5

individual narrative trajectories linear and causally organised. Sticking with the example of *Triangle*, we can observe that despite its highly non-linear storytelling and complex storyworld, the plot does in fact remain linear, following one protagonist progressing through the looping world. The non-linearity of the narrative structure is only presented in the form of inferred violations of natural laws (viewers' realisation of the looping time) and such violations' consequences on the diegetic world (like character and object duplications) that intrude on the otherwise predominantly linear storyline. Maintaining linearity in plot hereby provides viewers with an 'experienceable' entry point into an abstract and impossible storyworld, facilitating basic (embodied) cognitive viewing schemas – like SOURCE-PATH-GOAL continuity, PART-WHOLE causality and other narrative parameters deeply anchored in everyday experience.

In relation to this, Bordwell also notes how, on the level of the overall plot, forking paths are often unified by traditional cohesion devices known from classical narration. These serve to tighten the causal relations of these plotlines, for instance by setting appointments and deadlines around which the scattered story paths dovetail (ibid.: 95). Impossible puzzle films also occasionally use such traditional tactics to maintain some control over their intricately knotted plotlines. For instance, in *Reality*, Quentin Dupieux's tongue-in-cheek take on impossibly complex narrativity, one of the central characters, a cameraman who dreams of becoming a film director, is given a forty-eight-hour deadline by his producer to record the most terrifying scream he can come up with – or else he will not get funding for his planned movie. Such a deadline to a character's objectives (even if it is a rather absurd one) propels the entire story in a clear direction and ties the diffuse plotlines together. Not all impossible puzzle films include such common cohesion devices, but all do involve some form of goal-oriented chains of causality within individual plotlines. This common appeal to cause-and-effect logic discerns these films' experience from that which art-cinema narration invokes, as art films, in the words of Bordwell, often rely more on the 'sheer successiveness of events' (ibid.: 96), without forcing strong causal or temporal bonds among their presented segments.

Third, Bordwell observes that in forking-path films the scattered plotlines often cohere by certain pervasive conditions. Their multiple paths might intersect or only run parallel to each other, but contain recurrences in terms of settings, characters and events. After all, this way, 'even divergent futures are rendered more cognitively coherent, thanks to recurring characters and background conditions' (ibid.: 95). Likewise, many impossible puzzle films keep their conundrums manageable by restricting the number of characters, settings or timelines. They also maintain narrative logic by creating salient recurrences and other patterns and redundancies among these limited elements. For instance, films like *Triangle*, *Coherence* or *Timecrimes* make use of a constrained setting in which most of the action takes place (respectively: on a ship, within a single housing block and in and around one mysterious facility in a forest); they introduce a small, limited set of characters (no more than six); and they restrict the action to a short and specific timeframe (respectively roughly a single day; one night; or, in the case of *Timecrimes*, only around an hour – see Figure 3.1). As with forking-path films, '[o]ne consequence of sticking to a core situation, the same locales, and the same cast of characters is that certain components emerge as vivid variants of one another' (ibid.: 96). Even within ultimately unnavigable story structures, detecting narrative overlaps and recurrences can encourage viewers to speculate on the possible logical interrelation of otherwise often dissonant events, and incite them to make an effort to establish coherence among patterns and variations. Hereby, as Bordwell argues, complex plots like forking-path narratives can 'bring parallelisms to our notice quite vividly, thereby calling forth well-practiced habits of sense-making' (ibid.: 97).

Lastly, Bordwell also notes how popular forking-path plots often make use of clear signposting through establishing salient markers for their moments of bifurcation and other narrative transitions: 'each film's narration sets up a pattern that clearly indicates the branching-points – a kind of highlighted "reset" button' (ibid.: 94). Such signposting appears in impossible puzzle films too, whether as a tool of viewer orientation, or as a vehicle for showing off operational aesthetics. A film like *Timecrimes* presents its looping, forking and duplicating story through clear patterns and rather overt markers (by stylistic transitions, recurring shots, events, sounds or, in Vigalondo's film, even

Figure 5.6

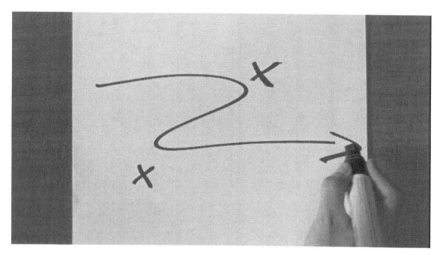

Figure 5.7

with the help of an explicit drawing – see Figures 5.6 and 5.7 – and the invitation to construct a 'precise' plot map of happenings, as seen in Figure 3.1). As the subtlety of the above discussed mirror scene from *Triangle* proves, other impossible puzzle films play more ambiguously with such orienting markers and signposting elements – see Figures 5.1–5.5.

Indeed, many impossible puzzle films not only present significantly recurring shots or events, but also use 'materialised' signposts such as diegetic props. Through their striking recurrence and foregrounded presentation, these objects appear salient; however, most impossible puzzle films leave uncertainty over what information these signposts are meant to convey. One can think here of central props like the crashed aeroplane engine in *Donnie Darko*, the blue key and box in *Mulholland Drive* or the (strikingly similar) blue videotape in *Reality*. Through their prominence, uniqueness and conspicuous recurrence in crucial moments of the story, these props all seem to say something that could help viewers orient themselves in these convoluted worlds, but what exactly they are signalling is usually kept unclear or ambiguous. Their possible status as narrative markers thus evokes speculation: what do they stand for, indicate or symbolise? An *engine* that delivers Donnie's fate, or propels a time-travel anomaly? A *key* to a portal that leads to alternative worlds of Betty Elms/Diane Selwyn? A *master tape* that rules mediated realities? Or are they just playfully indefinite red herrings, MacGuffin-like baits implying crucial information and suggesting coherence to the impossible puzzle?

In conclusion to the above strategies, we argue that these classical storytelling devices on both the micro- and macro-narrative levels work to 'counter' the high degree of complexity of impossible puzzle films. More precisely, these techniques do not so much reduce the confusing effect of these films' dissonances and impossibilities per se, but they do provide viewers with the sense that they could get a logical grip on the presented. These formal and stylistic strategies invite logical sense-making, first because they help to maintain local cohesion and conventional progression within a plot's development, and second because they provide the suggestion or illusion of possible logic and overall narrative coherence.

Regarding the first function, most impossible puzzle films keep large portions of the narrative (specific scenes and plotlines) comprehensible and in adherence to a linear narrative cause-and-effect logic. By contrast, 'puzzling' art movies, as Norman N. Holland noted, confuse viewers on all levels: 'They puzzle us as to their meaning in a total sense [and t]hey puzzle us scene-by-scene simply as to what is going on in a narrative' (Holland 1963: 18–19). Contemporary impossible puzzle films only use the first type of global confusion; on the scene-to-scene level they largely retain transparency and comprehensibility. Their complexity only arises when viewers try to piece together the (otherwise separately mostly sensible) plot trajectories, which do not seem to add up to a coherent whole, but form a dissonant and impossible constellation.

As for the second function, the appeal of these films to classical narration evokes certain expectations. Impossible puzzle films partially work by suggesting regular narrative logic and coherence. Their style and narration evoke aspects of classical narrativity without actually committing to it. And so these films provide the illusion of an unambiguous and coherent story, and encourage viewers to apply conventional inferential narrative logic. The viewing expectations and analytical routines that come with these formal strategies, however, often do not pay off, and viewers' rationalising efforts may prove futile.

5.2.5 Inclusion of quasi-rational frames of naturalisation

Lastly, the final formal strategy common to impossible puzzle films is that they frequently include quasi-rational or pseudo-scientific explanations and motivations for their complex stories and narrative structures. In section 4.2 we discussed the function of naturalisations (Culler 1975) as interpretive frames. Naturalisations can help viewers to make sense of narrative complexity by attributing motivations and explanations to it. As we noted there, viewers can naturalise narrative complexity in a great variety of ways (for instance by explaining it as a distorted subjective reality, as a dream or fantasy, as an aspect of the fictional storyworld, as an allegory, as communicating a specific thematic function, as a personal expression of the film's author and so on). What we see in many impossible puzzle films, however, is that these movies do not keep all these potential paths of naturalisation open. Rather, in their attempt to sustain their viewers' diegetic immersion, they include clues that usually point towards possible explanations and motivations on the level of the storyworld. Two such naturalisations are particularly prominent in this respect. First, many impossible puzzle films hint at explanations of their complexity or strangeness as the product of the mental state of one of the characters (see also the 'subjectification' principle discussed in section 4.2). Such clues suggest that a character's mental illness, distorted worldview, substance abuse or repressed dreams and desires cause the convoluted story presentation. Yet in impossible puzzle films, clues for subjectivity are often invoked without explicitly indicating how one could read them to establish cohesion and restore logic; these films, for example, hint at, but do not unambiguously reveal to viewers what is a dream or hallucination and what is real (see also our consideration of *Mulholland Drive* and *Enemy* as possible subjective narratives, discussed in subsection 4.4.1). Second, impossible puzzle films often include quasi-scientific or quasi-rational explanations that are aimed at convincing the viewer about a complicated but possible motivation behind their narrative complexity. Popular devices to suggest rational logic behind logical impossibilities are semi-scientific contemplations about time travelling (such as in *Primer*, *Timecrimes*), parallel universes (*Donnie Darko*, *Source Code*) and quantum mechanics (*Coherence*, or the television series *Fringe*). By pointing towards real-world scientific theory and freely adapted futuristic or fantastic versions thereof, these films suggest a 'rationally' motivating logic where a coherent narrative logic is absent. They advance the possibility that a rational theory may be able to account for their paradoxes, contradictions and impossibilities, but (quite understandably) without fully revealing what this logic would be.

In an interview, director James Ward Byrkit openly talks about the strategic inclusion of such quasi-scientific explanations in his movie *Coherence*:

> The big difference between us and *Primer* is that Shane [Carruth, writer and director] really did a great job of making *Primer* seem like it had plausible science in it, whereas we don't [laughs]. We don't have plausible science . . . We thought, wouldn't that be fun to have a completely ridiculous story, but have elements of it that sounded like plausible explanations? (Lincoln 2014)

In *Coherence*, we follow six people at a dinner party on a night that, so is suggested, a comet happens to be closely passing Earth. Following a power outage, the group starts witnessing strange and disturbing events, including mysterious disappearances, looping events and duplicating characters. Halfway into the movie, while the group is trying to make sense of the anomalies, they happen to come across a book of theoretical physics that one of the disappeared characters left behind. Upon inspection of the book, one of the remaining characters recalls the famous thought experiment of Schrödinger's cat, and the multiple-worlds interpretation of quantum mechanics – the suggestion of course being that (probably due to the strange influence of the comet) the characters are experiencing the interaction of different possible worlds that usually remain separated. By providing such internal 'scientific' motivations, however brief or thin, the film sends its viewers in a clear direction in terms of meaning-making: it emphasises diegetic and generic investigation, inspiring viewers to direct their sense-making at the internal laws of the storyworld (that is, solving the puzzle, cracking the code) rather than utilising authorial, allegorical, thematic or other hermeneutic and meta-fictional motivations. Providing quasi-scientific or psychological naturalisations for the challenges of their confusingly complex diegetic universes, impossible puzzle films thus encourage viewers to keep using their toolkit of interpretations and motivations trained on classical narratives.

To conclude, we argue that it is through a combination of formal and stylistic tactics, derived from both the art-cinema and classical narrative tradition, that impossible puzzle films achieve their distinct viewing effects. By strategically appealing to cognitive and habitualised dispositions from classical narration in particular, these films discourage the interpretive modes of sense-making associated with art cinema; instead, they encourage viewers' immersion and classical narrative engagement, and prompt them to make sense of the dissonances and other paradoxes on the diegetic, intratextual level. These formal, stylistic and diegetic tactics serve as a kind of unattainable 'red herring' to keep viewers in a cognitive loop of sense-making, tempting them to look for rational and logical solutions to these films' 'irrational' complexities – an effect that can account for the films' engaging potential. In our next, final chapter we will focus on this engaging capacity, and conclude our book by pondering about the possible reasons for the attractiveness of impossible puzzle films.

CHAPTER 6

Wallowing in Dissonance: The Attractiveness of Impossible Puzzles

If you're not confused, you're not paying attention.

Tom Peters

Throughout the preceding chapters, we have aimed to formulate an in-depth understanding of the effects and experiences of narrative complexity in contemporary cinema. We proposed a cognitive reconceptualisation of story and storytelling complexity in film, and directed our investigations at a distinct set of movies that we labelled 'impossible puzzle films'. Impossible puzzle stories, we argued, evoke pervasively confusing viewing experiences and undermine narrative comprehension by means of various complicating storytelling techniques and the eliciting of dissonant cognitions. We examined not only the ways in which these films create confusion, but also the (counter-) strategies by which they strive to keep viewers interested and immersed in their challenges and mysteries. This inquiry led us to further questions, such as what kinds of interpretive responses these films evoke and encourage, and how their viewing effects are different from other complex narratives (such as those in the tradition of art cinema). We have tried to discuss these issues and our proposed approach in the most comprehensive manner, and we will not aim to restate and reconstruct those findings in this closing chapter. Rather, in conclusion to this study, we would like to devote some attention to one fundamental question that has lurked around the past chapters, but has remained unaddressed all along: *Why would anyone be interested in confusing films or potentially unsolvable puzzles?*

In this final chapter, we take a step back from our previous theorising, and make room to freely ponder the question of what makes highly complex stories attractive, or at least engaging, for some viewers. We would like to make it clear that we do not claim to provide any definitive answers. Thinking about these films' potential for engagement or attractiveness implies other big questions that can be quite thorny (such as why people engage with art and fiction in the first place). Queries of this kind also generally resist easy or univocal explanations. Moreover, what people draw from these particular films is likely to vary significantly according to their individual film and media literacy, personal history, preferences, competences and attitudes. Undoubtedly, there is also a significant share of viewers who do not like or for whom this type of cinema simply does not resonate at all. Nevertheless, such constraints do not make the question irrelevant – on the contrary: understanding what draws some people to complex stories is a fundamental part of understanding these films themselves, both in terms of the viewing experiences of those who watch them and as cultural phenomena. We believe that the observations we have made in this book provide a stimulating basis to explore this question a bit further. Therefore, by way of opening up the discussion and looking ahead, we will devote the final pages of this book to ruminating the possible *attractiveness of complexity*. This means that we will loosen the scientific rigour, try to look beyond our theoretical framework and take a stance that is, admittedly, a speculative one.

Most of the impossible puzzle films we have discussed cannot be said to provide the type of gratifications that are commonly attributed to classical narrative film. From a cognitive and affective perspective, Nitzan Ben Shaul characterises the attractiveness of classical narrative cinema as follows:

> it seems that the challenging of the viewers' cognitive faculties in a manner that satisfyingly lets them construct out of the movies' compelling audio-visual flow a coherent story that leads to closure, along with the attendant arousal, regulation, and control of tension, mostly through suspense strategies, are the sine qua non components that account for the popularity of movies. (Ben Shaul 2012: 25)

Impossible puzzle films, however, apparently deny viewers much of this satisfaction. Although these films can involve suspense, tension and other attractive affects, they do not allow viewers clear-cut solutions to well-framed problems, and often deny narrative closure. Some of these films do not even allow the construction of any coherent narrative chain of events. Rather, impossible puzzle films are dissonant, ambiguous and open-ended, and may leave viewers searching for the story logic. Simply put, these films are confusing – a state of mind that, arguably, most people under most circumstances would prefer to avoid. However, what seems an undesirable sensation in real life might be an appealing experience in mediated art; impossible puzzle films have attracted a considerable audience, as well as critical acclaim. The question of what underlies the fascination with such films thus becomes a rather intriguing one. While working on this book, we have accumulated some ideas and hunches for potential reasons for the attractiveness of cognitively dissonant and highly complex stories. In the below, we will share eight of these ideas in the form of *explorative hypotheses*. No rigid factuality should be ascribed to these – they are not 'claims' as such; rather, we hope our reader will feel invited to think along, to bring in his or her own knowledge and experiences, and to reflect further on the possible pleasures and functions of this particular type of film.

6.1 HERMENEUTIC PLAY AND INTERPRETIVE MULTIPLICITY

One unique aspect of engaging with impossible puzzle films could lie in the peculiar meaning-making activities that they allow. In Chapter 4 we discussed the possible interpretive responses to dissonant stories, and noted that they can evoke what we call *hermeneutic play* through repeated frame-switching (see specifically section 4.4). Impossible puzzle films do not allow a single interpretive resolution to achieve full closure, but rather seem designed to keep viewers in a loop of sense-making (as also elaborated in section 5.2). They thereby evoke a perpetual sense of cognitive dissonance that encourages an enduring search for a satisfying resolution or a clear meaningfulness. This invites viewers to repeatedly try out different interpretations, frames of knowledge, analytical strategies and critical competences, without necessarily settling on a single outcome. This prolonged interpretive quest, we hypothesise, can maintain a distinct *interpretive multiplicity* that viewers may appreciate for various reasons.

First of all, this lack of closure and interpretive hierarchy may be deemed *liberating*. In terms of engaging with fiction, impossible puzzle films offer an appealing alternative to the closed, teleological cause-and-effect logic of classical film narratives.[1] They refuse to adhere to the singular logic and typical closure that characterises the vast majority of classical narratives with which contemporary audiovisual culture is saturated. Highly complex stories that challenge (but do not entirely break with) this familiar mode of classical narration may thus simply be attractive for their novelty, offering a refreshing variation on the very common ways of engaging with fiction. In more general terms, viewers may also appreciate these films' resistance to sense and meaning-making as a triumph over reason and order at large. For instance, one frequently heard argument is that highly complex film narratives form a critique of the Enlightenment values that determine much of the modern scientific worldview (for example, Panek 2006: 67). A work's noncompliance with being contained rationally can be appreciated as a liberation from modern Western scientism, or from the cultural dominance of qualities

---

[1] See also Nitzan Ben Shaul's analysis of how many classical narrative films induce a certain 'close-mindedness' in viewers, whereas some films do allow them the distinct pleasure of entertaining their ability for 'optional thinking', for instance by offering alternative narrative paths among which viewers can choose or can imagine different possibilities (Ben Shaul 2012).

such as objectivity, logic, clarity, purposefulness, prediction and explanation. Viewers may value complex classical narratives also for their emancipation of alternative qualities like subjectivity, irregularity, contingency, unpredictability, uncertainty and ambiguity. Indeed, such alternative value-attributions need not be exclusive to art cinema. Furthermore, some individuals may also simply take pleasure in being overwhelmed by an artwork that surpasses reason and cerebral comprehension. Arguably, the recognition that a work does not allow itself to be pinned down by a single reading is also held in high cultural esteem, as this quality is considered an artistic asset (signalling a work's depth or durability) in many forms of art criticism.

Second, viewers may also connect these qualities of interpretive multiplicity to *mimetic expressivity* – that is, they may see the complexity as mirroring aspects of the world we live in, or the ways in which we engage with this world. Some critics have argued that complex, unsolvable narratives reflect the decentralised or diffuse postmodern culture, or the complexity of contemporary socio-economic problems.[2] It is assumable that there are viewers who feel that artworks that evoke high complexity, dissonance or ambiguity as an effect (instead of merely depicting these conditions in their stories) do a better job at representing the inherent complexity or ambiguity of living in the real world. Moreover, films like *Mulholland Drive* or *Enemy* may likewise be appreciated for the reason that they do justice to the complexities of the human mind, finding ways of representing the (anti-)logic of dreams or the subconscious strata of the human psyche. In this sense, impossible and unresolvable puzzles may be attributed mimetic functions that can be characterised as rather existential. Jan Alber eloquently phrases such a position when pondering the appeal of 'unnatural' fiction (physically, logically or humanly impossible stories) that resists meaning-making:

> At the end of the day, all examples of unnaturalness can be read as saying something about us and the world we live in ... For me the unnatural addresses one fundamental aspect of our being in the world: the lack of

---

[2] For instance, cultural philosopher Thijs Lijster (2014) proposes such a view on the historical development of the detective/mystery genre. According to Lijster, the detective fiction evolved from the celebration of Enlightenment values and scientific reason (cf. Sherlock Holmes' ever-successful use of deductive logic and inference-making) to a genre riddled with paranoia, labyrinth-like enigmas and mysteries that can no longer be solved or understood by a single detective (cf. *Inherent Vice*). The detectives themselves, moreover, became increasingly unreliable, questionable and flawed throughout twentieth-century fiction. For Lijster, these shifts mirror the state of the (post-)modern condition from which the stories originate, such as the increasing cultural complexity and socio-economic decentralisation of our times. For another illustration of a narrative reading in light of socio-economic complexity, see Roger Ebert's review of *Syriana* discussed in subsection 2.2.3 (Ebert 2005).

order and meaning and the difficulties of coming to terms with this lack . . .
The unnatural . . . reminds us of the fact that we are never fully in control
of things: represented impossibilities challenge the search for order and
meaning in a radical way. At the same time, however, it is of course our
human predicament not just to stare into this abyss but also to try to come to
terms with it. (Alber 2016: 36–7)

This also points towards a third possible component behind the attractiveness of this type of hermeneutic play, namely *training a real-world skill* for
dealing with interpretive multiplicity. If the everyday world is complex and
characterised by a lack of clear order and meaning, then it follows that dealing
with the multiplicity and multi-stability of different meanings forms a key
aspect of dealing with that world. Connecting strategies trained in fictional
complexity to abilities for coping with real-world complexity, Ien Ang has
called for the nurturing of a kind of 'cultural intelligence'. According to her,

[f]inding a language to understand . . . complexities – that is, to describe
the specific ways in which things are 'complex and contradictory' . . . – is a
necessary step to generate the cultural intelligence with which to formulate
'solutions' in terms of strategic, flexible, emergent, non-simplistic simplifica-
tions, rather than the reductionist and mechanistic thinking (informed by
positivism) which still dominates much policy-making and problem-solving.
(Ang 2011: 788–9)

Artworks can exercise our ability to cope with complex situations in real life
by presenting complex stories or by foregrounding formal-structural complexity that requires viewers to juggle multiple, simultaneously reasonable
interpretive options. The tendency of impossible puzzle films to withhold
closure and unambiguous meaning can also be seen in this light. These films
may, for instance, train viewers in what Reuven Tsur has labelled 'negative
capability'. Tsur quotes Keats to characterise negative capability as a competence 'of being in uncertainties, Mysteries, doubts, without any irritable
reaching after fact and reason' (Tsur 1975: 776). This stands opposed to what
Tsur calls the 'quest for certitude': the urge to distill singular, unambiguous
meaning from an artwork and reach interpretive closure. These notions form
two poles in a spectrum, ranging from the appreciation of fixedness and certitude to the valuing of lingering ambiguity and interpretive multiplicity. One
may assume that a viewer's position on this spectrum will be determined by
personal attributes and dispositions (cf. an individual's psychological 'need
for closure' – see Webster and Kruglanski 1994), and that this position is
relevant in the degree to which one enjoys or values ambiguous artworks.
Nonetheless, it can be hypothesised that repeated exposure to narrative
artworks that highlight interpretive multi-stability may serve to train everyday

'negative capability'. By altering the shortcuts in an individual's meaning-making routines, repeated exposure to interpretive multiplicity may make him or her less prone to readily seeking interpretive closure.

Lastly, even if complex films do not necessarily form 'cognitive playgrounds' in which viewers can train and test the meaning-making skills demanded by an increasingly complex world, then they can still be said to simply entertain skills that viewers already possess. That is, complex stories can trigger the use of certain interpretive and analytic mental competences, the exercising of which viewers may enjoy simply for their own sake. Following Liesbeth Korthals Altes, we could call this aesthetic pleasure *Funktionslust*. According to her, there seems to be a

> pleasure and interest our minds seem to take in *complexity itself*, admittedly in different degrees. This pleasure seems akin to what the German psychologist Karl Bühler called *Funktionslust*. This eloquent term refers to the pleasure taken in exercising a mental or bodily function (Bühler 1965: 157). Such function-oriented pleasure can be observed in repetitive movements in animal and child play but also in adult behaviour, from a good physical workout to riddles or crosswords that engage the pleasure of puzzling and pattern-seeking minds. (Korthals Altes 2014: 23 – our emphases)

An impossible narrative puzzle may engage us in a similar pleasure by entertaining viewers' *Funktionslust* in repeatedly utilising their analytic and interpretive abilities. Complexity of narrative form, Korthals Altes notes, is particularly likely to become the target of such enjoyment, as 'the pleasure we may take in our skillfulness in understanding intricate form may also appear like the *Funktionslust* of puzzling and pattern-seeking minds' (Korthals Altes 2014: 131). To a degree, however, this could of course be said for many kinds of (if not all) aesthetic and narrative engagement. As David Bordwell notes,

> [i]n our culture, aesthetic activity deploys such [everyday cognitive] skills for nonpractical ends. In experiencing art, instead of focusing on the pragmatic results of perception, we turn our attention to the very process itself. What is nonconscious in everyday mental life becomes consciously attended to. Our schemata get shaped, stretched, and transgressed; a delay in hypothesis-confirmation can be prolonged for its own sake. And like all psychological activities, aesthetic activity has long-range effects. Art may reinforce, or modify, or even assault our normal perceptual-cognitive repertoire. (Bordwell 1985: 32)

In this respect, too, impossible puzzle films can be seen as having rather unique reflexive functions. Through their problematisation of narrative construction, as well as through their interpretive challenges, these films can have viewers experience and reflect on their cognitive involvement in narrative construction, or on different sense-making processes (perceptual, narrative, interpretive) more generally. Engaged viewers' repeated attempts to come to terms with the inherent dissonances of these stories may afford a gratifying *Funktionslust* in the pattern-seeking and other puzzle-solving activities of their hermeneutic play.

6.2 Orientation, navigation, mapping

Besides affording hermeneutic play, impossible puzzle films may also challenge other everyday cognitive skills and activities. One idea we would like to forward is that impossible puzzle films could provide special (embodied-) cognitive experiences by *challenging one's real-life skills of orientation and navigation*. Our hypothesis postulates that the pressure that such challenges exert on these skills might be a source of an enhanced viewer engagement. This first requires some explanation about the general function of orientation and navigation in relation to narrative fiction.

Earlier we argued that real-life skills of everyday, embodied orientation and navigation are relevant in processes of comprehending narrative structures (see sections 2.1 and 3.5; or Kiss 2013, 2015). Following previous embodied accounts of psychological and narrative continuity (cf. Slors 1998; Menary 2008), we have drawn a link between abilities of real-world orientation and navigation and analytical skills of plot segmentation in narrative comprehension.[3] We hypothesised that viewers use basic spatial schemas in 'mapping' narrative plot structures, for instance through the mental projection of image schemas, or by mapping one's own familiar action patterns onto the experiential paths of the fictional characters. This claim considers the idea that viewers and readers 'map' a story to be more than just a metaphor, and, therefore, 'mapping' is not tied to strictly topographic dimensions.[4] For instance, when viewers follow and trace stories by means of narrative plotting, mapping can involve spatial visualisations of temporal relations among events (by placing them on a timeline). Arguably, readers and viewers are willing to invest cognitive resources into creating mental models of narrative maps if their investment presumably contributes to their comprehension of

---

[3] For theoretical arguments (Johnson [1987] 1990; Slors 1998; Menary 2008) and neuroscientific proofs (Gallese and Lakoff 2005), consult the previously published article (Kiss 2013).

[4] As for such topographic mapping, because '[p]eople read for the plot and not for the map' (Ryan 2003: 238), it can be said that both film viewers and 'readers of print texts rarely maintain an "accurate map of spatial relations" in the represented storyworld' (Ciccoricco 2007: 54). It is obvious that the topographic practice of literary or visual cartography is a useful tool for creative artists, but it is rarely triggered as a 'natural' reader or viewer response. Yet there is empirical proof that adult viewers encode a more or less stable spatial layout 'even when there is no explicit demand for them to do so' (Levin and Wang 2009: 26).

a story. The challenges of (impossible) puzzle films seem to provide a cognitive playground that particularly encourages such mapping activity in one's narrative orientation.

Similar to real-world navigation, in fictional worlds the absence of a clear reference point can lead to disorientation. This reference point can be characterised as the *deictic centre*. In everyday navigation, the deictic centre refers to the embodied ego-reference point from which we navigate space and monitor time (establishing dimensions such as front, back, up, down, or before and after). When extended to narrative, the notion denotes our constructions of 'where we are' in the story, referring to the constructed spatio-temporal coordinates of 'here and now'. In any narrative text or film, this deictic centre is an essential feature of storytelling and a necessary reference point for reasoning. According to William F. Hanks, it 'is the indexical ground or *origo* relative to which relations of proximity, temporality, perceptual access, givenness in discourse, and prospection and retrospection are arrayed' (Hanks [2005] 2010: 99). It is 'the locus in conceptual space-time of the objects and events depicted or described by the sentences [and images] currently being perceived' (Rapaport et al. n.d.: 3). As such, the deictic centre is the starting point from which we can make inferences about the film's narrative and visual markers (or a written text's grammatical indications) concerning the when, where and who of the story.

In constructing a narrative plot, the deictic centre positions characters relative to the spatio-temporal progression of the storyline, advancing along with the unfolding narrative. This allows viewers to determine 'where they are' in the story, and enables them to determine not only the 'here and now' but also, for instance, what is a flashback to earlier or flash forward to upcoming events. In most narratives, the deictic centre is communicated clearly, providing a backbone for the smooth integration of narrative information: we know where we are in a story and can map flashbacks, flash forwards, changes of scenes and ellipses in relation to that point in space and time. In impossible puzzle films, however, determining a clear deictic centre may become problematic, or may even prove virtually impossible, as the result of palpable dissonances between cognitions or of a sheer lack of order. This is particularly evident with narratives that present impossible storyworlds, such as parallel universe stories (that obscure the spatio-temporal hierarchy among their multiple realities), and/or use complex non-chronological storytelling structures, particularly loops (which can severely destabilise a clear determination of the 'here and now' or the 'beginning and end'). We hypothesise that impossible puzzle films can disorient viewers by either denying the designation of a clear deictic centre, or by asking them to map the story from multiple deictic centres.

As for the first option, many impossible puzzle films challenge orientation by hiding or obscuring the deictic centre, leaving a high degree of uncertainty over the status of narrative information. It may for instance be left unclear whether scenes belong to the past, present or the future, or are a part of someone's hallucinations or dreams about the past, present or future. One may for instance think of the extensive sections in *Mulholland Drive* during which the film delves into a mysterious variety of uncanny scenes and storylines (including those of the Hollywood director, his casting and the mobsters, the nightmare story at the Winkie's diner, the cowboy, the hitman, as well as the ongoing story of Betty and Rita). While the film spirals into these different non-chronologically organised and ambiguously focalised story paths, it becomes increasingly difficult for a viewer to establish how events relate to each other, or how scenes might be connected at all – spatially, temporally, causally, or as a network. The film does not follow a single character who could have provided a navigable reference point through the succession of different scenes and settings; nor does *Mulholland Drive* include other clear spatial or temporal markers by which events could be readily placed in relation to each other. Moreover, the few recurring characters, like Betty and Rita, who could embody a focal(ising) centre point around which these events revolve, seem to have slippery identities as well, which further riddles the story with contradictions and incoherency. As the film progresses, this continuous lack of a clear centre of orientation, from which the story's dimensions could be mapped (for example, as past or present, or as a dream or reality) frustrates the engaged viewer's attempts to do so. The strategy of making a deictic reference point permanently elusive is arguably paramount to *Mulholland Drive*'s complex effects, and, along with the films' use of highly uncanny and estranging film style, leads to a palpable sense of disorientation.

With regard to the second option, impossible puzzle films frequently present multiple (sometimes contradictory or paradoxical) deictic centres from which the plot needs to be mapped. This is particularly apparent in narratives that feature time loops and/or duplicating characters, as in *Primer*, *Triangle*, *Timecrimes*, *Miraq* or *Reality*. In the convoluted time-travel logic of *Primer*, for instance, the multiplying – and for the viewer often indistinguishable – versions of the protagonists destabilise our ability to map past, present and future, because these versions all form different, simultaneously existing deictic centres active on different points of the film's timeline. As various incarnations of the protagonists co-exist within a single looping structure, the film's spatio-temporal markers become increasingly dislocated. Another interesting (albeit lesser known) example is Csaba Bollók's film *Miraq*, which presents a bi-directional story reminiscent of the temporal setup of Martin Amis' 1991 novel *Time's Arrow*: while the time of the telling (the time of the protagonist we follow) is chronological, the time of the told (the diegetic spatio-temporal reality that surrounds the protagonist's experience) runs backwards. Such narrative discrepancy allows the film to be mapped from two contradictory deictic centres within a single diegetic world, creating a dissonance that seriously hinders viewers' efforts to grasp the plot.[5]

The effect of an intensified need for orientation in complex story comprehension can also be observed in viewers' attempts at *graphically mapping* such plots. Drawing physical maps can function as a kind of 'prosthetic extension' of viewers' mental work. A physical map can unburden limited cognitive resources and working memory when coping with complex stories and plots. Visual maps of narratives might also reveal neglected clues, new semantic fields, overlooked relations and patterns, and other forms of internal logic, which otherwise could have escaped one's awareness (for example, the plot map of *Timecrimes* reveals a simple structure behind the complex experience – Figure 3.1).[6]

By creating visual models of the experience, narrative maps also offer illustrations of the process of understanding itself. Let's see how this works with regard to an impossible puzzle example. Figure 6.1 exhibits a narrative map of the film *Triangle*, sketched by a student.[7] This attempt not only illustrates the degree of narrative complexity, but also shows the mental struggle of coming to terms with the film's multiple and simultaneously existing plotlines. In *Triangle*, multiple versions of the protagonist Jess are simultaneously active within the plot's single time loop. The actions of each Jess cause events to happen to the other versions of Jess, while these actions were themselves the effect of the actions of earlier Jesses – a classic 'chicken or egg' causality paradox that follows from the story's impossible temporal loop. To make sense of this warped causation, as well as to grasp the larger plot structure, the viewer consequently has to establish the different versions of Jess as different deictic centres inhabiting the same diegetic space and time loop. This struggle is apparent in the student's mapping activity. The first three drawings

---

[5] *Miraq*'s bi-directionality should not be mistaken for that of David Fincher's *The Curious Case of Benjamin Button* (2008). While Fincher's fantastic storyworld, employing only a single deictic centre, introduces a *biological discrepancy* (a man who is aging backwards), Bollók's film, utilising two contradictory deictic centres, creates a perplexing *narrative discrepancy*.

[6] The method of graphical extension of mental mapping might be implemented into the creative practice of designing narrative experiences as well. For instance, Christopher Nolan is known for making such sketches, as revealed in the shooting script for his fairly complex film *Inception* (Nolan 2010).

[7] Between 2010 and 2014 (at the University of Groningen, the Netherlands) we led seminar conversations and carried out various pilot projects regarding students' graphical note-taking activities.

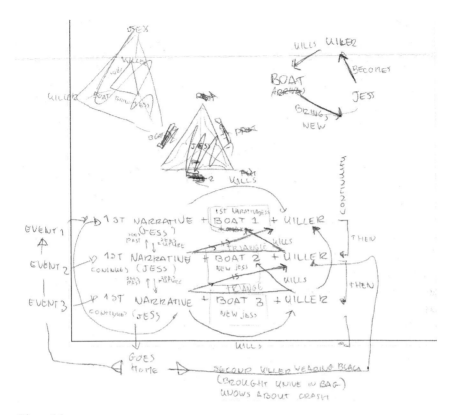

Figure 6.1

(on the top of the figure) show the initial unsuccessful attempts at mapping the looping plot from a single centre. The final drawing (at the bottom) ostensibly follows the realisation that the plot must be mapped from multiple deictic centres. This 'solution' shows a three-layered plot representation, allowing a single story to be constructed around three deictic centres that occasionally overlap and interact (although close reading would in fact reveal that, for a full overview, there must at least be four simultaneously active protagonists from whose perspectives the story should be mapped).

On the whole, we would not claim that these films' challenging of deeply engrained skills of orientation and navigation is attractive in itself. Instead, we could look at complexifying narrative tactics as invitational strategies that encourage heightened viewer activity, and, through that, even manage to pull some viewers into literally mapping the intricate plot at hand. Inspiring augmented analytical and interpretive activities, movies, especially the complex kinds, often provide models for such mapping practice themselves: from Robert Zemeckis' *Back to the Future Part II* (1989) through Mennan Yapo's

Figure 6.2

Figure 6.3

Premonition (2007) to *Timecrimes*, many films present pensive characters chalking diagrams or grabbing pen and paper (see Figures 6.2 and 6.3 and Figures 5.6 and 5.7 in Chapter 5, respectively). As the abundance of online available plot maps of complex films suggests, some (although definitely not all) viewers seem to engage in this activity, and, whether mentally or even graphically, play along with the puzzle-solving games of navigational challenge.

6.3 GAME LOGIC AND THE FASCINATION IN FAILURE

Another hypothesis to explain the popularity of contemporary puzzle films is frequently sought in the comparison of their viewing experiences to the *logic* of videogames. According to Jason Mittell, many contemporary complex narratives

> require the audience to learn the particular rules of a film to comprehend its narrative; movies like *The Sixth Sense*, *Pulp Fiction*, *Memento*, *The Usual Suspects*, *Adaptation*, *Eternal Sunshine of the Spotless Mind*, and *Run Lola Run* have all embraced a game aesthetic, inviting audiences to play along with the creators to crack the interpretive codes to make sense of their complex narrative strategies. But crucially, the goal of these puzzle films is not to solve the mysteries ahead of time; rather, we want to be competent enough to follow their narrative strategies but still relish in the pleasures of being manipulated successfully. (Mittell 2006: 37–8)

Similarly, Elliot Panek notes that

> [a]n element of non-filmic interactive storytelling exists in these [puzzle] films. Younger audiences that are increasingly comfortable with the burgeoning interactive medium of video games may find puzzle narratives appealing for this reason. It is not enough say that these characters are mentally unstable and that when the narration diverges from the classical mode, it is merely reflecting their fractured look on life. We seem to seek the nature of the instability even when we realize we are watching a psychological puzzle film, and take pleasure in trying to figure out the rules of the narration that presents the story to us. (Panek 2006: 87)

According to Warren Buckland, the narrative logic of contemporary puzzle films can be traced in the emerging logic of new media, specifically of videogames (see his analysis of Duncan Jones's *Source Code* in Buckland 2014c: 185–97). For him, the influence can be observed in puzzle films' promise of 'reliable rules' – a characteristic that is central to the logic of videogames (Gottschalk 1995).

> These rules, which are reliable in that they are systematic and unambiguous . . . constitute the video game's environment, or location, which is not restrained by the laws of the physical world. The game user can experience video pleasure primarily by attempting to master these rules – that is, decipher the game's logic. Moreover, the desire to attain mastery makes video games addictive, which at times can lead to the user's total absorption into the game's rules and environment. (Buckland 2014c: 187)

Although we believe a fundamental caution should be maintained with regard to claims crossing over from different media (film is, after all, still a non-interactive medium according to most definitions of interactivity), Mittell's, Panek's and Buckland's observations do offer an interesting angle. Indeed, we would agree that in highly complex films, viewers do not just experience complexity and dissonance, but are also often inclined to try to understand the underlying logic of it – in Panek's words, to 'seek the nature of the instability'. In many cases, this does indeed involve attempts to discern a set of logical rules in the narration – rules that the viewer could ultimately master. However, as we have noted before, impossible puzzle films do not seem to offer the 'reward' usually associated either with puzzle films or with games (in the forms of a revealing twist, resolution or outcome, or in the reaching of a new level). Impossible puzzle films do not just delay the viewer's access to the rules and logic that govern their narration, but sometimes even fully deny viewers such (or any) logic. Nonetheless, this does not need to make the game-logic analogy invalid for these films. There are two reasons for this. First, through various (post-)classical narrative strategies, impossible puzzle films seem designed to keep viewers inclined to search for a logic to their stories. Viewers may therefore still find in these films the 'promise of reliable rules' that Gottschalk and Buckland observe in games and cinematic puzzles. Second, it seems that failure forms an intrinsic, even pleasurable part of any gaming activity. As impossible puzzle films often evoke in viewers unsuccessful attempts to grasp their stories and story logic, a certain sense of 'failure' also seems to characterise their experiences. While the first reason has already been discussed in Chapter 5, let us now focus on the second.

An explanation for the appeal of impossible puzzle films could be found in human's seemingly paradoxical fascination with failure. Regarding impossible fictional worlds, Umberto Eco identified such appeal as 'the pleasure of our logical and perceptual defeat' (1990: 77 – see also subsection 3.3.2). But what is pleasurable about a cognitive and perceptual defeat? In his book on videogames (tellingly titled *The Art of Failure*), Danish ludologist Jesper Juul points out the initially somewhat counterintuitive fact that 'players prefer games in which they fail' (Juul 2013: 2). Drawing from his own experience, Juul notes that 'I dislike failing in games, but I dislike *not* failing even more' (ibid: 2). By means of some elegantly simple experiments, Juul demonstrates the importance of failure and feelings of inadequacy in the context of videogames. He observes that 'players who completed the game without failing gave it a *lower* rating than those who failed at least once' (ibid.: 35), and that 'players rated the game significantly higher when they felt responsible for failure than when they did not' (ibid.: 53–4).

Juul's observations seem to rhyme with the psychological workings of impossible puzzle films. Comparable to how a game 'promises us that we can remedy the problem if we keep playing' (ibid.: 7), impossible puzzle films may beguile viewers with a similar promise, as their highly complex (but seemingly logical) narration continuously encourages viewers to rationalise and narrativise the illogical. The prospect of the potential intelligibility of these films inspires viewers to keep trying to overcome their felt inadequacy – which, as Juul notes with regard to games, is 'an inadequacy that they produce in us in the first place' (ibid: 7). By arousing a sense of inadequacy, impossible puzzle films seem to trigger a similar motivational bias: viewers may feel that their competence or intelligence is being challenged in cracking the puzzle, and therefore submit to the urge to overcome 'their' failure through recurring attempts of problem-solving. To capture this recurring aspect of the process in gaming, Juul introduces a model of the *failure-improvement cycle* of videogame play (ibid.: 60). The cycle consists of four steps: (1) new goal is introduced; (2) failure presents the player as inadequate; (3) player searches for the cause of the failure and improves; (4) inadequacy gone in player; player has new skills. A similar mechanism seems to be active in impossible puzzle film viewing, with the key difference being that the viewer's 'improvement' may not be satisfyingly reached. Rather, viewers' ongoing lack of understanding and maintained feeling of inadequacy may become a drive that keeps them invested in comprehending the story, and, eventually, might contribute to their evaluating the experience as engaging. In sum, this hypothesis would assume that the engaging potential of impossible puzzle films is partly managed by strategies that continuously challenge viewers' feeling of competence, which can contribute to the framing of the failure in achieving full comprehension as a fascinating experience.

6.4 EFFORT JUSTIFICATION

Related to our fascination in failure, another possible reason behind the attraction of confusing and cognitively demanding narrative experiences could be sought in the psychological principle of *effort justification*. In social psychology, effort justification is understood as an everyday cognitive dissonance-reduction strategy – a mode of changing the value of existing cognitions. Simply put, the principle states that people tend to evaluate an outcome, reached goal or completed task as being more valuable when this outcome has cost them more effort to achieve. It has been suggested that this principle is active in many different social and behavioural patterns. It can, for example, help to explain phenomena such as hazing and initiation rituals: by having to go through hardships or having to make an effort to be allowed into a social group, an individual is likely to value this membership more highly, as he or she has to justify the effort made (valuing the outcome more highly reduces the dissonance with regard to the more unpleasant aspects of the experience). Drawing on Festinger's theory of cognitive dissonance, a classic study by Elliot Aronson and Judson Mills (1959) connected varying amounts of effort to evaluative judgements. Aronson and Mills hypothesised that the effort justification mechanism could be effective in any basic set of conditions regarding effort and evaluation: 'For example, one would expect persons who travel a great distance to see a motion picture to be more impressed with it than those who see the same picture at a neighborhood theater' (Aronson and Mills 1959: 177).

Cognitive scientist Jim Davies (2014) has extended the principle of effort justification to the realm of meaning-making. For him, discerned meaning becomes more valuable if it is attained through substantial cognitive effort. According to Davies, the pleasure of puzzles can also be related to this principle; after all, '[w]ith puzzles, the audience gets to appreciate so many things: the initial incongruity, the pleasure of knowing the solution, the pride of having discovered it themselves, and an increased value of the found solution due to idea effort justification' (Davies 2014: 143).

But how does this translate to an impossible puzzle? What is the mental payoff of a perpetually challenging experience that impossible puzzle films provide? It is apparent that the narrative comprehension of these films demands significantly more cognitive efforts than most classical stories or 'ordinary' puzzle films (which provide or allow a relatively easy access to a coherent and logical solution to their conundrum). As we noted earlier (particularly in chapter 4), impossible puzzle films allow cognitive operations and interpretive strategies that can compensate for viewers' fruitless efforts to find a coherent and logical solution. We would therefore hypothesise that Aronson and Mills' '*suffering-leading-to-liking*' thesis (Gerard and Mathewson 1966) can play a role in the appreciation of more pervasively complex films too: attributing a positive judgement to these films' rich affordances might tame the experienced dissonance with regard to the effort made. Simply put, one could presume that the general principle of effort justification still holds for films that do not necessarily offer narrative closure or a satisfying resolution. According to this, the appeal of impossible puzzle films may stem from these films' offered *analytical and interpretive richness*, the intensified *inspiration for forensic activities* the puzzles call forth, and from viewers' general *respect towards a highly challenging experience* that seems to outsmart them. These ideas and hypotheses could make an interesting subject for further empirical investigations.

6.5 Diegetisation of decoupling

According to cultural cognitivist Barend van Heusden, the appeal of cognitively dissonant narrative art comes from the amplification of a very general human disposition – one that characterises practically all our real-life and mediated narrative experiences (van Heusden 2009; and personal correspondence). Cognitively dissonant scenarios, he reasons, make us *re-experience* the act of *decoupling*, which is not only an integral part of our cognition, but also a core aspect of the general human condition.

As Merlin Donald has argued (1991; 2006), through the evolutionarily increased capacities of working memory, humans have become capable of decoupling memory from actuality:

> Donald equates the origins of modern humans to a transition from episodic to mimetic cultures, or the transition from lives that are bounded to the immediacy of experience to lives that are lived not only in the present but also in the simulation or representation of this experience. (Rochat [2001] 2004: 73)

In this sense, the act of decoupling is the source of human imagination: being able to 'decouple' from the actuality of our here-and-now experience, we can simulate, represent or even fantasise about alternative versions of our reality. Following this train of thought, decoupling allows mimesis, whereas 'art is an inevitable by-product of mimesis' (Donald 2006: 14). Hence, as a result of the cognitive evolution of the human species, and due to the developed capacity of decoupling, the nature of culture and the experience of mimetic art fundamentally bear elements of dissonance. This means that there is a fundamental, deep-seated (yet unconscious and rarely reflected) conflict between our actual and imagined experience: between the 'here and now' of actual perception (the reality context of reading or viewing, that is, our reality as real readers and viewers) and the 'there and then' virtual domain of narrative immersion (the diegetic world and its fictive population, which form the destination of our absorption and embodied identification). This 'cognitive dissonance' is a result of the transfer from our real-life existence to the mediated art experience.[8]

If art is the mimetic imitation of an experience through representation by mediated simulation, then 'metarepresentation' is a reflection on art's mimetic representation. Certain metarepresentational cinematic strategies may highlight the cognitive dissonance inherent to the experience of artistic representation. Films can thematise and manifest the act of decoupling through narrative diegetisation of this very fundamental dissonance. A notable example of this is provided by the abundance of character duplications in impossible puzzle films. Character splittings, doublings and multiplications

---

[8] In van Heusden's words, since '[w]e do not live in, and reality does not coincide with, our representations' (van Heusden 2009: 614), the possible awareness of the fundamental difference between our experiential domains of 'here and now' reality and 'there and then' simulation of this reality 'seems to be basic to human cognition' (ibid.: 614).

provide powerful instances for the diegetisation of decoupling's inherent dissonance. Looping narratives' character multiplications – such as in Roman Polanski's *The Tenant* (1976), Smith's *Triangle*, Vigalondo's *Timecrimes*, the Spierig brothers' *Predestination* (2014) or Lynch's *Lost Highway* – make us literally re-experience the underlying dissonance between our doubled presence of 'here and now' and immersed 'being there', which can be seen as a subtle addition to these films' attractiveness (beyond, and in case of Polanski's film, prior to the more obvious effects of digital lossless copying, videogames' multiple lives, social media avatars and other distinctly contemporary reasons that scholars and critics have attributed to the character-doubling 'trend' – discussed in more detail in section 4.2).[9]

6.6 Fascination in infinity

Certain impossible puzzle films owe part of their attraction to the arousal of what seems to be a deeply rooted human fascination in infinity. Whether encountered via mathematics or geometry, cosmology or theology, the idea of endlessness seems to exert a strong curiosity that is detectable throughout Western cultural history and the arts.[10] Like mathematicians, visual artists have repeatedly attempted to capture infinity in an aesthetic form, for instance through endlessly looping patterns (comparable to the famous steps by Lionel and Roger Penrose (1958) – Figure 6.4) or recursive mise-en-abymes (a picture of a picture in a picture in a picture – suggesting multiplication ad infinitum). Some impossible puzzle films similarly suggest 'infinity', using narrative versions of infinite loops (for example, *Triangle*, *Timecrimes*) or endless narrative mise-en-abymes through metalepses (for example, *Reality* and *Synecdoche, New York*). These peculiar 'endless' narrative structures seem to exert a curious fascination.

Why is it that pondering 'the infinite' is prone to evoke reactions of wonder or bewilderment? In a 1994 paper, psychologist Ruma Falk discusses how infinity seems to be 'infinitely challenging to the human mind' (Falk 1994: 35). She notes that 'people's intellectual attempts to cope with the puzzles posed by the infinite have been interwoven with a wide spectrum of emotional responses' (ibid.: 35). According to her, these emotions and fascinations are essentially triggered by the human inability to cope with the 'disturbing

[9] Beyond technology-fuelled allegories, character-duplication films like *Enemy* '[tap] into the root of our newfound doppelgänger obsession and fear. Many of us are afraid that we're simply not enough as we are – that we're not cool enough, pretty enough, passionate enough, or interesting enough' (Wilkinson 2014).

[10] For an eloquent historical overview, see Eli Maor's 1987 *To Infinity and Beyond: A Cultural History of the Infinite*.

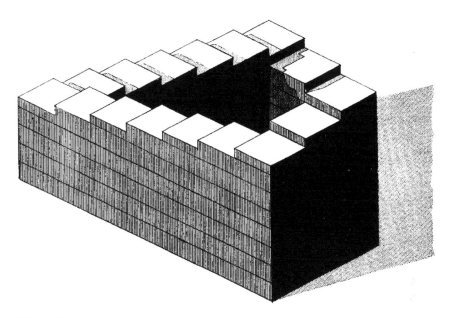

Figure 6.4

contradictions' that endlessness entails (ibid.: 36). This inability, Falk argues, is grounded in two particular cognitive moves – neither of which is compatible with our habitual strategies of reasoning. First, in order to grasp infinity one needs to practise 'the ability to *suppress* our imagination, at least the visual part of it' (ibid.: 54). This entails a conscious detachment from everyday experience and knowledge, common sense and the habitual formation of mental imagery, all of which imply (and depend upon) finiteness in the world around us. Coming to terms with infinity thus demands the challenge of *'unlearning* of old truisms' (ibid.: 53) about the laws and dimensions of the world we live in. Secondly, according to Falk, the infinite will always remain an abstraction – a concept that is beyond the reach of human experience and intuition, and that is best explained by scientific conceptualisation. Like quantum mechanics, infinity proves very difficult to comprehend in terms of the realm of everyday experience, yet its workings can ultimately be understood through (scientific) argumentation and description. Falk illustrates this by referring to examples of so-called 'super-task problems', borrowed from mathematical and psychological experiments: she asserts that as long as one tries to reconcile puzzles about the infinite rationally and commonsensically, they will elicit 'bizarre conclusions' (ibid.: 55). Hence, Falk argues,

> [n]o real-life experiment can ever model the infinite . . . Paradoxically, one needs a kind of (non-visual) vision that can accept the unimaginable. The key

to abstract thought is its detachment, not only from sensory perception, but even from imagery. Dissociation from familiar aspects of reality and from strongly held beliefs may enable human understanding to surpass intuition. (Falk 1994: 37, 54)

Arguably, infinity derives its fascinating aesthetic potential from this challenging of familiar aspects of our (beliefs about) reality. Illustrations like Penrose and Penrose's infinite steps or Escher's paradox loops (such as his 1959–60 lithograph *Ascending and Descending*) are examples of attempts 'to capture infinity in a "closed" composition' (Schattschneider [1990] 2005: 241).[11] In section 3.4, we compared the narrative structures of impossible puzzle films to depictions like Escher's, noting how these films also make the seemingly impossible perceptually and conceptually available. Some impossible puzzle films (not all, it must be noted) play with narrative mechanisms that suggest 'infinite' outcomes. Films like *Triangle* or *The Tenant* present stories that turn into endless loops without beginnings or ends; *Reality* constructs a mise-en-abyme in which different story levels are contained in each other, offering a continuous paradox; and *Synecdoche, New York* plays with another kind of mise-en-abyme, one that is implied through a constantly duplicating simulacrum: as protagonist Caden wants to direct a play that honestly and realistically captures his real, mundane life, he finds that his play must also include him making the play, which then needs to include a play about him making that play – a logic that ultimately points towards a potentially infinite recursion of plays within plays within plays.

These examples all use circular structures and recursive multiplications as narrative techniques to suggest endlessly looping or duplicating diegetic realities. Although such storyworlds exert a strong sense of 'impossibility', they are at the same time presented as coherent, 'inhabitable' and, up to a point, imaginable. In their totality, however, potentially 'infinite' story patterns like these indeed entail, as Falk noted, 'disturbing contradictions' – or, we would say, 'dissonant cognitions': they clash with common sense, reason and everyday experiential evidence. It seems that the challenge of coming to terms with the infinite pushes the limits of our embodied and situated cognition – which is not surprising, considering that our cognition emerges in and is directed at a seemingly 'finite' world (as our lived environment is characterised by apparent physical boundaries and limitations). The way in which infinity surpasses these everyday intuitions and defies our imagination may therefore be experienced as engaging, uncanny, enthralling or simply

---

[11] Penrose and Penrose's article in the *British Journal of Psychology* (1958) featured the impossible staircase, which then in fact inspired Escher's *Ascending and Descending*.

surprising. Some impossible puzzle films play on this effect, suggesting infinity to further fuel the fascination that viewers find in the narrative acrobatics and cognitive challenge of metalepses, loops and other intricately multiplying story patterns.

6.7 DESTABILISED ONTOLOGICAL CERTAINTY

Metalepses in narrative fiction collapse fictional boundaries among embedded narrative frames. While our fascination in infinity can be triggered by simulating the possibility of endless multiplication of embedded levels in a story (that is, stories within stories), metaleptic transgressions work by breaking the boundaries between story levels, often playing with the odd option of extending the fictional to the real (for example, real writers appearing in their fictional stories). Complex films and impossible puzzle films, we hypothesise, often seem to use such 'ontological metalepses' (see also our discussion in subsection 2.2.2) to arouse uncanny, potentially intriguing emotional and intellectual effects.

Contemporary complex films frequently employ ontological metalepses to present fictional transgressions between their diegetic and embedded hypodiegetic story levels. Examples may include Marc Forster's *Stranger Than Fiction*, in which Harold Crick (Will Ferrell) becomes aware that he is a fictional character in a still-developing book of an author, with whom he even shares the narrative level; or Spike Jonze's *Adaptation*, where the film's real screenplay writer Charlie Kaufman writes himself into his film script of *Adaptation*, which becomes the film that the viewer is watching (details in section 4.2, and below). A compelling literary case is provided by the short story by Cortázar that we discussed in the opening paragraphs of this book, *Continuity of Parks*, wherein the protagonist is apparently threatened by a character *from* a book he is reading. In 2011 Spanish photographer Miguel Angel Lozano Bonora took inspiration from Cortázar's story, and visualised the 'threat' of ontological metalepsis, making the otherwise strictly drawn boundary between embedded narrative levels permeable (Figure 6.5).

Due to the logic that such porous narrative structures allow, ontological metalepses may have the potential to awaken in readers or viewers a certain 'sense of logical unease' (Eco 1979: 234). Stories like Cortázar's collapse very basic ontological boundaries – not only between different story layers, but also between fictional and real-life levels of the experienced fiction and experiencing context. As for the latter, the 'ontologically threatening' potential of metalepsis was acknowledged already in the theorising of Gérard Genette ([1972] 1980: 236). Genette quoted Jorge Luis Borges – himself a master of narrative metalepsis – who, being fascinated by such deep ontological uncertainties,

Figure 6.5

noted that 'if the characters in a story can be readers or viewers, then we, their readers or spectators, can be fictitious' (Borges 1964: 46). According to this, an ontological metalepsis might 'amount to a double catharsis, a *representational* and an *existential* one' (Meister 2003 – our emphases).

Impossible puzzle films, with their tangled complexity and ambiguous hierarchies among different levels and multiple plots, are especially prone to arousing a certain ontological uncertainty in viewers. These films frequently play with vague or transgressed boundaries between dream and reality, fiction and real life, or telling and told. In a rare but registered effect, ontological metalepses might even lead to a psychologically identified disorder that is tellingly called the Truman Syndrome (Fusar-Poli et al. 2008), in which the patient suffers from a delusion that his or her life is part of a fictional story, staged as a play or reality show and controlled by unseen powers.[12] Although we would not want to claim that impossible puzzle films' narrative tactics instil such degrees of psychological (truly existential) anxiety in their viewers, it is reasonable to say that some playful metalepses are able to set in motion the idea (and subsequent feelings) of ontological uncertainty, adding to the fascination and perhaps appreciation of their ambiguous, paradoxical and dissonant experience while maintaining their stories' stubborn mysteries.

Take, for instance, *Adaptation*'s playful destabilisation of its viewers' ontological positions and assumptions. The film's narration revolves around a fictionalised version of the actual screenplay writer Charlie Kaufman. It shows Kaufman's (Nicolas Cage) struggle to adapt a book, and a decision to write a film about this struggle, which turns out to be the film we are

---

[12] The term stems from the story of Truman Burbank (Jim Carrey), who unknowingly participates in a reality television programme in Peter Weir's 1998 *The Truman Show*.

watching. Director Jonze and screenwriter Kaufman do not only play with these transgressions within the film's narrative levels (writer/written), but further utilise the destabilising potential of their metalepsis by letting the fiction 'leak' into the film's paratextual as well as actual contexts: for example, *Adaptation*'s credits mention Charlie Kaufman's fictional brother from the film, Donald Kaufman (also played by Nicolas Cage), as a co-writer of the film's real screenplay.[13] Also, the film further plays with its own reality status by including scenes about the making of Jonze's and Kaufman's previous movie, *Being John Malkovich* (1999), as part of *Adaptation*'s fiction. Such strategies do not only obfuscate the relation between the adapted and adaptation in the film, but also undercut viewers' 'uppermost' controlling position regarding the fictional and the real. This involvement of the viewer through an ultimate metaleptic pop can be seen as a device that heightens this kind of cinema's engaging capacity, making viewers part of the film's complex game.

6.8. EUDAIMONIC MOTIVATIONS AND INTRINSIC NEEDS

In this book we have discussed how complex and 'impossible' cinematic stories work, how viewers make sense of them and, now, finally, why such experiences may be found attractive. At the start of this study, we characterised the attractiveness of confusing stories as somewhat 'paradoxical'. Similar to the well-known *sadness-paradox* in art and media studies ('people willingly engage with artworks that evoke negative emotions, such as sadness, that they would normally avoid'), we encountered what resembled a '*confusion-paradox*': it seems that in narrative art and fiction, the negative valence of being confused can be considered enjoyable. However, as this final chapter has argued, viewers' willing engagement with impossible puzzle films appears less problematic; after all, the above hypotheses all assume that highly complex movies are capable of engaging and fascinating viewers in a variety of ways. How, then, should this 'paradox of the confusion-paradox' be resolved?

One way of getting out of the confusion-paradox is by emphasising the so-called *eudaimonic motivations* that viewers may have for engaging with fiction. Addressing the issue of negative emotions in art, media psychologists Mary Beth Oliver and Arthur A. Raney have argued that 'people consume media entertainment in the pursuit of pleasure and amusement (*hedonic* motivations) *and* as a part of their general need to search for and ponder life's meaning, truths, and purposes – motivations that we characterise as "*eudaimonic*"' (Oliver and Raney 2011: 985 – our emphases). Indeed,

---

[13] This even resulted in an Oscar nomination for 'Charlie Kaufman and Donald Kaufman' (for Best Adapted Screenplay), making Donald the first ever entirely fictitious Oscar nominee.

the attraction to highly complex stories becomes less paradoxical if one drops the (arguably erroneous) assumption that the engagement with fiction should be conceived of as only 'hedonically' motivated – that is, strictly in terms of bringing 'entertaining pleasure'. Most of the hypotheses developed in this chapter concern cognitive and interpretive reflections that are better characterised as driven by eudaimonic motivations (reflection, truth-seeking or self-development) than as strictly hedonically motivated. However, postulating a distinction between 'hedonic' and 'eudaimonic' drives still implies a basic difference between 'fun' and 'meaningful' experiences that seems problematic. After all, can hedonic pleasures not be found in the gratification of eudaimonic concerns as well?

Having the same dilemma, Ron Tamborini and his colleagues (2010) suggested that it would be better to approach eudaimonic motivations for media consumption in relation to the satisfaction of people's intrinsic needs. Conceptualising these 'intrinsic needs', the researchers used Edward L. Deci and Richard M. Ryan's *self-determination theory* (1985). This seminal theoretical model assumes three basic psychological needs in individuals, namely *autonomy*, *competence* and *relatedness*:

> autonomy [is] a sense of volition or willingness when doing a task (Deci and Ryan 2000); competence [is] a need for challenge and feelings of effectance (Deci 1975); and relatedness [is] a need to feel connected with others (Ryan and Deci 2001). (Tamborini et al. 2010: 761)

Working with experiments involving a videogame, the researchers confirmed the role of these needs in relation to media consumption. Yet they also noted that there is 'no basis to believe that our definition of enjoyment as the satisfaction of needs is limited to video games' (Tamborini et al. 2010: 771). Therefore, our final hypothesis concerns the enjoyment and engagement of impossible puzzle films in light of these intrinsic psychological needs. We would suggest that the attractiveness of complex films should not be seen as strictly hedonic (pleasurable or entertaining) or merely eudaimonic reflections (pondering life's complexities or achieving personal development), but should be understood as appealing to viewers' psychological intrinsic needs. For some people, impossible puzzle films may resonate with their need for *autonomy* (as the interpretive freedom and playfulness of these films leaves a relatively high amount of choice and authority to the individual viewer), or may be a means to establish *relatedness* (for instance through collective forensic fan activities, or the social rewards of sharing of interpretations, plot maps, or explanatory videos online). Yet the key notion for the enjoyment of impossible puzzle films seems to lie in the notion of *competence*. On the basis of the above hypotheses and arguments, we would argue that highly complex films – by challenging and entertaining a variety of cognitive, analytic and interpretive skills – engage viewers by appealing to their intrinsic needs for competence and effectance. Whether it is about finding an interpretation that works, grasping a story's intricate mechanisms, dealing with ontological uncertainties or mapping a plot, enjoying these films usually entails engaging in simulated challenges that playfully (and safely) address viewers' needs to feel competent and skilled.[14] As Jason Mittell noted, viewers of complex narratives 'relish in the pleasures of being manipulated', but, ultimately, 'want to be competent enough to follow their narrative strategies' (Mittell 2006: 38). The urge to 'keep up' with a complex story arguably tickles viewers' self-esteem and engages their potential for effectance.

In conclusion to our study, we would propose that feeling 'challenged' by complex movies may be more important than solving their puzzles. In this light, the success of impossible puzzle films can be seen as the result of a narrative audacity that takes its viewers' 'empowered' positions into consideration; these films dare to enduringly confuse viewers, and boldly leave large chunks of the interpretive and analytic work up to their cognitive and interpretive competences. The narrative and psychological pressures on viewers to resolve dissonances and achieve comprehension make room for all kinds of creative, intellectual, analytic and interpretive skills and processes. This, especially in a mainstream context, is quite novel, but, as the trend proves, not inconceivable. Surely, our proposition presupposes viewers' resonance with this kind of cinema, and entails that varying degrees of competency (in terms of film and media literacy) will form a key factor in terms of their varying enjoyment of such highly complex films. Impossible puzzle films may in this sense be seen as the product of a specific moment in our media- and narrative-saturated time: films like these are able to cognitively challenge and intellectually intrigue a share of viewers who may have already grown accustomed to ever-increasing amounts and forms of mediacy, narratives and complication – whether in popular fiction or in culture at large. Thereby, cinematic versions of impossible puzzles seem to reflect the larger cultural shifts behind their emergence: not only do they appeal to a deep-seated human hunger to solve puzzles, they also embrace our life's complexities, providing enigmatic journeys into the impossible.

---

[14] Of course, formally complex stories are not the only types of fiction that play on this. For instance, in his 1991 model of mystery enjoyment, Dolf Zillmann argued for the role of competence in all mystery fiction, noting that 'the enjoyment of certain forms of mystery is motivated by self-esteem needs akin to competence' (Tamborini et al. 2010: 771). Although impossible puzzle films do not offer coherent and explicit answers that much of mystery fiction requires and provides (such as a clear answer to the 'whodunit' question in detective stories), they do seem to tease a similar viewing disposition.

References

Abbott, Porter H. 2008. 'Unreadable Minds and the Captive Reader', *Style* 42 (4): 448–67.

Alber, Jan 2009. 'Impossible Storyworlds – and What to Do With Them', *StoryWorlds: A Journal of Narrative Studies* 1, 79–96.

Alber, Jan 2010. 'Hypothetical Intentionalism: Cinematic Narration Reconsidered', in Jan Alber and Monika Fludernik (eds) *Postclassical Narratology: Approaches and Analyses*. Columbus, OH: Ohio State University Press, pp. 163–85.

Alber, Jan 2013a. 'Unnatural Narratology: Developments and Perspectives', *Germanisch-Romanische Monatsschrift* (special issue, ed. Ansgar Nünning) 63 (1): 69–84.

Alber, Jan 2013b. 'Unnatural Narrative Theory: The Systematic Study of Anti-Mimeticism', *Literature Compass* 10 (5): 449–60.

Alber, Jan 2016. *Unnatural Narrative: Impossible Worlds in Fiction and Drama*. Lincoln, NE: University of Nebraska Press.

Alber, Jan, Stefan Iversen, Henrik Skov Nielsen and Brian Richardson 2010. 'Unnatural Narratology, Unnatural Narratives: Beyond Mimetic Models', *Narrative* 18 (2): 113–31. Available online at http://projects.au.dk/fileadmin/www.nordisk.au.dk/forskning/centre__grupper_og_projekter/narrative_research_lab/unnatural_narratology/Alber__Iversen__Nielsen__Richardson_2010.pdf (retrieved 20 March 2016).

Anderson, Joseph D. 1998 [1996]. *The Reality of Illusion: An Ecological Approach to Cognitive Film Theory*. Carbondale, IL: Southern Illinois University Press.

Andrew, Geoff (n.d.). 'Blow-Up', *Time Out London*. Available online at www.timeout.com/london/film/blow-up–1966 (retrieved 20 March 2016).

Andrews, David 2010. 'Art Cinema as Institution, Redux: Art Houses, Film Festivals, and Film Studies', *Scope* 18 (October): 1–21. Available online at www.nottingham.ac.uk/scope/documents/2010/october–2010/andrews.pdf (retrieved 20 March 2016).

Ang, Ien 2011. 'Navigating Complexity: From Cultural Critique to Cultural Intelligence', *Continuum* 25 (6): 779–94.

Aristotle 1902 [350 BC]. *Poetics*. Translated by S. H. Butcher. London: Macmillan and Co.

Aronson, Elliot and Judson Mills 1959. 'The Effect of Severity of Initiation on Liking for a Group', *Journal of Abnormal and Social Psychology* 59 (2): 177–81.

Bal, Mieke 1977. *Narratologie. Essais sur la signification narrative dans quatre romans modernes*. Paris: Klincksieck.

Bal, Mieke 1997 [1985]. *Narratology. Introduction to the Theory of Narrative*. 2nd edition. Toronto: University of Toronto Press.

Bálint, Katalin, Frank Hakemulder, Ed Tan, Moniek Kuijpers and Miruna Doicaru (under review). 'A Wide Spectrum View of Literariness: An Interview Study on Responses to Deviation in Absorbing Literary and Cinematic Narratives', *Scientific Study of Literature*.

Baroni, Raphaël 2011. 'Tellability', in Peter Hühn et al. (eds) *the living handbook of narratology*, Hamburg: Hamburg University, revised in 2014. Available online at www.lhn.uni-hamburg.de/article/tellability (retrieved 20 March 2016).

Barratt, Daniel 2009. '"Twist Blindness": The Role of Primacy, Priming, Schemas, and Reconstructive Memory in a First-Time Viewing of *The Sixth Sense*', in Warren Buckland (ed.) *Puzzle Films: Complex Storytelling in Contemporary Cinema*. Oxford: Wiley-Blackwell, pp. 62–86.

Bartlett, Frederic Charles 1932. *Remembering: A Study in Experimental and Social Psychology*. New York: Cambridge University Press.

Bellour, Raymond 1987 [1984]. 'The Pensive Spectator', *Wide Angle* 9 (1): 6–10.

Ben Shaul, Nitzan 2012. *Cinema of Choice: Optional Thinking and Narrative Movies*. New York and Oxford: Berghahn.

Berg, Charles Ramírez 2006. 'Taxonomy of Alternative Plots in Recent Films: Classifying the "Tarantino Effect"', *Film Criticism* 31 (1–2, Fall/Winter): 5–61.

Bjornson, Richard 1981. 'Cognitive Mapping and the Understanding of Literature', *SubStance* 10 (1): 51–62.

Booth, Wayne C. 1983 [1961]. *The Rhetoric of Fiction*. Chicago, IL: Chicago Univerity Press.

Bordwell, David 1979. 'The Art Cinema as a Mode of Film Practice', *Film Criticism* 4 (1): 56–64.

Bordwell, David 1985. *Narration in the Fiction Film*. Madison, WI: University of Wisconsin Press.

Bordwell, David 1989. 'Historical Poetics of Cinema', in R. Barton Palmer (ed.) *The Cinematic Text: Methods and Approaches*. New York: AMS Press, pp. 369–98.

Bordwell, David 1991 [1989]. *Making Meaning. Inference and Rhetoric in the Interpretation of Cinema*. Cambridge, MA: Harvard University Press.

Bordwell, David 2002a. 'Film Futures', *SubStance* 31 (1): 88–104.

Bordwell, David 2002b. 'Intensified Continuity: Visual Style in Contemporary American Film', *Film Quarterly* 55 (3): 16–28.

Bordwell, David 2006. *The Way Hollywood Tells It*. Berkeley, CA and Los Angeles, CA: University of California Press.

Bordwell, David 2008. *Poetics of Cinema*. London and New York: Routledge.

Bordwell, David 2009. 'Cognitive Theory', in Paisley Livingstone and Carl Plantinga (eds) *The Routledge Companion to Philosophy and Film*. New York: Routledge, pp. 356–67.

Bordwell, David 2012. 'Tinker Tailor: A guide for the perplexed', *Observations on Film Art*. 23 January. Available online at www.davidbordwell.net/blog/2012/01/23/tinker-tailor-a-guide-for-the-perplexed (retrieved 20 March 2016).

Bordwell, David 2013. 'The Viewer's Share: Models of Mind in Explaining Film', in Arthur P. Shimamura (ed.) *Psychocinematics: Exploring Cognition at the Movies*. New York: Oxford University Press, pp. 29–52.

Bordwell, David, Janet Staiger and Kristin Thompson 1985. *The Classical Hollywood Cinema*. London: Routledge.

Bordwell, David and Kristin Thompson 2013. *Christopher Nolan. A Labyrinth of Linkages*. Madison, WI: Irvington Way Institute Press.

Borges, Jorge Luis 1964 [1960]. *Other Inquisitions 1937–1952*. Austin, TX: University of Texas Press.

Boyd, Brian 2009. *On the Origin of Stories. Evolution, Cognition, and Fiction*. Cambridge, MA: The Belknap Press of Harvard University Press.

Boyd, Brian, Joseph Carroll and Jonathan Gottschall 2010. 'Introduction', in Brian Boyd, Joseph Carroll and Jonathan Gottschall (eds) *Evolution, Literature, and Film*. New York: Columbia University Press, pp. 1–17.

Branigan, Edward 1992. *Narrative Comprehension and Film*. London and New York: Routledge.

Branigan, Edward 2002. 'Nearly True: Forking Plots, Forking Interpretations: A Response to David Bordwell's "Film Futures"', *SubStance* 31 (1): 105–14.

Branigan, Edward 2014. 'Butterfly Effects Upon a Spectator', in Warren Buckland (ed.) *Hollywood Puzzle Films*. London: Routledge, pp. 233–64.

Brown, William 2014. 'Complexity and Simplicity in *Inception* and *Five Dedicated to Ozu*', in Warren Buckland (ed.) *Hollywood Puzzle Films*. London: Routledge, pp. 125–39.

Bruner, Jerome Seymour 1987. *Actual Minds, Possible Worlds*. Cambridge, MA: Harvard University Press.

Bruner, Jerome Seymour 1991. 'The Narrative Construction of Reality', *Critical Inquiry* 18 (1): 1–21.

Buckland, Warren 2003. 'Orientation in Film Space: A Cognitive Semiotic Approach', *Recherches en communication* 19: 87–102.

Buckland, Warren (ed.) 2009a. *Puzzle Films: Complex Storytelling in Contemporary Cinema*. Oxford: Wiley-Blackwell.

Buckland, Warren 2009b. 'Introduction: Puzzle Plots', in Warren Buckland (ed.) *Puzzle Films: Complex Storytelling in Contemporary Cinema*. Oxford: Wiley-Blackwell, pp. 1–12.

Buckland, Warren 2009c. 'Making Sense of *Lost Highway*', in Warren Buckland (ed.) *Puzzle Films: Complex Storytelling in Contemporary Cinema*. Oxford: Wiley-Blackwell, pp. 42–61.

Buckland, Warren (ed.) 2014a. *Hollywood Puzzle Films*. London: Routledge.

Buckland, Warren 2014b. 'Introduction: Ambiguity, Ontological Pluralism, and Cognitive Dissonance in the Hollywood Puzzle Film', in Warren Buckland (ed.) *Hollywood Puzzle Films*. London: Routledge, pp. 1–14.

Buckland, Warren 2014c. '*Source Code*'s Video Game Logic', in Warren Buckland (ed.) *Hollywood Puzzle Films*. London: Routledge, pp. 185–97.

Cameron, Allan 2008. *Modular Narratives in Contemporary Cinema*. Basingstoke: Palgrave Macmillan.

Campora, Matthew 2014. *Subjective Realist Cinema: From Expressionism to* Inception. New York and Oxford: Berghahn.

Canjels, Rudmer 2011. *Distributing Silent Film Serials: Local Practices, Changing Forms, Cultural Transformation*. New York: Routledge.

Caracciolo, Marco 2013. 'Patterns of Cognitive Dissonance in Readers' Engagement with Characters', *Enthymema* VIII: 21–37.

Caracciolo, Marco 2014. *The Experientiality of Narrative: An Enactivist Approach*. Berlin: de Gruyter.

Carroll, Noël 1982. 'The Future of Allusion: Hollywood in the Seventies (and Beyond)', *October* 20 (Spring): 51–81.

Carroll, Noël 1988. *Mystifying Movies: Fads and Fallacies in Contemporary Film Theory*. New York: Columbia University Press.

Carroll, Noël 1998. 'Film Form: An Argument for a Functional Theory of Style in the Individual Film', *Style* 32 (3): 385–401.

Carroll, Noël 2009. 'Narrative Closure', in Paisley Livingstone and Carl Plantinga (eds) *The Routledge Companion to Philosophy and Film*. New York: Routledge, pp. 207–16.

Chandler, Daniel 1997. 'An Introduction to Genre Theory'. Available online at http://visual-memory.co.uk/daniel/Documents/intgenre/chandler_genre_theory.pdf (retrieved 20 March 2016).

Chatman, Seymour 1978. *Story and Discourse: Narrative Structure in Fiction and Film*. Ithaca, NY and London: Cornell University Press.

Chatman, Seymour 1990. *Coming to Terms: The Rhetoric of Narrative in Fiction and Film*. Ithaca, NY and London: Cornell University Press.

Chisholm, Brad 1991. 'Difficult Viewing: The Pleasures of Complex Screen Narratives', *Critical Studies in Mass Communication* 8 (4): 389–403.

Ciccoricco, David 2007. *Reading Network Fiction*. Tuscaloosa, AL: University of Alabama Press.

Cilliers, Paul 1998. *Complexity & Postmodernism: Understanding Complex Systems*. London: Routledge.

Coëgnarts, Maarten and Peter Kravanja 2014. 'A Study in Cinematic Subjectivity: Metaphors of Perception in Film', *Metaphor and the Social World* 4 (2): 149–73.

Coëgnarts, Maarten and Peter Kravanja (eds) 2015a. *Embodied Cognition and Cinema*. Leuven: Leuven University Press.

Coëgnarts, Maarten and Peter Kravanja 2015b. 'Embodied Cinematic Subjectivity: Metaphorical and Metonymical Modes of Character Perception in Film', in Maarten Coëgnarts and Peter Kravanja (eds) *Embodied Cognition and Cinema*. Leuven: Leuven University Press, pp. 221–44.

Coëgnarts, Maarten and Peter Kravanja 2015c. 'With the Past *in Front of* the Character: Evidence for Spatial-Temporal Metaphors in Cinema', *Metaphor and Symbol* 30 (3): 218–39.

Coëgnarts, Maarten, Miklós Kiss, Peter Kravanja and Steven Willemsen 2016. 'Seeing Yourself in the Past: The Role of Situational (Dis)continuity and Conceptual Metaphor in the Understanding of Complex Cases of Character Perception', *Projections* 10 (1): 114–38.

Coleridge, Samuel Taylor 1975 [1817]. *Biographia Literaria*. London: J. M. Dent.

Cooper, Joel 2007. *Cognitive Dissonance. Fifty Years of Classic Theory*. Los Angeles: Sage.

Cooper, Joel and Russell H. Fazio 1984. 'A New Look at Dissonance Theory', in Leonard Berkowitz (ed.) *Advances in Experimental Social Psychology*, vol. 17. Orlando, FL: Academic Press, pp. 229–64.

Cowan, Michael 2010. 'Moving Picture Puzzles: Training Urban Perception in the Weimar "Rebus Films"', *Screen* 51 (3): 197–218.

Culler, Jonathan 1975. *Structuralist Poetics. Structuralism, Linguistics and the Study of Literature*. London: Routledge and Kegan Paul.

Cuonzo, Margaret 2014. *Paradox*. Cambridge, MA: MIT Press.

Currie, Gregory 1995. 'Unreliability Refigured: Narrative in Literature and Film', *The Journal of Aesthetics and Art Criticism* 53 (1/Winter): 19–29.

Currie, Gregory 2004. *Arts and Minds*. Oxford: Clarendon Press.

Danesi, Marcel 2002. *The Puzzle Instinct: The Meaning of Puzzles in Human Life*. Bloomington, IN: Indiana University Press.

Davies, Jim 2014. *Riveted: The Science of Why Jokes Make Us Laugh, Movies Make Us Cry, and Religion Makes Us Feel One With the Universe*. New York: Palgrave Macmillan.

Deci, Edward L. 1975. *Intrinsic Motivation*. New York: Plenum Press.

Deci, Edward L. and Richard M. Ryan 1985. *Intrinsic Motivation and Self-Determination in Human Behaviour*. New York: Plenum.

Deci, Edward L. and Richard M. Ryan 2000. 'The "What" and "Why" of Goal Pursuits: Human Needs and the Self-Determination of Behavior', *Psychological Inquiry* 11 (4): 227–68.

Deren, Maya 1960. 'Cinematography: The Creative Use of Reality', *Daedalus* 89 (1): 150–67; republished in P. Adams Sitney (ed.) 1978. *The Avant-Garde Film: A Reader of Theory and Criticism*. New York: Anthology Film Archives, pp. 60–73.

Diffrient, David Scott 2006. 'Alternative Futures, Contradictory Pasts: Forking Paths and Cubist Narratives in Contemporary Film', *Screening the Past*, 20. Available online at http://tlweb.latrobe.edu.au/humanities/screeningthepast/20/alternate-futures.html (retrieved 20 March 2016).

Doležel, Lubomír 1976. 'Extensional and Intensional Narrative Worlds', *Poetics* 8: 193–212.

Doležel, Lubomír 1988. 'Mimesis and Possible Worlds', *Poetics Today* 9: 475–96.

Doležel, Lubomír 1998. *Heterocosmica: Fiction and Possible Worlds*. Baltimore, MD: Johns Hopkins University Press.

Donald, Merlin 1991. *Origins of the Modern Mind: Three Stages in the Evolution of Culture and Cognition*. Cambridge, MA: Harvard University Press.

Donald, Merlin 2006. 'Art and Cognitive Evolution', in Mark Turner (ed.) *The Artful Mind. Cognitive Science and the Riddle of Human Creativity*. New York: Oxford University Press, pp. 3–20.

Dulac, Germaine 1993 [1926]. 'Aesthetics, Obstacles, Integral Cinégraphie', in Richard Abel (ed.) *French Film Theory and Criticism*. Princeton, NJ: Princeton University Press, pp. 389–97.

Dzialo, Chris 2009. '"Frustrated Time" Narration: The Screenplays of Charlie Kaufman', in Warren Buckland (ed.) *Puzzle Films: Complex Storytelling in Contemporary Cinema*. Oxford: Wiley-Blackwell, pp. 107–28.

Ebert, Roger 1997. 'The Big Sleep', *RogerEbert.com*, 22 June. Available online at www.rogerebert. com/reviews/great-movie-the-big-sleep-1946 (retrieved 20 March 2016).

Ebert, Roger 1998. 'Blow-Up', *RogerEbert.com*, 8 November. Available online at www.rogerebert. com/reviews/great-movie-blow-up–1966 (retrieved 20 March 2016).

Ebert, Roger 2005. 'Syriana', *RogerEbert.com*, 8 December 8. Available online at www.rogerebert. com/reviews/syriana–2005 (retrieved 20 March 2016).

Eco, Umberto 1979. *The Role of the Reader: Explorations in the Semiotics of Texts*. Bloomington, IN: Indiana University Press.

Eco, Umberto 1994 [1990]. *The Limits of Interpretation*. Bloomington, IN: Indiana University Press.

Eig, Jonathan 2003. 'A Beautiful Mind(Fuck): Hollywood Structures of Identity', *Jump Cut*, 46. Available online at www.ejumpcut.org/archive/jc46.2003/eig.mindfilms/index.html (retrieved 20 March 2016).

Elsaesser, Thomas 2009. 'The Mind-Game Film', in Warren Buckland (ed.) *Puzzle Films: Complex Storytelling in Contemporary Cinema*. Oxford: Wiley-Blackwell, pp. 13–41.

Elsaesser, Thomas 2011. 'James Cameron's *Avatar*: Access for All', *New Review of Film and Television Studies* 9 (3): 247–64.

Elsaesser, Thomas and Warren Buckland 2002. *Studying Contemporary American Film*. London: Arnold.

Everett, Wendy 2005. 'Fractal Films and the Architecture of Complexity', *Studies in European Cinema* 2 (3): 159–71.

Eysenck, Michael W. and Mark Keane 2005. *Cognitive Psychology. A Student's Handbook*. 5th edition. Hove: Psychology Press.

Falk, Ruma 1994. 'Infinity: A Cognitive Challenge', *Theory & Psychology* 4 (1): 35–60.

Fauconnier, Gilles and Mark Turner 2002. *The Way We Think: Conceptual Blending and the Mind's Hidden Complexities*. New York: Basic Books.

Festinger, Leon 1957. *A Theory of Cognitive Dissonance*. Evanston, IL: Row.

Festinger, Leon, Henry W. Riecken and Stanley Schachter 1956. *When Prophecy Fails: A Social and Psychological Study of a Modern Group that Predicted the Destruction of the World*. New York: Harper and Row.

Fludernik, Monika 1996. *Towards a 'Natural' Narratology*. London and New York: Routledge.

Forceville, Charles and Marloes Jeulink 2011. 'The Flesh and Blood of Embodied Understanding: The Source-Path-Goal Schema in Animation Film', *Pragmatics & Cognition* 19 (1): 37–59.

Fusar-Poli, Paolo, Oliver Howes, Lucia Valmaggia and Philip McGuire 2008. '"Truman Signs" and Vulnerability to Psychosis', *The British Journal of Psychiatry* 193: 167–9.

Gallese, Vittorio 2009. 'Mirror Neurons, Embodied Simulation, and the Neural Basis of Social Identification', *Psychoanalytic Dialogues* 19: 519–36.

Gallese, Vittorio and Michele Guerra 2012. 'Embodying Movies: Embodied Simulation and Film Studies', in Patrícia Silveirinha and Castello Branco (eds) *Cinema: Journal of Philosophy and the Moving Image. No.3. Embodiment and the Body*, pp. 183–210.

Gallese, Vittorio and George Lakoff 2005. 'The Brain's Concepts: The Role of the Sensory-Motor System in Conceptual Knowledge', *Cognitive Neuropsychology* 21 (0): 1–25.

Gallese, Vittorio, Luciano Fadiga, Leonardo Fogassi and Giacomo Rizzolatti 1996. 'Action Recognition in the Premotor Cortex', *Brain*, 119: 593–609.

Genette, Gérard 1980 [1972]. *Narrative Discourse*. Ithaca, NY: Cornell University Press.

Gentner, Dedre, Mutsumi Imai and Lera Boroditsky. 2002. 'As Time Goes By: Evidence For Two Systems In Processing Space > Time Metaphors', *Language and Cognitive Processes* 17 (5): 537–65.

Gerard, Harold B. and Grover C. Mathewson 1966. 'The Effects of Severity of Initiation on Liking for a Group: A Replication', *Journal of Experimental Social Psychology* 2 (3): 278–87.

Ghislotti, Stefano 2009. 'Narrative Comprehension Made Difficult: Film Form and Mnemonic Devices in *Memento*', in Warren Buckland (ed.) *Puzzle Films: Complex Storytelling in Contemporary Cinema*. Oxford: Wiley-Blackwell, pp. 87–106.

Ghosal, Torsa 2015. 'Unprojections, or, World Under Erasure in Contemporary Hollywood Cinema', *Media-N, Journal of the New Media Caucus* 11 (1): 75–81. Available online at http://median.newmediacaucus.org/the_aesthetics_of_erasure/unprojections-or-worlds-under-erasure-in-contemporary-hollywood-cinema (retrieved 20 March 2016).

Gilbey, Ryan 2015. 'Should Critics See Films More Than Once?', *The Guardian*, 29 January. Available online at www.theguardian.com/film/filmblog/2015/jan/29/should-critics-see-films-more-than-once-inherent-vice (retrieved 20 March 2016).

Gillian, Jennifer 2010. *Television and New Media: Must-Click TV*. New York: Routledge.

Gladwell, Malcolm 2005. 'Brain Candy: Is Pop Culture Dumbing Us Down or Smartening Us Up?', *The New Yorker*, 16 May 16. Available online at www.newyorker.com/archive/2005/05/16/050516crbo_books (retrieved 20 March 2016).

Goffman, Erving 1974. *Frame Analysis: An Essay on the Organization of Experience*. Cambridge, MA: Harvard University Press.

Gottschalk, Simon 1995. 'Videology: Video-Games as Postmodern Sites/Sights of Ideological Reproduction', *Symbolic Interaction* 18 (1): 1–18.

Greenberg, Clement 1940. 'Towards a Newer Laocoon', *Partisan Review* 7 (July–August): 296–310.

Greimas, Algirdas Julien 1966. *Sémantique structurale: recherche de méthode*. Paris: Larousse.

Grodal, Torben 2002 [1997]. *Moving Pictures. A New Theory of Film Genres, Feelings, and Cognition*. New York: Oxford University Press.

Grodal, Torben 2007. 'Bio-Culturalism: Evolution and Film', in Joseph D. Anderson and Barbara Fisher Anderson (eds) *Narration and Spectatorship in Moving Images*. Newcastle: Cambridge Scholars Publishing, pp. 16–28.

Grodal, Torben 2009. *Embodied Visions. Evolution, Emotion, Culture, and Film*. New York: Oxford University Press.

Hanks, William F. 2010 [2005]. 'Deixis', in *Routledge Encyclopedia of Narrative Theory*, ed. David Herman, Manfred Jahn and Marie-Laure Ryan, London and New York: Routledge, pp. 99–100.

Hansen, Per Krogh 2007. 'Reconsidering the Unreliable Narrator', *Semiotica* 165 (1/4): 227–46.

Harris, Neil 1973. *Humbug: The Art of P.T. Barnum*. Chicago, IL: University of Chicago Press.

Hawking, Stephen 1988. *A Brief History of Time: From the Big Bang to Black Holes*. New York: Bantam.

Hayles, N. Katherine and Nicholas Gessler 2004. 'The Slipstream of Mixed Reality: Unstable Ontologies and Semiotic Markers in *The Thirteenth Floor*, *Dark City*, and *Mulholland Drive*', *PMLA: Publications of the Modern Language Association of America* 119 (3): 482–99.

Herman, David 2002. *Story Logic. Problems and Possibilities of Narrative*. Lincoln, NE: University of Nebraska Press.

Herman, David 2003. 'Stories as a Tool for Thinking', in David Herman (ed.) *Narrative Theory and the Cognitive Sciences*. Stanford, CA: CSLI, pp. 163–192.

Holland, Norman N. 1963. 'The Puzzling Movies: Their Appeal', *The Journal of the Society of Cinematologists* 3: 17–28.

Hughes, Sarah 2015. 'Woody Allen, House of Cards . . . What's Next for the Television Revolution?', *The Guardian*, 18 January. Available online at www.theguardian.com/media/2015/jan/18/woody-allen-television-revolution-amazon-internet (retrieved 20 March 2016).

Hutto, Daniel D. and Patrick McGivern 2014. 'How Embodied Is Cognition?', unpublished paper. Available online at www.academia.edu/9614435/How_Embodied_Is_Cognition (retrieved 20 March 2016).

Jahn, Manfred 2003. 'A Guide to Narratological Film Analysis', May 2015. Available online at www.uni-koeln.de/~ame02/pppf.htm (retrieved 20 March 2016).

Johnson, Mark 1990 [1987]. *The Body in the Mind. The Bodily Basis of Meaning, Imagination, and Reason*. Chicago, IL and London: University of Chicago Press.

Johnson, Steven 2006 [2005]. *Everything Bad is Good for You*. London: Penguin Books.

Johnson-Laird, Philip N. 1983. *Mental Models: Towards a Cognitive Science of Language, Inference, and Consciousness*. Cambridge: Cambridge University Press.

Juul, Jesper 2013. *The Art of Failure. An Essay on the Pain of Playing Video Games*. Cambridge, MA: MIT Press.

Kael, Pauline 2010. 'Tourist in the City of Youth', *NewRepublic.com*, 23 September. Available online at https://newrepublic.com/article/77842/tourist-in-the-city-youth (retrieved 20 March 2016).

Kinder, Marsha 2002. 'Hotspots, Avatars, and Narrative Fields Forever – Buñuel's Legacy for New Digital Media and Interactive Database Narrative', *Film Quarterly* 55 (4): 2–15.

Kiss, Miklós 2003. '"Mintha beakadna Isten bakelitlemeze" – Időutazásos filmek narratív vizsgálata', *Metropolis* (2): 28–38. Republished In. H. Nagy Péter (ed.) 2008. *Idegen (látvány)-világok*. Dunajská Streda: Lilium Aurum, pp. 51–70.

Kiss, Miklós 2010. 'The Perception of Reality as Deformed Realism', in Annie van den Oever (ed.) *Key Debates: Ostrannenie*. Amsterdam: Amsterdam University Press, pp. 165–72.

Kiss, Miklós 2012. 'Narrative Metalepsis as Diegetic Concept in Christopher Nolan's *Inception*', *Acta Film and Media Studies* (5): 35–54.

Kiss, Miklós 2013. 'Navigation in Complex Films: Real-life Embodied Experiences Underlying Narrative Categorisation', in Julia Eckel, Bernd Leiendecker, Daniela Olek and Christine Piepiorka (eds) *(Dis)Orienting Media and Narrative Mazes*. Bielefeld: Transcript, pp. 237–56.

Kiss, Miklós 2015. 'Film Narrative As Embodiment', in Maarten Coëgnarts and Peter Kravanja (eds) *Embodied Cognition and Cinema*. Leuven: Leuven University Press, pp. 43–61.

Klecker, Cornelia 2011. 'Chronology, Causality . . . Confusion: When Avant-Garde Goes Classic', *Journal of Film and Video* 63 (2): 11–27.

Klecker, Cornelia 2013. 'Mind-Tricking Narratives: Between Classical and Art-Cinema Narration', *Poetics Today* 34 (1–2): 119–46.

Klein, Paul L. 1971. 'Why You Watch What You Watch When You Watch', *TV Guide*, 24 July, 6–9.

Klinger, Barbara 2006. *Beyond the Multiplex: Cinema, New Technologies, and the Home*. Berkeley, CA and Los Angeles, CA: University of California Press.

Korthals Altes, Liesbeth 2014. *Ethos and Narrative Interpretation: The Negotiation of Values in Fiction*. Lincoln, NE: University of Nebraska Press.

Kovács, András Bálint 2007. *Screening Modernism. European Art Cinema, 1950–1980*. Chicago, IL: University of Chicago Press.

Laass, Eva 2008. *Broken Taboos, Subjective Truths: Forms and Functions of Unreliable Narration in Contemporary American Cinema. A Contribution to Film Narratology*. Trier: WVT.

Lakoff, George 1987. *Women, Fire, and Dangerous Things*. Chicago, IL and London: University of Chicago Press.

Lakoff, George and Mark Johnson 1999. *Philosophy in the Flesh: The Embodied Mind and its Challenge to Western Thought*. New York: Basic Books.

Lakoff, George and Mark Johnson 2003 [1980]. *Metaphors We Live By*. Chicago, IL: University of Chicago Press.

Lavik, Erlend 2006. 'Narrative Structure in *The Sixth Sense*: A New Twist in "Twist Movies"?', *The Velvet Light Trap* 58 (Fall): 55–64.

Leiendecker, Bernd 2013. 'Leaving the Narrative Maze. The Plot Twist as a Device of Re-orientation', in Julia Eckel, Bernd Leiendecker, Daniela Olek and Christine Piepiorka (eds) *(Dis)Orienting Media and Narrative Mazes*. Bielefeld: Transcript, pp. 257–72.

Levin, Daniel T. and Caryn Wang 2009. 'Spatial Representation in Cognitive Science and Film', *Projections* 3 (1): 24–52.

Lewis, Hilary 2014. '*Enemy* Director on Jake Gyllenhaal's Identical Characters: "It's Maybe Two Sides of the Same Persona"' (interview with Denis Villeneuve), *The Hollywood Reporter* 13 March. Available online at www.hollywoodreporter.com/news/enemy-director-jake-gyllenhaals-identical–688439 (retrieved 20 March 2016).

Lijster, Thijs 2014. 'Watching the Detectives', *De Groene Amsterdammer*, 27 May. Available online at www.groene.nl/artikel/watching-the-detectives (retrieved 20 March 2016).

Lim, Dennis 2015. 'Lim on Lynch: Mulholland Dr', *The Criterion Collection* 3 November. Available online at www.criterion.com/current/posts/3776-lim-on-lynch-mulholland-dr (retrieved 20 March 2016).

Lincoln, Kevin 2014. 'How to Make a Convincing Sci-Fi Movie on a Tight Budget?' (interview with James Ward Byrkit), *Pacific Standard* 30 July. Available online at www.psmag.com/books-and-culture/make-convincing-sci-fi-movie-tight-budget–87062 (retrieved 20 March 2016).

Lotz, Amanda D. 2007. *The Television Will Be Revolutionized*. New York: New York University Press.

Mackie, John Leslie 1973. *Truth, Probability, and Paradox*. New York: Oxford University Press.

Magliano, Joseph P., Jason Miller and Rolf A. Zwaan. 2001. 'Indexing Space and Time in Film Understanding', *Applied Cognitive Psychology* 15 (5): 533–45.

Mandler, Jean M. 1984. *Stories, Scripts and Scenes: Aspects of Schema Theory*. Hillsdale, NJ: Lawrence Erlbaum Associates.

Manovich, Lev 2001. *The Language of New Media*. Cambridge, MA: MIT Press.

Maor, Eli 1987. *To Infinity and Beyond. A Cultural History of the Infinite*. Princeton, NJ: Princeton University Press.

McHale, Brian 1984. *Postmodernist Fiction*. London and New York: Routledge.

McLuhan, Marshall 1964. *Understanding Media: The Extensions of Man*. New York: McGraw-Hill.

Meister, Jan Christoph 2003. 'The *Metalepticon*: A Computational Approach to Metalepsis'. Available online at http://publikationen.ub.uni-frankfurt.de/files/10444/MEISTER_Stack_overflow_toward_a_co.pdf (retrieved 20 March 2016).

Menary, Richard 2008. 'Embodied Narratives', *Journal of Consciousness Studies* 15 (6): 63–84.

Minsky, Marvin 1975. 'A Framework for Representing Knowledge', in Patrick Winston (ed.) *The Psychology of Computer Vision*. New York: McGraw-Hill, pp. 19–91.

Mittell, Jason 2006. 'Narrative Complexity in Contemporary American Television', *The Velvet Light Trap* 58: 29–40.

Mittell, Jason 2009. '*Lost* in a Great Story: Evaluation in Narrative Television (and Television Studies)', in Roberta Pearson (ed.) *Reading Lost*. London and New York: I. B. Tauris, pp. 119–28.

Mittell, Jason 2010. *Television and American Culture*. New York: Oxford University Press.

Mittell, Jason 2013. 'Haunted by Seriality: The Formal Uncanny of *Mulholland Drive*', 4 January. Available online at http://justtv.wordpress.com/2013/01/03/haunted-by-seriality-the-formal-uncanny-of-mulholland-drive (retrieved 20 March 2016).

Mittell, Jason 2015. *Complex TV. The Poetics of Contemporary Television Storytelling*. New York: New York University Press.

Morrow, Daniel G., Gordon H. Bower and Steven L. Greenspan 1989. 'Updating Situation Models during Narrative Comprehension', *Journal of Memory and Language* 28 (3): 292–312.

Mulvey, Laura 1975. 'Visual Pleasure and Narrative Cinema', *Screen*, 16 (3): 6–18.

Mulvey, Laura 2006. *Death 24x a Second. Stillness and the Moving Image*. London: Reaktion Books.

Murray, Janet H. 1997. *Hamlet on the Holodeck: The Future of Narrative in Cyberspace*. New York: The Free Press.

Nannicelli, Ted and Paul Taberham 2014. 'Introduction: Contemporary Cognitive Media Theory', in Ted Nannicelli and Paul Taberham (eds) *Cognitive Media Theory*. London: Routledge, pp. 1–23.

Neale, Steve 1981. 'Art Cinema as Institution', *Screen* 22 (1): 11–40.

Nielsen, Henrik Skov 2004. 'The Impersonal Voice in First-Person Narrative Fiction', *Narrative* 12 (2): 133–50.

Nielsen, Henrik Skov 2013. 'Naturalizing and Un-naturalizing Reading Strategies: Focalization Revisited', in Jan Alber, Henrik Skov Nielsen and Brian Richardson (eds) *A Poetics of Unnatural Narrative*. Columbus, OH: Ohio State University Press, pp. 67–93.

Nolan, Christopher 2010. *Inception: The Shooting Script*. San Rafael, CA: Insight Editions.

Nünning, Ansgar 1997. '"But why will you say that I am mad?" On the Theory, History, and Signals of Unreliable Narration in British Fiction', *Arbeiten aus Anglistik und Amerikanistik* 22 (1): 83–105.

Nünning, Ansgar 2005. 'Reconceptualizing Unreliable Narration. Synthesizing Cognitive and Rhetorical Approaches', in James Phelan and Peter J. Rabinowitz (eds) *A Companion to Narrative Theory*. Malden, MA: Blackwell, pp. 89–107.

Oliver, Mary Beth and Arthur A. Raney 2011. 'Entertainment as Pleasurable and Meaningful: Identifying Hedonic and Eudaimonic Motivations for Entertainment Consumption', *Journal of Communication* 61 (5): 984–1004.

Olson, Greta 2003. 'Reconsidering Unreliability: Fallible and Untrustworthy Narrators', *Narrative* 11 (1/January): 93–109.

Oxford Advanced Learner's Dictionary 2000. Oxford: Oxford University Press.

Panek, Elliot 2006. 'The Poet and the Detective: Defining the Psychological Puzzle Film', *Film Criticism* 31 (1–2): 62–88.

Pasolini, Pier Paolo 1966. 'The Cinema of Poetry', *Cahiers du Cinéma in English* (6/December): 34–43.

Patrick, Brian D. 2008. 'Metalepsis and Paradoxical Narration in *Don Quixote*: A Reconsideration', *Letras Hispanus* 5 (2): 116–32.

Pehla, Karen 1991. 'Joe May und seine Detektive: Der Serienfilm als Kinoerlebnis', in Hans-Michael Bock and Claudia Lenssen (eds) *Joe May: Regisseur und Produzent*. München: edition text + kritik, pp. 61–72.

Penrose, Lionel S. and Robert Penrose 1958. 'Impossible Objects: A Special Type of Visual Illusion', *British Journal of Psychology* 49 (1): 31–3.

Pier, John 2011. 'Metalepsis', *The Living Handbook of Narratology*. Available online at http://wikis.sub.uni-hamburg.de/lhn/index.php/Metalepsis (retrieved 20 March 2016).

Plantinga, Carl 2009. 'Emotion and Affect', in Paisley Livingstone and Carl Plantinga (eds) *The Routledge Companion to Philosophy and Film*. New York: Routledge, pp. 86–96.

Poulaki, Maria 2011. *Before Or Beyond Narrative? Towards a Complex Systems Theory of Contemporary Films*. Amsterdam: Rozenberg Publishers.

Poulaki, Maria 2014. 'Puzzled Hollywood and the Return of Complex Films', in Warren Buckland (ed.) *Hollywood Puzzle Films*. London: Routledge, pp. 35–54.

Prince, Gerald 1999. 'Revisiting Narrativity', in Walter Grünzweig and Andreas Solbach (eds) *Grenzüberschreitungen: Narratologie im Kontext / Transcending Boundaries: Narratology in Context*. Tübingen: Narr, pp. 43–51.

Radvansky, Gabriel A. and Jeffrey M. Zacks 2011. 'Event Perception', *WIREs Cogni Sci* 2: 608–20.

Rapaport, William J., Erwin M. Segal, Stuart C. Shapiro, David A. Zubin, Gail A. Bruder, Judith F. Duchan, Michael J. Almeida, Joyce H. Daniels, Mary Galbraith, Janyce M. Wiebe and Albert Hanyong Yuhan n.d. 'Deictic Centers and the Cognitive Structure of Narrative Comprehension'. Available online at www.cse.buffalo.edu/~rapaport/Papers/dc.pdf (retrieved 20 March 2016).

Rescher, Nicholas 2001. *Paradoxes: Their Roots, Range, and Resolution*. Chicago, IL and La Salle, IL: Open Court.

Richardson, Brian 2001. 'Denarration in Fiction: Erasing the Story in Beckett and Others', *Narrative* 9 (2): 168–75.

Richardson, Brian 2005. 'Denarration', in David Herman, Manfred Jahn and Marie-Laure Ryan (eds) *Routledge Encyclopedia of Narrative Theory*. London and New York: Routledge, pp. 100–1.

Richardson, Brian 2011. 'What is Unnatural Narrative Theory?', in Jan Alber and Rüdiger Heinze (eds) *Unnatural Narratives, Unnatural Narratology*. Berlin: de Gruyter, pp. 23–40.

Rizzolatti, Giacomo, Luciano Fadiga, Vittorio Gallese and Leonardo Fogassi 1996. 'Premotor Cortex and the Recognition of Motor Actions', *Cognitive Brain Research* 3: 131–41.

Rochat, Philippe 2004 [2001]. *The Infant's World*. Cambridge, MA: Harvard University Press.

Ronen, Ruth 1994. *Possible Worlds in Literary Theory*. Cambridge: Cambridge University Press.

Ronen, Ruth 1996. 'Are Fictional Worlds Possible?', in Calin-Andrei Mihailescu and Walid Hamarneh (eds) *Fiction Updated: Theories of Fictionality, Narratology and Poetics*. Toronto: University of Toronto Press, pp. 21–9.

Ros, Vincent and Miklós Kiss (under review). 'Disrupted PECMA Flows: A Cognitive Approach to the Affect of Narrative Complexity in Film'.

Rumelhart, David 1975. 'Notes on a Schema for Stories', in Daniel Gureasko Bobrow and Allan Collins (eds) *Representation and Understanding: Studies in Cognitive Science*. New York: Academic Press, pp. 211–36.

Ryan, Marie-Laure 1991. 'Possible Worlds and Accessibility Relations: A Semantic Typology of Fiction', *Poetics Today* 12 (3): 553–76.

Ryan, Marie-Laure 1992. 'Possible Worlds in Recent Literary Theory', *Style* 26 (4): 528–54.

Ryan, Marie-Laure 2003. 'Cognitive Maps and the Construction of Narrative Space', in David Herman (ed.) *Narrative Theory and the Cognitive Sciences*. Stanford, CA: CSLI, pp. 214–42.

Ryan, Marie-Laure 2005. 'Possible-Worlds Theory', in David Herman, Manfred Jahn and Marie-Laure Ryan (eds) *Routledge Encyclopedia of Narrative Theory*. London and New York: Routledge, pp. 446–50.

Ryan, Marie-Laure 2006a. *Avatars of Story*. Minneapolis, MN: University of Minneapolis Press.

Ryan, Marie-Laure 2006b. 'From Parallel Universes to Possible Worlds: Ontological Pluralism in Physics, Narratology, and Narrative', *Poetics Today* 27 (4): 633–74.

Ryan, Marie-Laure 2009. 'Cheap Plot Tricks, Plot Holes, and Narrative Design', *Narrative* 17 (1): 56–75.

Ryan, Marie-Laure 2010a. 'Narratology and Cognitive Science: A Problematic Relation', *Style* 44 (4): 469–95.

Ryan, Marie-Laure 2010b [2005]. 'Tellability', in David Herman, Manfred Jahn and Marie-Laure Ryan (eds) *Routledge Encyclopedia of Narrative Theory*. New York and London: Routledge, pp. 589–91.

Ryan, Marie-Laure 2013. 'Impossible Worlds and Aesthetic Illusion', in Walter Bernhard and Werner Wolf (eds) *Aesthetic Illusion in Literature and Other Media*. Amsterdam and New York: Rodopi, 131–48.

Ryan, Richard M. and Edward L. Deci 2001. 'On Happiness and Human Potentials: A Review of Research on Hedonic and Eudaimonic Well-Being', *Annual Review of Psychology*, ed. Susan T. Fiske, vol. 52. Palo Alto, CA: Annual Reviews, pp. 141–66.

Sainsbury, Mark R. 2009 [1995]. *Paradoxes*. 3rd edition. Cambridge: Cambridge University Press.

Schank, Roger C. and Robert P. Abelson 1977. *Scripts, Plans, Goals, and Understanding: An Inquiry into Human Knowledge Structures*. Hillsdale, NJ.: Lawrence Erlbaum Associates.

Schattschneider, Doris 2005 [1990]. *M.C. Escher. Visions of Symmetry*. London: Thames and Hudson.

Schlickers, Sabine 2009. 'Focalization, Ocularization and Auricularization in Film and Literature', in Peter Hühn, Wolf Schmid and Jörg Schönert (eds) *Point of View, Perspective, and Focalization: Modeling Mediation in Narrative*. Berlin: de Gruyter, pp. 243–58.

Sebeok, Thomas A. 1994. *An Introduction to Semiotics*. London: Pinter Publishers.

Shen, Dan 2013. 'Unreliability', *The Living Handbook of Narratology*, Available online at www.lhn.uni-hamburg.de/article/unreliability (retrieved 20 March 2016).

Shirky, Clay 2010. *Cognitive Surplus: Creativity and Generosity in a Connected Age*. London: Penguin Books.

Simons, Jan 2008. 'Complex Narratives', *New Review of Film and Television Studies* 6 (2): 111–26.

Slors, Marc 1998. 'Two Concepts of Psychological Continuity', *Philosophical Explorations* 1 (1): 61–80.

Smith, Gavin 1999. 'Inside Out. Gavin Smith Goes One-On-One with David Fincher', *Film Comment* 35 (5): 58–68.

Smith, Murray 2003. 'A Reasonable Guide to Horrible Noise (Part 2): Listening to *Lost Highway*', in Lennard Højberg and Peter Schepelern (eds) *Film Style and Story: A Tribute to Torben Grodal*. Copenhagen: Museum Tusculanum Press, pp. 153–70.

Smith, Murray 2011. 'On the Twofoldness of Character', *New Literary History* 42 (2): 277–94.

Sontag, Susan 1967 [1964]. *Against Interpretation*. London: Eyre & Spottiswoode.

Spolsky, Ellen 2007. *Word vs. Image: Cognitive Hunger in Shakespeare's England*. New York: Palgrave Macmillan.

Staiger, Janet 2006. 'Complex Narratives, An Introduction', *Film Criticism* 31 (1–2): 2–4.

Steele, Claude M., Steven J. Spencer and Michael Lynch 1993. 'Self-Image Resilience and Dissonance: The Role of Affirmational Resources', *Journal of Personality and Social Psychology* 64 (6): 885–96.

Sterling, Bruce 1989. 'Slipstream', *SF Eye* 5 (July). Available online at https://w2.eff.org/Misc/Publications/Bruce_Sterling/Catscan_columns/catscan.05 (retrieved 20 March 2016).

Sternberg, Meir 1978. *Expositional Modes and Temporal Ordering in Fiction*. Baltimore, MD: Johns Hopkins University Press.

Sternberg, Meir 1990. 'Telling in Time (I): Chronology and Narrative Theory', *Poetics Today* 11 (4): 901–48.

Sternberg, Meir 1992. 'Telling in Time (II): Chronology, Teleology, Narrativity', *Poetics Today* 13 (3): 463–541.

Stockwell, Peter 2002. *Cognitive Poetics: An Introduction*. London: Routledge.

Stone, Jeff 1999. 'What Exactly have I Done? The Role of Self-Attribute Accessibility in Dissonance', in Eddie Harmon-Jones and Judson Mills (eds) *Cognitive Dissonance: Progress on a Pivotal Theory in Social Psychology*, Washington, DC: American Psychological Association, pp. 175–201.

Tamborini, Ron, Nicholas David Bowman, Allison Eden, Matthew Grizzard and Ashley Organ 2010. 'Defining Media Enjoyment as the Satisfaction of Intrinsic Needs', *Journal of Communication* 60 (4): 758–77.

Tarantino, Quentin 1994. 'Interview, on The Charlie Rose Show', 14 October, transcript. Available online at www.industrycentral.net/director_interviews/QT02.HTM (retrieved 20 March 2016).

Thanouli, Eleftheria 2006. 'Post-Classical Narration: A New Paradigm in Contemporary Cinema', *New Review of Film and Television Studies* 4 (3): 183–96.

Thanouli, Eleftheria 2009a. *Post-Classical Cinema: An International Poetics of Film Narration*. London: Wallflower.

Thanouli, Eleftheria 2009b. 'Looking for Access in Narrative Complexity. The New and the Old in *Oldboy*', in Warren Buckland (ed.) *Puzzle Films: Complex Storytelling in Contemporary Cinema*. Oxford: Wiley-Blackwell, pp. 217–32.

Thanouli, Eleftheria 2009c. 'Art Cinema Narration: Breaking Down a Wayward Paradigm', *Scope* 14 (June): 1–14. Available online at www.nottingham.ac.uk/scope/documents/2009/june–2009/thanouli.pdf (retrieved 20 March 2016).

Thompson, Evan 2010. *Mind in Life: Biology, Phenomenology, and the Sciences of Mind*. Cambridge, MA: Harvard University Press.

Thompson, Kristin 1977. 'The Concept of Cinematic Excess', *Ciné-Tract* 1 (2): 54–64.

Thomson, David 2010 [1997]. *The Big Sleep*. London: British Film Institute.

Todorov, Tzvetan 1975. *The Fantastic: A Structural Approach to a Literary Genre*. New York: Cornell University Press.

Truffaut, François 1976 [1954]. 'A Certain Tendency of the French Cinema', in Bill Nichols (ed.) *Movies and Methods: an anthology. Vol. 1*. Berkeley, CA: University of California Press, pp. 224–37.

Tsur, Reuven 1975. 'Two Critical Attitudes: Quest for Certitude and Negative Capability', *College English* 36 (7): 776–88.

Tsur, Reuven 2008. *Toward a Theory of Cognitive Poetics*. Brighton and Portland, ME: Sussex Academic Press.

Turner, Mark 1996. *The Literary Mind*. Oxford and New York: Oxford University Press.

Tykwer, Tom 1999. *Cours, Lola, cours*. Paris: Fleuve noir.

Van den Berg, Thomas and Miklós Kiss 2016. *Film Studies in Motion: From Audiovisual Essay to Academic Research Video*. Available online at http://scalar.usc.edu/works/film-studies-in-motion

Van der Pol, Gerwin 2013. 'Cognitive Dissonance as an Effect of Watching *Amator*', *New Review of Film and Television Studies* 11 (3): 354–73.

Van Heusden, Barend 2009. 'Semiotic Cognition and the Logic of Culture', *Pragmatics and Cognition* 17 (3): 611–27.

Variety staff 1965. 'Review: Blow-Up', *Variety*, 31 December. Available online at http://variety.com/1965/film/reviews/blowup-1200421140 (retrieved 20 March 2016).

Verrone, William E. B. 2012. *The Avant-Garde Feature Film: A Critical History*. Jefferson, NC: McFarland and Company.

Verstraten, Peter 2008. *Handboek Filmnarratologie*. Nijmegen: Uitgeverij Vantilt.

Walton, Kendall 1990. *Mimesis as Make-Believe: On the Foundations of the Representational Arts*. Cambridge, MA: Harvard University Press.

Warhol, Robyn R. 2005. 'Neonarrative; or How to Render the Unnarratable in Realist Fiction and Contemporary Film', in James Phelan and Peter J. Rabinowitz (eds) *A Companion to Narrative Theory*. Malden, MA: Blackwell, pp. 220–31.

Webster, Donna M. and Arie W. Kruglanski 1994. 'Individual Differences in Need for Cognitive Closure', *Journal of Personality and Social Psychology* 67 (6): 1049–62.

Wheat, Alynda, Julie Jordan, Andra Chantim, Rennie Dyball and Mary Green 2010. 'Surprise Endings!' *People*, 10 March, 39.

Wilkinson, Alissa 2014. 'What's With All the Movies About Doppelgängers?' *The Atlantic*, 14 March. Available online at www.theatlantic.com/entertainment/archive/2014/03/whats-with-all-the-movies-about-doppelg-ngers/284413 (retrieved 20 March 2016).

Wojciehowski, Hannah Chapelle and Vittorio Gallese 2011. 'How Stories Make Us Feel: Toward an Embodied Narratology', *California Italian Studies Journal* 2 (1). Available online at http://escholarship.org/uc/item/3jg726c2 (retrieved 20 March 2016).

Wolf, Werner 2003. 'Narrative and Narrativity: A Narratological Reconceptualization and its Applicability to the Visual Arts', *Word & Image: A Journal of Verbal/Visual Enquiry* 19 (3): 180–97.

Wolf, Werner 2009. 'Illusion (Aesthetic)', in Peter Hühn, John Pier, Wolf Schmid and Jörg Schönert (eds) *Handbook of Narratology*. Berlin: de Gruyter, pp. 144–60.

Wyatt, Justin 1994. *High Concept: Movies and Marketing in Hollywood*. Austin, TX: University of Texas Press.

Yacobi, Tamar 1981. 'Fictional Reliability as a Communicative Problem', *Poetics Today* 2 (2): 113–26.

Young, Kay 2002. '"That Fabric of Times": A Response to David Bordwell's "Film Futures"' *SubStance* 31 (1): 115–18.

Zillmann, Dolf 1991. 'The Logic of Suspense and Mystery', in Jennings Bryant and Dolf Zillmann (eds) *Responding to the Screen: Reception and Reaction Processes*. Hillsdale, NJ: Erlbaum, pp. 281–303.

Zwaan, Rolf A. and Carol J. Madden 2004. 'Updating Situation Models', *Journal of Experimental Psychology: Learning, Memory, and Cognition* 30 (1): 283–88.

Filmography

+1. 2013. Dir. Dennis Iliadis. USA.
12 Monkeys (TV series). 2015– . Creat. Travis Fickett and Terry Matalas. USA.
2001: A Space Odyssey. 1968. Dir. Stanley Kubrick. USA, UK.
2046. 2004. Dir. Kar-wai Wong. Hong Kong, China, France, Italy, Germany.
A Beautiful Mind. 2001. Dir. Ron Howard. USA.
Abre los ojos (Open Your Eyes). 1997. Dir. Alejandro Amenábar. Spain, France, Italy.
Adaptation. 2002. Dir. Spike Jonze. USA.
Amator (Camera Buff). 1979. Dir. Krzysztof Kieślowski. Poland.
Annie Hall. 1977. Dir. Woody Allen. USA.
Back to the Future. 1985. Dir. Robert Zemeckis. USA.
Back to the Future Part II. 1989. Dir. Robert Zemeckis. USA.
Back to the Future Part III. 1990. Dir. Robert Zemeckis. USA.
Being John Malkovich. 1999. Dir. Spike Jonze. USA.
Birdman: or (The Unexpected Virtue of Ignorance). 2014. Dir. Alejandro González Iñárritu. USA.
Blow-Up. 1966. Dir. Michelangelo Antonioni. UK, Italy, USA.
Cet obscur objet du désir (That Obscure Object of Desire). 1977. Dir. Luis Buñuel. France, Spain.
Chasing Sleep. 2000. Dir. Michael Walker. Canada, USA, France.
Chinatown. 1974. Dir. Roman Polanski. USA.
Chung Hing sam lam (Chungking Express). 1994. Dir. Kar-wai Wong. Hong Kong.
Citizen Kane. 1941. Dir. Orson Welles. USA.
Cloud Atlas. 2012. Dir. Tom Tykwer, Andy/Lilly Wachowski and Larry/Lana Wachowski. Germany, USA, Hong Kong, Singapore.
Coherence. 2013. Dir. James Ward Byrkit. USA, UK.
Community (TV series). 2009–15. Creat. Dan Harmon. USA.
Copie conforme (Certified Copy). 2010. Dir. Abbas Kiarostami. France, Italy, Belgium, Iran.
Crash. 2004. Dir. Paul Haggis. Germany, USA.
Dark Country. 2009. Dir. Thomas Jane. USA.
Das Cabinet des Dr. Caligari (The Cabinet of Dr. Caligari). 1920. Dir. Robert Wiene. Germany.
Das Verschleierte Bild von Groß-Kleindorf. 1913. Dir. Joe May. Germany.
Deja Vu. 2006. Dir. Tony Scott. USA, UK.
Det sjunde inseglet (The Seventh Seal). 1957. Dir. Ingmar Bergman. Sweden.
Die Hard. 1988. Dir. John McTiernan. USA.
Donnie Darko. 2001. Dir. Richard Kelly. USA.
Dreamscape. 1984. Dir. Joseph Ruben. USA.
Edge of Tomorrow. 2014. Dir. Doug Liman. USA, Canada.
Enemy. 2013. Dir. Denis Villeneuve. Canada, Spain, France.
Enter Nowhere. 2011. Dir. Jack Heller. USA.
Eternal Sunshine of the Spotless Mind. 2004. Dir. Michel Gondry. USA.
eXistenZ. 1999. Dir. David Cronenberg. Canada, UK.

Fa yeung nin wa (In the Mood for Love). 2000. Dir. Kar-wai Wong. Hong Kong, France.
Fight Club. 1999. Dir. David Fincher. USA, Germany.
Five Dedicated to Ozu. 2003. Dir. Abbas Kiarostami. Iran, Japan, France.
Fringe (TV series). 2008–13. Creat. J. J. Abrams, Alex Kurtzman, Roberto Orci. USA, Canada.
Funny Games. 1997. Dir. Michael Haneke. Austria.
Funny Games. 2007. Dir. Michael Haneke. USA, France, UK, Austria, Germany, Italy.
Groundhog Day. 1993. Dir. Harold Ramis. USA.
High Fidelity. 2000. Dir. Stephen Frears. UK, USA.
Hiroshima mon amour. 1959. Dir. Alain Resnais. France, Japan.
House of Games. 1987. Dir. David Mamet. USA.
Hurok (Loop). 2016. Dir. Isti Madarász. Hungary.
Inception. 2010. Dir. Christopher Nolan. USA, UK.
Inherent Vice. 2014. Dir. Paul Thomas Anderson. USA.
Inland Empire. 2006. Dir. David Lynch. France, Poland, USA.
Interstellar. 2014. Dir. Christopher Nolan. USA, UK.
Irréversible (Irreversible). 2002. Dir. Gaspar Noé. France.
Jacob's Ladder. 1990. Dir. Adrian Lyne. USA.
Janghwa, Hongryeon (A Tale of Two Sisters). 2003. Dir. Jee-woon Kim. South Korea.
Jeanne Dielman, 23 Quai du Commerce, 1080 Bruxelles (Jeanne Dielman, 23 Commerce Quay, 1080 Brussels). 1975. Dir. Chantal Akerman. Belgium, France.
La commare secca (The Grim Reaper). 1962. Dir. Bernardo Bertolucci. Italy.
La double vie de Véronique (The Double Life of Véronique). 1991. Dir. Krzysztof Kieślowski. France, Poland, Norway.
La moustache. 2005. Dir. Emmanuel Carrère. France.
L'année dernière à Marienbad (Last Year at Marienbad). 1961. Dir. Alain Resnais. France, Italy.
Laura. 1944. Dir. Otto Preminger. USA.
L'Avventura. 1960. Dir. Michelangelo Antonioni. Italy, France.
Le doulos. 1962. Dir. Jean-Pierre Melville. France, Italy.
Le locataire (The Tenant). 1976. Dir. Roman Polanski. France.
Le sang d'un poète (The Blood of a Poet). 1932. Dir. Jean Cocteau. France.
Lola rennt (Run Lola Run). 1998. Dir. Tom Tykwer. Germany.
Looper. 2012. Dir. Rian Johnson. USA, China.
Los cronocrímenes (Timecrimes). 2007. Dir. Nacho Vigalondo. Spain.
Lost (TV series). 2004–10. Creat. J. J. Abrams, Jeffrey Lieber and Damon Lindelof. USA.
Lost Highway. 1997. Dir. David Lynch. France, USA.
Memento. 2000. Dir. Christopher Nolan. USA.
Miraq. 2006. Dir. Csaba Bollók. Hungary.
Mr. Nobody. 2009. Dir. Jaco van Dormael. France, Germany, Canada, Belgium.
Mulholland Drive. 2001. Dir. David Lynch. France, USA.
Now You See Me. 2013. Dir. Louis Leterrier. France, USA.
Oldeuboi (Oldboy). 2003. Dir. Chan-wook Park. South Korea.
Otto e mezzo (8½). 1963. Dir. Federico Fellini. Italy, France.
Paradox. 2016. Dir. Michael Hurst. USA.
Partner. 1968. Dir. Bernardo Bertolucci. Italy.
Persona. 1966. Dir. Ingmar Bergman. Sweden.
Person of Interest (TV series). 2011–16. Creat. Jonathan Nolan. USA.
Pierrot le fou. 1965. Dir. Jean-Luc Godard. France, Italy.
Post Tenebras Lux. 2012. Dir. Carlos Reygadas. Mexico, France, Netherlands, Germany.
Predestination. 2014. Dir. Michael Spierig and Peter Spierig. Australia.
Premonition. 2007. Dir. Mennan Yapo. USA.
Primer. 2004. Dir. Shane Carruth. USA.

Przypadek (Blind Chance). 1987. Dir. Krzysztof Kieślowski. Poland.
Psycho. 1960. Dir. Alfred Hitchcock. USA.
Pulp Fiction. 1994. Dir. Quentin Tarantino. USA.
Rashômon. 1950. Dir. Akira Kurosawa. Japan.
Reconstruction. 2003. Dir. Christoffer Boe. Denmark.
Réalité (Reality). 2014. Dir. Quentin Dupieux. France, Belgium, USA.
Sans toit ni loi (Vagabond). 1985. Dir. Agnès Varda. France.
Shutter Island. 2010. Dir. Martin Scorsese. USA.
Sliding Doors. 1998. Dir. Peter Howitt. UK, USA.
Slumdog Millionaire. 2008. Dir. Danny Boyle and Loveleen Tandan. UK, USA.
Source Code. 2011. Dir. Duncan Jones. USA.
South Park (TV series). 1997– . Creat. Trey Parker, Matt Stone and Brian Graden. USA.
Stage Fright. 1950. Dir. Alfred Hitchcock. UK.
Star Wars: Episode IV – A New Hope. 1977. Dir. George Lucas. USA.
Stay. 2005. Dir. Marc Forster. USA.
Stranger Than Fiction. 2006. Dir. Marc Forster. USA.
Suzhou he (Suzhou River). 2000. Dir. Ye Lou. Germany, China.
Synecdoche, New York. 2008. Dir. Charlie Kaufman. USA.
Syriana. 2005. Dir. Stephen Gaghan. USA, United Arab Emirates.
The Big Sleep. 1946. Dir. Howard Hawks. USA.
The Curious Case of Benjamin Button. 2008. Dir. David Fincher. USA.
The Double. 2013. Dir. Richard Ayoade. UK.
The Final Countdown. 1980. Dir. Don Taylor. USA.
The Following (TV series). 2013–15. Creat. Kevin Williamson. USA.
The Future. 2011. Dir. Miranda July. Germany, USA, France.
The Hours. 2002. Dir. Stephen Daldry. USA, UK.
The Jacket. 2005. Dir. John Maybury. USA, Germany.
The Locket. 1946. Dir. John Brahm. USA.
The Machinist. 2004. Dir. Brad Anderson. Spain, USA.
The Nines. 2007. Dir. John August. USA.
The Prestige. 2006. Dir. Christopher Nolan. USA, UK.
The Secret Life of Walter Mitty. 1947. Dir. Norman Z. McLeod. USA.
The Secret Life of Walter Mitty. 2013. Dir. Ben Stiller. USA, Canada.
The Sixth Sense. 1999. Dir. M. Night Shyamalan. USA.
The Truman Show. 1998. Dir. Peter Weir. USA.
The Usual Suspects. 1995. Dir. Bryan Singer. USA, Germany.
The Wizard of Oz. 1939. Dir. Victor Fleming. USA.
Time Lapse. 2014. Dir. Bradley King. USA.
Tinker Tailor Soldier Spy. 2011. Dir. Tomas Alfredson. France, UK, Germany.
Trance. 2013. Dir. Danny Boyle. UK.
Triangle. 2009. Dir. Christopher Smith. UK, Australia.
Trois couleurs: Blanc (Three Colors: White). 1994. Dir. Krzysztof Kieślowski. France, Poland, Switzerland.
Trois couleurs: Bleu (Three Colors: Blue). 1993. Dir. Krzysztof Kieślowski. France, Poland, Switzerland.
Trois couleurs: Rouge (Three Colors: Red). 1994. Dir. Krzysztof Kieślowski. France, Poland, Switzerland.
True Detective (TV series). 2015 (second season). Creat. Nic Pizzolatto. USA.
Twin Peaks (TV series). 1990–1. Creat. Mark Frost, David Lynch. USA.
Vanilla Sky. 2001. Dir. Cameron Crowe. USA, Spain.
Zodiac. 2007. Dir. David Fincher. USA.

Index

Printed and bound by CPI Group (UK) Ltd, Croydon, CR0 4YY

11/04/2025

01843608-0001